# More Than a Haircut

To Penny & Joe.

I'm sure you will enjoy the book.

Ugo Petriana

# More Than a Haircut

Ugo Patriarca

ATHENA PRESS
LONDON

ISBN  978  1  84748  271  6




First published 2008 by
ATHENA PRESS
Queen's House, 2 Holly Road
Twickenham TW1 4EG
United Kingdom

Printed for Athena Press

THE BARBER IS YOUR FATHER CONFESSOR

*TELL ME ALL – I SHAN'T TELL*

*I would like to thank my wife for editing this book and for correcting my punctuation.*

*Thanks also go to my publisher for the all their help.*

# Contents

# Introduction

**W**hat do I remember? On retirement I had time to write, but found that I'd lost it all; not that I had it before. So off to college I went, somewhat apprehensive at first, but I was soon enjoying the experience.

Mrs Saunders was my English teacher at Norfolk College. I joined when I was seventy years old, and my spelling was atrocious. I had not written for years: my late wife, Marie, had paid all the bills and written all the correspondence and banked my money. I had had no time for these chores, as I worked late in my barbershop and played sports in the evenings and at the weekends. In retrospect I was selfish. Now my present wife, Norma, pays my bills, writes my letters and fills in forms. She is also in charge of my finances. I don't know what a bill is! We both play golf – I'm a lucky boy.

After a few months at the college, the younger students would feed off me for ideas to help with their essays. Mrs Saunders wanted me to take the GCSE, but I would not pay the forty pounds for the privilege – silly sod! 'Why don't you write about your time in Italy?' said Mrs Saunders. I replied, 'I was too young to remember, as I was only five or six years old when we came back to England.' She said, 'The more you write, the more you remember.' I should have stayed. I was always impetuous. As you read this, you will find the name 'prat' suits me to the ground!

A few years later I said, 'Why not?'

Mrs Saunders tried her best to get me to do another term. I said to her that I was not as bad as I had thought, compared to the younger students. As I said, they used to feed off me for ideas for their essays. What my family forgets is that I'm self-taught. I did not realise that I spoke poor English, more cockney, know what I mean? I realised that if I spoke correctly I would be able to spell better. When I've tried to correct my speech, my clients in

Leytonstone and E17 would say, 'Who do you fink you are?' But that's enough excuses.

I later continued my English studies at the King's Lynn Learning Centre under Elizabeth Richards. I very much appreciate her encouragement of my meagre efforts.

# An Italian Childhood

**M**y first recollections of this world are of Italy. Although I was conceived in Larkhall, Scotland, I was born in Italy – then reared in London from the age of six. (Who was chasing us?) I spent much of my early life in Walthamstow.

## Scotland

My Grandfather, Luigi Patriarca, went to Glasgow in the late 1890s – it may have been earlier. The tradition of the Italians those days was for the father to go first and get settled in; then he would bring the family over, one by one. Luigi's son Salvatore came with him, followed later by Giovanni, then my father, Silvio, and lastly by Vincent. My grandmother, Francesca, never left Italy until she arrived in England as a widow after the Second World War.

*Luigi Patriarca*

I feel I must put down what I have been told about my father's side of the family. My grandfather, Luigi, had more than one fish and chip shop in Glasgow, and did well. My Uncle Salvatore had a ladies' hair salon which my mother remembered well. It was on the second floor, and the stairs leading to the shop had on the wall photos showing stylish perms. He also did well. I don't know how Salvatore became a ladies' hairdresser! My father and Uncle Johnny became barbers and after the Great War had their own shops. I presume that their father helped them. There is a gap: I don't know how the boys travelled to Scotland. The answer must be in the story as told to me by Uncle Vincent, the youngest of the boys.

My Uncle Vincent told me that his father had called him to Scotland. An Italian family, friends of my grandfathers, were on their way to Italy from Glasgow, visiting Castelforte. On returning to Scotland, they would bring Uncle Vincent back with them. This they did (this was before the 1914 war). On arriving at Liverpool Street Station, as they were not going further, they stitched Vincent's father's name and address on to his jacket and put him on the train to Glasgow. He was only ten years old. On arriving in Glasgow Station, lost and not knowing a word of English, he stood on the platform, not knowing which way to turn. A porter took pity and on reading the note stitched to his jacket, put him on a tram telling the conductor where to drop him off (in retrospect the porter must have also paid for his fare). Lucky for him the fish shop was on the main route. Stopping the tram, the driver pointed to a fish shop across the road. On crossing the cobbled street Vincent knocked on the door. His father, a big burly man with an upturned moustache, opened the door and said, 'There you are!' Promptly putting an apron around him, he pointed to a pile of potatoes in the corner of the room. Handing Vincent a knife, Luigi told him to peel them. Vincent must have felt as I did in later years on arriving in Aldgate – very lonely.

My mother would say, 'The only good one of the boys was Salvatore.' When the 1914 war broke out the boys went back to Italy and the three eldest joined the Italian army. I don't know why they went back. My cousin, Olga, not forthcoming with information, did say that there was some racial tension in Glasgow at the time. That may have been the case. Salvatore joined the *Arditi*, the commandos of that time. I'm told that they would glue their eyelids so that they would not blink. After the Austrians and Germans were driven back over the Alps, he was reported missing, presumed killed in action. His body was never found. He was awarded a posthumous medal. I tried to get information from Olga, as she lived with our father's mother in Italy. She wrote and said, 'Don't think of the past, think of the future.' She did mention a medal but did not know who had it. His name appears on the war memorial at the town hall in Castelforte.

I remember my father telling me of his experience of the war. He had been in the machine gun corps and fought in the Alps. He and Uncle Johnny returned unharmed. I don't know what part of the army Uncle Johnny was in. My father met my mother, Maria, while on leave. By all accounts, her father gave him a lift on his cart, as he was visiting his mother who lived next door to Maria's father. My mother, who happened to be sitting with her father, took to him; a sad day for her! However, I must say that he was a good-looking man. After the war he went back to Scotland, but kept up a correspondence with her. In 1921 he came back and married Maria. I presume that my grandfather opened the shops for my Father and Uncle Johnny; Vincent was not yet of age.

It was not a happy time for my mother, from sunny Italy, to have to put up with the cold in Scotland, and without knowing a word of English. My father had a shop in Larkhall, a small mining village. The shop was in the front with one room at the back, and that was it – no electricity or gas – and what was the toilet? A hole in the ground, behind the house. The light was by a lantern and the floor was of stone. My mother lost twin boys – I should not say how, but I will. My Father kicked her in the stomach and she had a miscarriage. What had my mother done? She had left a land with sun, the best of foods and loving parents. I said to my mother that she should have gone back to Italy, but no, the stigma! My Uncle Vincent also married an Italian girl, Antoneta, from Napoli. Antoneta told me that at her wedding they were all kissing her when Uncle got uptight and shouted, 'Leave some for

*Silvio Patriarca in the Italian army*

me!' He looked after his wife better than my father, who ill-treated my mother. Mum went back to Italy, or was sent back. My sister Frances had been born in Larkhall and my mother was four months pregnant with me. Is this why she was sent back – he could not be bothered with the fuss of a birth nor the expensive upbringing of a child? Send her back to her father! This tells you what a bastard the old man was, always putting the burden on my grandad Romano's shoulders!

With all this going backwards and forwards to Italy, where did the money come from? In those days, people almost never left their villages. After all, it was not a trip to Southend! Cough up – who's got the money? Where's my share? (Your share was in Italy.) When my grandad died I remember my mother saying to me in Aldgate, 'You did not want the farm, did you?' I was only seven years old! I remember the farm was shared between her sisters. Maybe she made sure that Father did not get a share.

## Uncle Johnny's Family

My Aunt Rosa, Uncle Johnny's first wife, is buried just outside Larkhall – the weather killed her. She lies with my unborn twin brothers. Aunt Rosa had two children, Gino and Olga, who were born in Glasgow, After the death of their mother, they were sent to live in Italy with their grandmother, Francesca. Gino and Olga returned to England while we were still living in Aldgate. Gino went to live with his dad, (Uncle Johnny) and Olga stayed with us in Aldgate under the care of Auntie Antoneta. During the war, Gino was called up and was stationed in Scotland. The army gave him the surname of 'Boswell', in case he was captured by the enemy. While serving, he was promoted to sergeant.

He told me that he went to Larkhall to find his mother's grave. Having found the cemetery, he looked for the tombstone but couldn't find it. On enquiring, he was given the plot number. He found it – no tombstone, nothing! There had never been one. He cursed his father. The family were all hard people – if you were no more use to them, then goodbye. I wished I'd said goodbye when I had the chance, and I've had a few.

In later years, it was my duty to go and cut my uncles' hair and visit them once a month. I'd visit Uncle Johnny after I'd gone to Uncle Vincent in Aldgate to give him a haircut. I always seemed to be at the families' beck and call. Uncle Johnny had a shop at

*Sergeant Gino Boswell (Patriarca)*

the Borough, near Blackfriars Bridge. The buildings in the back streets around Borough Station were very Victorian and soot-stained. The shop and its surroundings had a heavy, sombre atmosphere – I doubt if you would hear anybody laughing. The shop was small and dingy. Uncle Johnny could play the guitar well and made up ditties about his second wife, Angelina, whom he disliked. Why he married her no one knows. She never did see England. One ditty that I remember went: '*Chi te la fata, la barber su peto, oi figlia de Giuseppe.*' It translates, 'Who shaved the hairs of your chest, O daughter of Joseph?' After the war he returned to Italy to his flat; only mother's flat was badly damaged. Sod's law! Two years later he died a lonely man. If I remember correctly, he tried to get back with his wife – to express myself better in English, she told him to get lost!

# Uncle Vincent

My aunt told me this about Uncle Vincent. When young (and old), he was a vicious man. I know those days in Scotland were not easy and you had to be on your toes. Vincent was involved in a card game with a group of Italians. The bet was for a bottle of wine. The winner had his bottle, and for some reason he gave everyone a drink out of it, bar Vincent. Those who won did the same thing, and left Uncle out. Eventually Uncle won his bottle of wine. He poured himself a glass, went to the sink and poured the rest away – as you would! It was not taken well by one of the players. He came after Uncle, who drew a razor from his top pocket and slashed the other man across his face. The man still came forward and Uncle gave him a few more across his face, before they overpowered him. My aunt said that the poor man Uncle attacked could hardly speak. The police put Vincent in jail. I don't know if they kept him in until the trial. (I later found that they had.) Uncle Vincent got away with it, as the solicitor said that it was self-defence and that the razor he was carrying was the tool of his trade. The razor was well used in Scotland those days! The Italians loved to play cards; it seemed that at every spare moment, they would be at it, and invariably the game would end in a punch-up. If they were anything like my family, they would cheat if possible. My cousin had all his fingers broken in his right hand for cheating at cards. In hospital at Elephant and Castle, while under the gas, he started to swear in Italian. They were taken aback – as he was fair-haired and in uniform, they presumed that he was English, or maybe a spy.

*Silvio and Vincent Patriarca*

# Castelforte, Italy

The Commune di Castelforte is on the edge of the hills of Mount Auranci. Before it lies the Plain of the Garigliano. The rivers Garigliano and Sesse divide the provinces of Latina and Caserta, and the regions of Lazio and Campania. The people who lived there pre-1900 had to cross the fast-flowing river on a raft (*scafo*) pulled by horses or by buffalo (*bui*) from the banks of the rivers transporting people and fertilisers from bank to bank. The fertilisers were for the cultivation of the farming lands (*campi*). A dam was constructed at Suio, to control the fast-flowing river. The Garigliano played a major part in delaying the Allied push for Rome in the Great War!

The origins of Castelforte, a small town, lie in pre-medieval times. It still has the original entrance gates to the town. A tower that has withstood bombardments from 1079, survived an earthquake in 1349 and repelled the French in 1812 was nearly destroyed by the British assault on the Gustav Line centred on nearby Monte Cassino on the push by the British to Rome. Castelforte was badly damaged at that time. My mother's flat and all her family heirlooms were lost. I think that my mother would have gone back to Italy had the flat been intact. I accused those of my hairdressing clients who had been in that campaign of blowing up my mother's flat. They all denied it! Actually, the damage was mostly done by naval bombardment.

The lovely house of our grandma Francesca was no more. Apparently you had to rebuild first, and then claim compensation from the government. My father was too grand and full of self-importance – and bloody lazy – so all was lost. Mum did manage to sell her plot of ground for a pittance.

My widowed grandmother, Francesca, had Germans billeted in her house, and got on well with them. When the Gustav Line was broken and the Germans evacuated the town, they took Francesca with them out of harm's way. When the war was over, she was found in northern Italy in good health. Her sons brought her to England. She was then in her late seventies and died a few years later in Uncle Vincent's house in Kingston-upon-Thames.

*Castelforte Old Town*

She is buried in the local cemetery. I hope her age saved her from being molested – or worse. I think she was all right. In England, her sons continued to move her around – two weeks with Dad, two weeks with Vincent; no one wanted to do more than the other. Uncle Johnny did not want to know. Don't it make you proud?

My family had returned to Castelforte in 1924, in the Italian province of Latina, situated between Rome and Naples. Frances was a year or so old, my mother was six months pregnant with me. We loved it there.

I was thrust into this world in our house on the Via Risorgimento, which was on the left-hand side (above) in Castelforte at five o'clock in the afternoon on 20 February 1925 while my father was in Scotland.

Castelforte lies south of Rome. It is a country town in Latina, but at the time we were there, it was in the province of Rome. It had a town hall, a theatre and a market; it also had a convent where the nuns taught, and a school. There was a huge building with a gigantic wine press. Everybody took their grapes to be pressed and it was always overflowing into the gutter; the sweet smell of wine was rich and strong. I lived there with my family from 1925 until 1931, when I was six years old and we left Italy for England for good. Only flashes of Italy come to mind, though my sister, Frances, has filled in some gaps. I remember sunlight – never the darkness, only the sun. I had tremendous freedom, running like a hare and as agile as a monkey, up to all sorts of tricks.

I recall running, my little feet hitting the ground and making clouds of dust. We wore no shoes in the summer. I entered a narrow lane and saw a garden of cactus plants (prickly pears), full of fruits standing out from their big green ears, like warts. With my mouth watering and greedy for the juice I entered the garden, picking the succulent ripe fruit in their green and yellow casings.

The fruit had many pips and the skin of the fruit was covered in prickles; it made your hands itch and made me miserable, but I overcame that and took my pick. All of a sudden I was lifted aloft by this man whom to me was a giant. He threw me over his shoulder while I screamed and shouted and swore (I have never lost the art of it!) and bore me to my mother who promptly smacked me across my legs and carried me in while I was crying; by all accounts I did a lot of that too!

*Castelforte, as it is now*

I remember a man coming out of the wine press with a huge snake; Frances and I ran away. We also found a skin that had been shed by a snake behind our aunt's well in San Rocco, just down the road. Our village (*Comune*), had a church that was supposed to be haunted. We would run past it very quickly! I remember our mother telling us of a worker on the roof of the church who thought it was funny to put some of his lunch into the statue's mouth. Later that day, he fell off the roof and was killed. In his mouth was a lump of bread! Mother told us that a tramp regularly slept in an empty stone coffin outside the church. I suppose if he arose from his slumber, and you saw him easing himself out of his bed, in the twilight, you'd lose a few drops of pee (was that the ghost?).

We formed our own band and I remember how the kids followed it. My sister and I had tin cans, with a stick that you pushed up and down through a hole in the skin that was stretched across the bottom: they made a weird noise. We would follow the occasional prisoner going to jail. It was all fun to us.

*Panorama di Castelforte*

The posh shops for us were the grocery shop and the sweet shop. We had a cousin who was a soldier or *carabinieri*; he was in the armed branch of the police force. We would make such a fuss of him, as he always bought us sweets. There was also a photographer's shop. The families would be in set poses for photographs, the husband always with his hand on the shoulder of his wife. Another favoured shot was the mother with her male baby on her lap, in the nude, showing his wedding tackle.

There was a big man, the grandfather of our neighbour, called Almirinda, who would always sit outside his front door. He seemed a giant to our five and six year old eyes. He was big, ugly and used to scare us just by talking. He only had to look at us and we'd scatter away. He had a habit of farting, so loud it made our hearts beat faster. We'd run away to a roar of his laughter and the bellowing of his fart!

Frances tells me that I was made a fuss of, by my mother's side of the family, as I was the first male. Frances was the favourite of our father's mum and dad. We lived next door to my father's parents, so it was not too bad. Frances loved her lovely Nonno Luigi; to her he was the greatest and she was his shadow. But he died early. Our Nonna Francesca, after whom my sister was named, was left on her own and she and my sister were always together. (These are my sister's recollections.) It seems that my family were connected to the police. My uncle was a marshal in the *Carabinieri* in Rome; in later years I was to visit him. My cousins were also in the *Carabinieri*. The ones in America were also connected.

## Nonno Domenico and Nonna Antoneta Romano

When my mother returned to Italy in late 1924, she lived with her parents, Nonno Domenico and Nonna Antoneta. Our grandad, Domenico, was a really hard-working man. He had a farm and a chalk pit; he used to hire workers to gather olives, grapes, and so on. He was very comfortable in material ways and had a farm-house, situated at the end of the town. When spring was in the air the weather became warmer and enticed people to walk outdoors. The older people sat outside their homes in their chairs, chatting with a glass of wine that was always on hand in my grandfather's house.

*Antoneta and Domenico Romano with Ugo*

The front door to the farmhouse opened in two sections, big and wide, and led you into a large room with a stone floor. It was also a dining room that saw many a good meal on the long table near the fireplace. It was a rich house for food. The food always seemed to be on hand, as the room was also a larder. Hanging from the ceiling was a trestle decorated with hams, sides of pork, sausages, salamis and smoked meats, near a massive open fireplace you could sit in. The smoked meats would be dark with the smoke from the fire. *Baccala* (salted cod) was stiff with the salt. You had to soak it overnight, drain it well, steam or boil it with garlic, pour plenty of olive oil over it, add good bread and it would put hairs on your chest!

In all the corners of the big room were tall Ali Baba jars, filled with olives (all shades of green and black) oil, olive oil in large containers and cheeses so mature that the maggots would crawl in and out of them. When you bit the cheese, it would bite you back. The Italians love strong cheese. I recall an old man sitting on a chair outside his house, a plate of goat's cheese on his knees swimming with maggots. It did not bother him, as he continued to push both cheese and maggots into his mouth, a flask of wine at his side – to drown the maggots on their way down?

Flagons of wine lined the stairs leading to the next floor. The wine press was set up in the kitchen for the harvest once a year. I remember pressing the grapes with my feet in the press and a crowd of people around the tub, people holding my hands, as I crushed the grapes with my little feet – or so I was told. The neighbours came to taste the wine straight from the press. I'm told that my grandmother would moan about it. My grandad sold the wine and kept a good bit for himself, for our own use. This was the time of the witches (*Bufana*) and people hung dolls at their windows to keep bad luck away. Others came around in masks similar to the trick-or-treaters of today, and asked for wine. I would shout with fear, and I would also drink the wine. Everyone was happy, coming and going, eating food, drinking – very tiring. We all ate together with our grandparents. Frances and I used to dip bread in the wine, which I suppose was watered down. I remember Frances saying that I always had more wine than her. She would pretend that one piece of the bread was cheese. I don't know if she tasted the flavour from it, but she said that she did!

We had a bedroom that Frances and I slept in with Mum. I think there were three bedrooms in all. Off to bed; climbing the stairs lined with those big jars all in formation led you to the bedroom. Mother would always say, 'Close your mouth,' as there were lizards crawling on the walls. I always slept with my mouth closed. They were not big!

I loved my maternal grandparents, Antoneta and Domenico Romano, who denied me nothing. Their farm provided for the whole of their family, three girls and one boy. My *tadiglio* (Grandad) had a longish ride to his *campi*. I know they were not situated together. He had vineyards where he grew his own grapes and a chalk pit, from which he would sell construction material to the builders. He employed people and his daughters to clear his land of rocks. He worked them hard. The *campi* were very fertile. My mother said that when it rained it rained like rods being driven into the ground. She said that the morning after the rain, the sown seeds would start to shoot up. The produce would then be sold.

Grandad was a small-built man, but worked like a giant. I can see him now: quite bald and working from dawn until dusk. The donkey (it could have been a mule) he rode to work had two big baskets, one on each side, always full to the brim when he returned from work with fruits and all types of vegetables. I remember waiting for him outside the town where I would get a nice piece of fruit and lead the mule home.

Sometimes I used to take the mule for a walk, maybe to feed him on new grass. One day, instead of walking, I rode him! Climbing on from a milestone, I was on his back. The mule did no more than turn around and return to his stable, but the ceiling was low and I was pressed against it. Luckily for me, a neighbour heard my cries and ran to call my mother, who calmed the mule down and then proceeded to give me a good hiding. They did not spare the rod in those days! She would leave me weeping on the ground. I'm told that I was a right *bastardo*.

Nonno Domenico had plenty to eat, but his house was not so big. Mum used to go and do her washing in the garden of Nonna

Francesca's big house, when she married the son. Before then, she used to take the washing to the stream on the back road. The earlier you went, the better the washing stone you got. The clothes were always washed well, as it was a running stream, and formed a good meeting place to chatter and gossip. This was after the Great War – no washing machine in those days!

Sometimes Frances and I were taken on our Nonno Domenico's mule and cart to get some *aqua seffuria* (fizzy water) from the mountainside, but always under supervision. I don't know where the horses were kept; they must have been with our uncle, Ernesto.

We were very lucky in lots of ways: barefoot in the summer and with plenty of freedom. Frances once cut her foot badly, when Dad was due to come home, and could not put on her new shoes, for which she got a big slap from our mother. In another incident, I was playing with the boys with big stones I fell with one big stone and hurt myself, with my willy bleeding badly. Mum was upset and took me to *la farmecia* (the chemist). I have been firing on one ever since! This is what Frances said. But I recall me hitting the edge of the pavement, missing – and hitting myself!

We also went to Scauri (a seaside resort) – the Mediterranean was only six miles away. As Frances was weaker than me and used to faint, Mother took us to special hot baths that had healing minerals. The baths were circular in shape, with marble all round, and steps leading you into the water (Roman baths). The bathing was beneficial, according to the locals. Frances was also made to dip bread into the yolks of fresh eggs, to build up her strength – and hated it!

I remember Frances and I made a pet of Nonno Domenico's pig. (More Frances than me.) We used to sing to him (or her?), and to ask which trotter he wanted us to shake; he (or she) would lift up a foot so that we could. We never knew if he was killed for salami and we ate him, or hanging on the trestle near the fire, had been smoked. (He was loved in life as he was in death!)

My Nonna Antoneta was also small. I can recall the dresses she wore, more like a uniform, with a lace mantle on her small shoulders, billowing skirt with many petticoats and a large starched hat that was more like a nun's hat. Mother also wore the same outfit. In retrospect, I think they wore them on special occasions (at *fiesta*). My mother being the youngest, and just five feet tall, was spoilt and did not do any farm work. Her two sisters, Francesca and Damiana, were each nearly six feet in height and her brother, Donato, was over six feet. He was sent to America by my grandad, who, not short of a few bob, also paid for our fare to Italy. He sent his son to America, employed men and women to work the farm, plus kept his family. I still can't understand Mum giving all this up, and settling for the hard life in Scotland.

My mother used to tell me stories of her sisters and of their strength. Clearing big rocks from the fields they would make a ring from cloth and place it on their heads, then lift and place the rocks on to it, putting many a man to shame with their strength. Being country folk, they had a broad outlook and were not shy in telling you the facts of life. They would tease me a lot – so my mother said.

If I translated my mother's cussing into English, she would put a fishwife to shame. It was very explicit. Mind you, it does not sound so bad in Italian. As for punishing me – she would leave me screaming on the street pavement. I still remember my mouth being open, trying to catch my breath. She said that she loved me. I think in retrospect that we were a burden to her – or I was!

One story that my mother told me concerned her sisters when they were working on the farm. One of them went to lie down in the hut to shelter from the sun. Another sister went looking for her, found her asleep and saw that keeping her company was a snake coiled on her chest. She did not wake her sister but ran and got some milk in a container, then laid it to the side of her sister. When the snake slithered off her sister's chest to drink the milk, she gave it a nasty blow and killed the snake. My mother would tell these tales as if I should have remembered them. My *tadiglio* took his produce to towns to sell, and would sleep rough overnight in an old ruin. There were plenty of Roman ruins around us. On one occasion he awoke suddenly to find Roman ladies dancing around him. He jumped through the window opening, threw himself on his cart and did not stop until he got home. My mother swore it was the truth!

My mother always told me that Nonno Domenico, after whom I was given my second Christian name, promised to leave the farm to me. So what happened? It was shared between her sisters. Did Mother get anything? Where is my FARM? There's a thought! Is it too late?

## Nonno Luigi and Nonna Francesca Patriarca

I remember when my grandfather, Luigi, died in 1929: his body was lying on the bed, on the second floor of his house. A group of females was around it. I presume that they were related. My Grandmother was prostrated over him. A sound of sadness hung in the air, as the women were crying and praying; I can't recall any men being there. My sister, Frances, felt the loss badly, as he was her favourite. While the lamentations were going on around her, she ran to the balcony, shouting that her grandad was beckoning her! It was some time before she calmed down.

Nonna Francesca decided the house where she lived was too big for her, now that she was on her own. She made it into four apartments, one for each of her sons and their respective families. Eventually, my mother moved from Nonno Romano's house, just a short walk to the apartment that Nonno Luigi died in. (Silly boy that I was, I thought my Father had sent money from England to buy the flat.) It had a balcony that overlooked the main street. We lived there with Frances. My younger brother, Elmo, had arrived after a brief visit from my father, who would come from Scotland now and then. I would fear him.

Uncle Vincent's apartment was across the landing to us, although at that time Vincent was in Scotland and let it out – it was used as a classroom. The stairs on the left of his door led you to Uncle Johnny's apartment on the top floor. Nonna was on the ground floor and had the best apartment with a beautiful loggia full of grapes – grapes were everywhere – and big pots of geraniums and parsley – I presume she let off Nonno Luigi's *cantina* on the ground floor, which he opened on coming back from Scotland, when retiring from running fish and chip shops. I don't think a fish and chip shop would have done well in Italy.

It was on the landing of our flat that I found my Father on one of his rare visits, trading blows with Nonno Domenico. I recall kicking Dad's leg. Maybe my grandfather was asking my father for help towards the upkeep of his wife and kids, whom he had supported from the time we had arrived from Scotland. Well – you know what happens when you ask for your money back from this family? Read on!

When the carnival and processions came through our part of the town, the two homes were on the main road. Frances and I used to collect flowers from the hillsides, then pull off the petals and throw them from the balcony on to our favourite saint, Santo Antonio, as he came by. The gaiety and colour was lovely. Mother used to bake fancies. We used to look up at the tightrope artist with our mouths open. Everyone joined in the fun.

My mother worked as a seamstress, using a sewing machine, late into the night. Our aunt said that she was the village's fashion trendsetter. When she was young, the boys and girls would go a *passegada* in the evening, eyeing each other up – all under their mums and dads' eyes, of course! Our Nonna Francesca used to do the most beautiful lace work, with extra special detail for brides. She had some put away for Frances, but the war came and Dad never went back to collect the big chest of lovely linen. All was lost before the war ended. It's lucky that we can remember the house, as there are no photos of it. The garden had its own beautiful fruit trees, and grapes of course, huge melons, lemons, apples: you name it, it was there!

Nonna Francesca also had two big concrete washtubs and her own well. It was fun to play in the water. Nonna Francesca's house was big, as was the door. We would go up the steps into a hall then up more steps to a vast landing and our apartments, which had stairs at the back that led into the garden. There were also shops on the ground floor. Though my Nonna had this house, money was short, and she managed with the help of a pension that she received for the loss of her son Salvatore.

By all accounts, I was a noisy baby and Mother would say, '*Tu sei un vero bastardo!*' (You are a real bastard.) She really loved me! There was a rope maker opposite our flat and from our balcony, we would watch him making his rope from hemp. He would tie his hemp to a post, pull the hemp tight and gradually plait it,

*Nonna Francesca and Ugo*

pulling hard at the rope. It gave off a funny smell as it got longer. One day a very long *serpe* (snake) was caught among the ropes and they killed it. Or perhaps it was in the *cantina* on the ground floor of our house? Memory plays funny tricks.

My Uncle Ernesto, Mum's favourite, used to take me with

him to gather fodder for the horses. I can recall that the fodder was carob beans, which when dried became dark brown and sweet. I remember buying the same thing in England as a sweet. We gathered it in a sloping valley. I see it now, very quiet and only us two, though there were probably others – I could not help him much. I also remember tending sheep – another flash of memory: there were sheep all around me on the meadow – whose were they? They must have belonged to the family. Shame I can't remember more. More shame that I did not keep in touch when I grew older.

My uncle drove standing up and would set off at a gallop. The sudden jerk would make me hold on tight to the rail on the side of the cart, as it crashed along the cobbled roads. Through the villages, the cart was swaying, the harness creaking with the strain, just waiting for the reins to snap and wrap themselves around my uncle's neck. I hung on like grim death to the rail. Every bit of wood that made the cart, plus the nails and bolts on the floor of the cart, seemed to move up to meet my feet coming down. Driving through the small villages, we would get abuse from the kids; they hurled stones at the cart and swore at us. I returned the compliment; after all, swearing was my game – so they tell me.

When my father made one of his visits from Scotland, I would fear him. Even in those days, he took my freedom away from me. I recall the local men shouting, 'Here comes your dad!' I would run as if my arse was on fire, to their laughter behind me.

There was one episode I recall vaguely – a lady shouting at a boy who was running away and my pants down. I don't know what happened but Mother was very upset. Maybe I should be saying, 'Hello sailor?' I was only four or five! I think it was the call of nature, in someone's garden. The women all wore billowing black skirts, but no knickers! They would pee while talking, and a river of water would flow from under their long skirts.

What was that tree from which we would pick and eat the leaves called? I wish I could recall more. I seemed to be out and about a lot, but some memories come second-hand from my mother, who related them to me as if I were there all the time.

The milkman came daily, driving his flock of sheep in front of him. He sat on a three-legged stool, pulling the teats of the ewes and squirting the milk into cans the old girls held. They would also form a queue when the herdsman came with his bullocks. You would hand a can to the herdsman who would make a slit in the side of a bullock's neck and squirt blood into the can. He stopped the flow by pressing his fingers into the slit – 'Next please.' I suppose it was used to make some form of black pudding. (I read a book on Africa, with tribes who also drew blood from the neck of their cattle.) Not as bad as the Irish, who would slice meat off a ramp of a bullock, and then pack the cavity with clay! Hunger is a terrible thing! The fishmonger would also sell his stock daily straight from his cart. There were no refrigerators in those days but the Mediterranean was only six miles away. The fish had to be fresh as in the heat of the day it would not take long for it to go off!

## Games

The games that I played were in a piazza. I'm sure it was Piazza San Rocco. The boys and girls formed a circle and a *saraga* (herring) was put into the centre. A boy or girl was left outside the circle and would have to fight to break into the centre and pick up the herring. Then they had to get out. The one who let him through would then take his place, and so on. The games were rough. Boys would line up, and one boy would stand in front with one hand under his armpit, palm showing, the other hand covering his eye, so he could not see one of the boys leave the line, and whack the palm under the armpit! If the boy could not point out who hit him, he would have to stay there until he picked the right one. Not only would your palm be sore; the hand covering your eye would give your head a nasty knock too.

Here is another one you can try: put two fingers together and wet them with your tongue. A partner does the same, then taking turns, one player brings his two fingers down on the two fingers of his partner with force. The game is not to give up. It was somewhat painful.

I remember marching with a boys' band, down the main road. We were all dressed in black, each with a black hat that had a tassel. A boy was beating a drum, and in time to the beat, I was pushing a stick through a hole in a skin covering a tin, making an 'ooh-ooh' sound. Who knows what I would have become if we stayed in Italy? Most likely a farmer like my grandad. I would have loved it.

Some customs I've been told of or recall of Sardinia. If a male became seriously ill, his kinfolk would take him to the village square and lay him on the grass, on his back. Seven village virgins would leap over his face. He would see that they were without their knickers! On realising what he would be leaving behind, he would make a remarkable recovery! I think it's a good custom made up by a dirty old man! This next one was the most common one. The morning after the wedding night, the bed sheet would be hung from the window and show the blood to prove that the bride was a virgin. I think it was quite common in Europe. Do they still do it now? I don't think so. Was tomato sauce about in those days?

# Leaving Italy for England

My brother Elmo was also born in Italy. Frances was upset when Elmo was born and kept asking our mother when she was going to get a sister. She could not forgive our mother for having Elmo and shut herself outside on the balcony. They had a hard time with her, but she got over it and got to love him, and had to look after him even when she was too young and small to be his second mum, carrying him on her hip. Our mother treated us very hard, and was very demanding. Even when much older, she would not let go; she would cause me a lot of pain with her demands in later years.

Dad got fed up after Elmo was born, told Mum he was not coming to Italy any more, and that she was to make her mind up whether she was coming to England or not. She said she came for our sakes – she would have been happier if she had stayed in Italy, and so would we!

Anyway, the day neared for departure to London. We had to go to San Lorenzo to buy some clothes, as that was our nearest big town. I was dressed up in velvet short trousers, and Frances had the most gorgeous turquoise shawl, or so she thought. When

Uncle Vincent met us at Victoria Station, he told her to take her lovely shawl off. She told me she cried because he said, 'They wear coats in London!' I don't remember how I was dressed. Only arriving at the front door in Aldgate.

From those happy days of my childhood, we were uprooted and transported to London. At the age of six, I and my sister, Frances, aged seven, and my brother, Elmo, only one year old, were taken from sunlight to the dark city of London.

Goodbye happy childhood!

# Aldgate

It was Uncle Vincent who met us at the station, and ushered the family on to another train to Aldgate Station. It was 26 September 1931. I can't recall the journey. We did not have far to walk as it only a few minutes to No. 27 Aldgate. It was the home of Uncle Vincent and Auntie Antoneta. A recess led you to the front door of a big building. The door was open, and I looked up at a high and dark stairwell; no sunlight probed its dark corners, and it had a foreboding feeling. Little did we know what was in store for us. It must have been a Sunday, as the shops were closed. I remember the Aldgate pump with the water trough at its base, separating Fleet Street and Leadenhall Street. In the earlier years, it quenched many a horse's mouth. We were to hate living there! We must have left Mum and Uncle behind, as we rushed up the stairs shouting '*Zia! Zia!*' to greet our aunt, who was overjoyed and made a fuss over us.

On the risers to the steps leading from the recess were written slogans, which you could read as you went up, advertising cosmetics sold in the barbershop. On a small landing was a tall mirror advertising a hairdressing salon; a few more steps and you were facing my Uncle Vincent's salon. On this landing, a bespoke tailor faced the barber's shop. To the right of my uncle's shop a row of wooden steps wound around the building to the second floor, where we were to live. On the left of the landing was a large room that would be our bedroom; in fact, the family's bedroom, which had French windows leading to a flat roof, that had lead ridges that we'd trip on when we played there. To the right of our door was a big cupboard that stretched across the landing. It was divided in two. The family had the first half; the bookmakers kept their coal at their end of the cupboard. (God knows what was kept in our half, most likely the bookmakers' coal.) A wide door led you into the betting shop; and to the right of it were more steps that led up to the third floor where our aunt would be looking over the banister, as my mother would also do waiting for their husbands to come up for their dinners. On the third floor, my auntie and uncle had two rooms on the right-hand side, a dining room-cum-lounge, and a bedroom. To our eyes, it was posh.

Across the landing on the left was a door that led to a shared scullery and the eating room. On the right as you entered was an iron stove, with an iron pipe at the back where the smoke escaped the building. The stove was set in a recess in the wall, to give more space to the room. It was also used for cooking our food as Mum had to share the gas cooker with Aunty. The scullery was on the left as you entered the door from the landing. It was only big enough to have the gas cooker and a sink plus a sideboard. Aunty always cooked first, as Uncle, like his brother, came before us. They were strong on the pecking order! On the side of the kitchen door on the landing, a passage ran along the back of our kitchen/eating room, which led to the toilet. We all used the same toilet, as did the betting shop people and their clients from the floor below. You heard their heavy tread walk down the passage, opening the door and closing it with a bang! Then you heard the pee hit the water in the bowl and them relieving themselves with a loud fart! To the right of the landing were my aunt's rooms and the stairs that led you to the fourth and top floor, where a mother and daughter lived. They were very nice people who always gave us treats. When my young sister was born, Mum named her after their daughter, Ena. They had a dog, called Biff; he was very old and would take ages to huff and puff his way up the stairs. I don't recall carpets anywhere... Hold on! My dad had one beside his bed, so he could put his feet down off the cold floor.

On the ground floor of the building beside the main door, there was a jewellers-cum-toy shop, an Aladdin's cave with all sorts of things. The proprietor, who liked or took pity on me, gave me a tank that shot out sparks as it went along: I was over the moon. He also used to give me lead solders. Mischievous Elmo broke off their heads and stuck matchsticks in the holes, so that he could turn their heads round. On the other side, there was a restaurant that cooked food in the window: sausages, beans, tomatoes, potatoes, onions – all quick food for the city folks. It was fascinating for us, who had never seen it before. The cook also lived above his workplace on the fourth floor. His rear window overlooked the roof that we played on. Past the restaurant on the corner was a music shop, which had brass instruments shining in the window when the sunrays caught them.

Our bedroom was big and we all slept there. It had two beds. Father's bed was near the front door and ours near the French windows. I think there were three of us sleeping in the bed. We were not happy living there. From open fields and plenty of food we had ended in a dark hole with nowhere to run! Father would slap me and once threw a chair at me in the bedroom; I remember the leg making a hole in the wall. What did I do or say? Another time I was sleepwalking and picked up the key that he kept on a chair beside his bed. He awoke saying, 'Where are you going?' I said that I was going swimming. He slapped my face and told me to get to bed. To go swimming was like a holiday, getting away from the entombed claustrophobic atmosphere that surrounded us from morning until night.

My father would always send me to get the Sunday papers, with the sleep still in my eyes, while he stayed in bed. There would be hardly anyone about. The elderly paper man had his pitch just in the entrance of Aldgate Station. Opposite the trolley bus station, I recall a big billboard advertising Tommy Trinder, the comedian with a Tilbury hat, a cheeky smile and a longish chin. I would see workmen with pads on their knees, kneeling down, spreading the hot tarmac with the hot irons out on the silent roads beside the Aldgate pump, which still stands.

On Sunday, when the City was quiet, the roads would be maintained. There was a man with a long pole with a hook and a hood at the top; the hood was to snuff the gaslight out, the hook was to pull down a lever to release the gas, and relight the lamps in the side alleys at night. I also had the job of bringing the milk bottles up for Mum and Aunty. Four bottles up three flights of stairs and I never dropped one – until one Christmas, or a few days before, when there were two big cream cartons with the milk. It was a Christmas gift from the dairy to their clients. I tried to carry the lot and dropped one, as you would! Luckily, the

*Aldgate Pump*

cream was just outside the main door. I threw the other one in the road, in the hope they would not find out that they would have had something free – they did! But I did not get a good hiding: they thought it was funny! It made an awful mess on the road.

I also remember most weeks, when we had a penny, going into the sweet shop and having a lucky dip. If we were lucky, we would end up with four ounces of sweets. I liked pop-eyes, tobacco (coconut covered with chocolate), gobstoppers, sherbet dabs, and so on. Dad also gave us a penny Nestlé's chocolate bar every Friday; sometimes we would flake it with a knife to make it last longer. So Dad used to treat us here and there, and then spoil it when he got drunk.

I was afraid of my father, who had us all by the balls and felt good about it. I recall him coming home in a good mood and putting all the money he had won at the dogs on the bed. It seemed to cover it! But nothing for my mother or the kids; it was all back in the bookmaker's pocket within the week. I got a hiding when he lost. The more Mum moaned, the more hidings I got.

My mother gave birth to a daughter, Ena. So I had another sister. But four kids for Dad were too much. Not all Italians were family men. He had got used to being single, gambling, drinking and fornicating where he worked in the West End. He was always short of money, because he was betting on anything that moved. Mum had a rough time as he had started to hit her. Frances used to try to pull him off; then he would start on me. I don't think I was that bad a boy, but Dad knew that Mum would be hurt more by seeing me being hit. (So I'm told.) It was a bad time. Elmo was smacked sometimes but not like me, whom Dad hit for nothing. Maybe he read my thoughts. Dad had a split personality. When I look back, I can see why we were so scared of him.

On Thursdays, Dad's half day off from work, Frances and I used to stand on the landing, looking down over the banisters, wondering if he was coming home drunk. She often cried before things happened. I would wet myself just when Dad looked at me. When we saw him appear, we would run in and tell Mum. The meal would be ready on the table by the time he reached the flat. We would hear him walk along the passage to the toilet, hear it gashing into the pan, while we were around the table waiting to eat. Not a word of greeting passed his lips. When he wore his bowler hat, he must have thought he was a city gent. He thought a lot of himself, and was opinionated. He must have known what I thought of him, as even at that tender age, I showed what I felt with my eyes. Hatred!

When Dad was in a good mood, we'd get Elmo to ask him to take us out, usually along the Thames, to Tower Bridge. Frances had school friends who lived in the married quarters in the Tower. Her friend Queenie often used to ask us to tea. We knew a secret stretch of the Thames where, when the tide was out and it was sandy, we would swim, Frances said. (I don't remember that, nor swimming in the Thames – uck!)

*Pool of London*

We loved to see the bridge open up to let the boats through. I recall Frances and I had a really nice and juicy triangular lolly from the Walls ice cream man who rode around on a tricycle. (Did I pinch the money? I really can't recall my father ever giving me money, taking but never giving.)

I can recall going to the cinema with him and Frances once. It must have been Caruso who was singing – *Foniculi, Fonicula*. We would never ask him directly, but would use Elmo as a go-between. Dad did take us to the Italian quarter in Clerkenwell.

We would just follow him and not speak to anyone. Leaving us on our own, to meander around, he would see his friends, popping into a club down the hill beside the church, us not far behind. We saw men playing *Morre*, an Italian game like paper and scissors. They played it with passion, banging their fists with fingers extended on the table. The glasses tinkled, keeping in time with the bottles of wine jumping about to avoid a collision. Very noisy!

Every year a religious festival was held there. All the Italian families would come from far and wide and gather around the Catholic church in Clerkenwell, and have a good time. They liked to squirt water over you! People used to live in the basement; every bit of space was used. Looking down from the pavement, I saw this chap stirring a big pot of polenta; using both hands to move the yellow mash he looked up and gave me a wink. It was full of Italians in those days; now they have all gone into the melting pot. Nothing is for ever. Why he took me with him, I don't know. On coming home, we would run for the train, hearing it drawing in; while running he would ask if I wanted to go to the lavatory. I was too scared to say yes, so once on the train I'd pee myself. On getting home, he would give me a good hiding.

The bookies office was on the other side of the landing from us. Sometimes we would hear money being dropped, and at night, when they had gone home, we'd look for it! It was our secret – we did not tell a soul. I had a big find once, six pence! It was a fortune. Frances and I kept the sweet shop busy the next day.

# A Growing Family

Things changed when my younger sister, Ena arrived. She was able to understand English and Italian before she could speak. Who spoke English? Not I, nor the family. Aunty spoke English diabolically. I did not realise that my father and uncles spoke with a Scottish accent. Frances had the job of washing my uncle's shop on Saturday afternoon, when the shop was closed. She never got any money, my mother took it, as she needed every penny – my Father kept her short (he was never short for his gambling or drinking!). I would get the comics that were in Uncle's Saturday paper that he would give me as if it was something grand. Uncle Vincent gave it to us with a bad heart after Frances washed the barbershop's floor. In retrospect, I think he hated or resented us. I would cut out the comic figures and play with them, and hide them from Elmo under the lino. I knew Uncle resented us, but made use of us and gave nothing. Never a coin crossed our grubby hands.

## The Sabini Mob

(This is what I've read and been told.)

Here in Clerkenwell drama once occurred! Roughly, around 1934, the Sabini mob were getting a name for gambling, extorting money from bookmakers, paying off the police and other vices. They were well liked around Clerkenwell. Their favourite tool was the razor. It's a wonder that Uncle Vincent was not in the mob since as you know, he was quite handy with one! The Elephant and Castle Mob were getting nervous, as the Sabini Mob was becoming a threat to their domain.

I assume an arrangement was made for them to sort it out, or word got about that they would meet in Clerkenwell. They clashed and blood ran heavily in the gutters. As it was written in the daily papers, the Italians were being overwhelmed, but what happened next was unexpected – the local Italian residents came and helped to turn the tide. They got stuck in – no shouting, just silence – and set about each other; no guns, only knives and razors. The Elephant Mob scattered to tend their wounds. The Sabini's had control of all London. The Italian mob ruled the race meetings, fixing races as far as the north of England, and they had the police in their pockets – so I'm told. It lasted for quite a few years. Eventually it seems that Darby Sabini made enough, or had enough aggro, and retired to Brighton. Of course, it did not stop there; other Italians moved in – Jack Diamond, to name one. They were quite strong in London around the 1950s. Then the Maltese came and took over.

One Christmas, many years later, I met Sabini's granddaughter. My wife Norma and I had gone to our friends near Epping Forest for the festivities. Our friend's son was courting Sabini's granddaughter, and my friends invited her family to join us. There were quite a few of us around the table, the wine and conversation flowing. Being polite, I asked her name and where she came from. She said, 'I'm Sabini.' I replied, 'That's an Italian name,' and asked had he not been a gangster. Her mother got agitated and said, 'Who told you?' I passed it over as quickly as I could, as my friend was a CID inspector! The funny thing is that nothing else was said about it. I got on well with the girl's family, who treated Norma and me with respect. (Most likely it was because I was Italian, and they were of Greek background) I knew that they did not have much respect for my friends, who always treated them well. I also have noted that money does not always bring respect – just jealousy and envy. I'm sorry to have lost touch with my good friends, who were very good to Norma and me. Ann, I shan't forget. Who else would have given me a substantial loan without a blink of the eye?) I can think of just one other. That was Norma, who secured the shop in Gosport Road E17, by buying the freehold.

Frances, Elmo and I used to wait for Father returning from his drinking spree or what other things he got up to in the West End. We looked down over the banner rails into the dark and gloomy stairwell in Aldgate. How many times had we looked down, waiting for him to come home? Was he in a good mood? Was he drunk? That would have been bad news! We would see him emerging from the gloom of the stairway with his Tilbury hat, or sometimes a bowler hat. He thought that he and Uncle were City gents. We'd rush in and tell Mum, who would quickly finish the cooking so it would be waiting for him. This was a weekly event, not only the weekend but a ritual every night! The dinner would be waiting for him on entering the dining room/part-time bedroom. He would be served first, before we could eat. I suppose those days we were not the only ones in that situation. This time all was happy now that Frances not only had Elmo to carry on her hip but also Ena, an addition to the family. Three storeys was a long way to climb up for a young girl of ten, either with Elmo or Ena on her hip – I don't think she tried one on each hip.

Our randy Uncle Vincent had a roving eye. He would waylay Ena going to her flat as she passed the door of the shop and pester her. He must have become very persistent, as there was terrible shouting and screaming directed at Uncle by Ena's mother, shouting from the top floor. Every one in the building heard what a bastard my uncle was, as she was very explicit! Poor Aunty had no choice but take Uncle's side. I remember her saying to Mum that Vincent was enticed by Ena. It was a shame, as they were very nice to us. On Guy Fawkes' day, they would buy the fireworks and give a display on their roof for us. They always gave something for Christmas, but I can't recall a present from my Father or Uncle. Aunty would sneak in a small present when she could. The brothers were made of the same tree, rotten inside. I must say, thank you Uncle, for what you did for us – bastard! (My English teachers were right when they said, 'The more you write, the more you will remember.) It makes me somewhat bitter when I recall past events.

My sister, Ena, became ill, and was taken to hospital. I don't know what was wrong with her. When Mother and Father visited her, she cried and would not let go of Dad when he picked her up. This was the thing that made him closer to her, someone who really wanted him. He brought her home. She was the only one who was not afraid of him and the only one he really cared for. In E17, he was always proud of her, when she walked through the shop in her grammar school uniform, after school. She always had a smile.

As I have said, Mother and Auntie shared the gas stove, and Aunty was first in the pecking order. They would eat in their dining room. Uncle did not like to eat with us; I don't blame him. I'll always remember the scullery. It was while Frances was washing my feet that she poured boiling water on my feet! I yelled with pain, Mum came running and I watched the blisters rise like golf balls. I never knew what I had done to upset Frances so much she would do that.

We would be sent by my mother to pinch lumps of coal from the bookmakers' cupboard that ran the length of the landing. It was big! I did not like the stealing as they gave Frances and me sixpence now and then. I think one was called Mr Lippie, a nice Jewish man. I would sneak a look into his office just to see his tape machine spewing the coils of tape. I was mesmerised. Mr Lippie had six or so men working for him. I can't remember much of the bespoke tailor opposite my uncle's. I do recall Frances going on holiday with Auntie and her friend, and with the school to the Isle of Wight. I, poor sod, only got good hidings. Ahh!

I slept everywhere in Aldgate. I remember sleeping with my sister in the kitchen on a put-you-up; being ill falling out of bed, and sleeping on the sofa in my aunt's front room, but not too well, as I could hear the trams and trolley buses all night. Always the same dream: a man following me. I quickly start to run... he also runs. I run faster, and he is gaining on me, I turn as he catches up with me; and awake in a sweat on the floor! I never did see his face. My Nonna Antoneta Romano died in 1934 while we were in Aldgate. That was sad, as she was still fresh in my mind and my hopes of escaping and returning to Italy were fading fast.

I remember once hearing a horrible noise. Fran and I ran to the window and saw this big airship. I said, 'Get the broom, so we can touch it.' The Zeppelin was so huge that it seemed to be just over the window. I thought it was going to fall on our heads! I got on the windowsill, stepping up from the chair. Frances handed me the broom. I was going to hit it with the broom as I held on to the side of the window frame, Frances holding my legs. It seemed so near just missing the chimneys; I did try! We saw it disappear over the horizon. I was always an idiot, later a prize prat.

My father, bless him, bought some pictures of Italian solders whose bodies were cut about by the Abyssinians. Their scrotums hung around their necks, their private parts sown into their mouths and other things. It was not nice to show us. The paper smelt like Swan Vestas when lit; I would be sick if anything had that smell. It took a while before I lost that feeling.

I did get up to mischief, such as removing the light cover in the kitchen, and not being electrocuted – I received a good hiding for that (I suppose it was because I was not electrocuted). But the worst thing that I remember is taking half a crown from my mother's purse. I used to see the other kids spending their pennies, and we never had any! I don't know if I or we spent it all, but Mother was very upset, as it was a lot of money those days. I can't remember if I got a good hiding or not. I don't think that Mother told Dad. I still feel guilty about it.

My mother and my aunt would go to Petticoat Lane – I should say that Aunty would take Mother! It became a treat when we were taken. The people were packed like sardines. Salted herring's were sold in abundance. The stallholders were Jews and Cockneys. The Jews mostly sold food, fish, poultry and clothes. The salted fish were packed in barrels: anchovies and smoked fish of every description. Smoked salmon was cut with a sharp knife to the quantity that was required. The Cockneys sold vegetables, groceries and kitchenware. They would throw the plates up in the air, shuffle them like a packet of cards and make them sound like expensive china! It was a happy experience for us to go shopping with Mum, to help her with her English, instead of being stuck on the roof where we lived in Aldgate.

It was still the same in later years, when I'd come up from Walthamstow with my late wife Marie. I'd return to Petticoat Lane and, being older, loved to push myself along until I got to the end of the road. On the main road was Aldgate East Station. I'd stop opposite Tubby Isaac's jellied eels stall at the end of the lane, and have a bowl of jellied eels, with pepper, vinegar and stale bread (the bread was free!). There were cardsharps, playing 'pick the ace'. Marie and I would return a few more times to the lane from E17. Stopping at an auction that was taking place I told Marie not to buy or put her hand up, as we went in – just to have a look. But you know how it is; you get drawn in with the patter, and before I knew it, Marie was bidding with the lot of them. Mind you, I did not stop her, I nearly bid against her, as we fell into the mood of the crowd. We ended up with a brush and mirror set that we did not need and paid over the top for them. Nostalgia – it has a price.

## Swan Street School

We went to Swan Street School in the Minories. We entered through an iron gate; the house where the caretaker lived was on the right, and opposite stairs led you down into the playground. Frances loved Swan Street School. We arose early for our coffee and bread: I can't remember having anything else. We'd toast the bread, break it up in pieces, put them in a bowl and pour the hot coffee over it that was our daily food for the morning. I can't recall who took us first to school. I recall that Frances was shown the way once then we were on our own. The school was always deserted; either Mum or Aunty did not know the time of school hours, or she got rid of us as there was no room for us to hang around indoors.

We were glad to get away from where we lived. It was a bit hairy going to school, weaving in and out of the crowd going to work. We were afraid of the traffic, as it was very busy, so we obeyed our mother's orders and only crossed the road where the police were. She never did take us to school – shame; she would have seen that we went too early. To get to our school we had to cross two busy roads at Aldgate and the Minories. There was a policeman whom to us looked like Mussolini, and I would shout, 'Mussolini!' until he heard us. He would cross very quickly and take us over. I think it was to stop us shouting, and embarrassing him. (On reflection, I'd love to have known what he was thinking.) On arriving there would be no one there – God knows what time it was, silent as a concrete tomb. I don't remember coming home for lunch: surely, we had a sandwich? I don't think so. I really think that we were not wanted, we were a drain on their resources. We definitely weren't showered with money – we were never given any!

One morning on our way to school, we heard this tintinnabulation. A beautiful red shining fire engine flew past, the brass helmets of the firemen gleaming in the sunlight like gold, and us jumping up and down with excitement. It was the first time we had seen anything like it. So school was our outlet, but even there Mr Honeyford, who was Frances's teacher, was called the wicked monster because he would whack the boys hard. Frances was nearly in tears many times when I got mine. I'd say, 'I did not cry', But we used to shed a tear going back to our class. There were always two of us.

I had a tough time at first with a bully called Dawson, who used to wait for me and punch me really hard, calling out, 'Ugo where I go!' But I soon joined the football team and really enjoyed it (the football team consisted of the teachers and those who did not go home for lunch). The fighting stopped – maybe I was beginning to punch back harder. My friend Morris would also be there early in the mornings. I remember one bitter cold morning, I was teaching Morris how to fight. I remember it well because he hit me on my cold ear – I could have cried with the pain! I don't think that I taught him again.

I recall a brewer's dray drawn by four shire horses, all well groomed and shining. The driver and his mate perched on their high seat with the barrels of beer piled high behind them. They had a long whip beside them to reach the front horses. I, a small lad, would gaze and wonder at this sight. Maybe it brought back memories of me riding in my uncle's cart in Italy, hanging on for dear life. The Aldgate pump, on the divide between Leadenhall Street and Fenchurch Street, had a stone trough at its base at which the horses drank from in years gone by. I can't remember ever seeing a horse drinking from the trough or anybody using the hand pump. I saw people with a bucket and brush sweeping the horse droppings into a bucket with a shovel, then dodging back on to the pavement. Later I'd see this repeated when we moved to Walthamstow, where it was the old girls with a bucket following the horses on either the milk cart or the coal cart. (The milkman used to push the milk bottles on a trolley around the streets to their customers; the horse came later. It was bloody hard work for the milkman!)

On one occasion, I was halfway across the main road in the Minories, and stopped on the centre island. A bloke rushed by me and was knocked down by a car. I just stood there looking at his head beating a tattoo of blood on the ground – I remember it well – the blood was coming from his mouth and ears. Another man ran up and placed a bundle of cloth under his head, which lifted his head off the ground. I know that I was spewing my heart up.

In school, a part of the playground was under the main building supported by stout pillars. A high wall surrounded the main playground. We used to linger in the playground, since at home, we were cooped in and the only outlet was the roof. It was not big and had a small wall that we would climb by hauling ourselves up to look three storeys down over a small wooden fence into the playground of a school that faced us. That school had a second playground on top of the building, from where the kids would shout down at us, and I would reply swearing in Italian – I was good at that! The roof was lead lined and had ridges.

The school always started the morning assembly with prayers and singing with gusto 'God save the King'. The headmaster wore false teeth and now and then, they would slip down. I always waited for a repeat performance; I was not let down.

The lady teacher put Frances and me together. I did not know what it was all about and would copy Frances, who had been to school in Italy and was a bright girl. The teacher soon parted us. One day she accused Frances of cheating and Frances burst into tears. I stood up and gave the teacher a mouthful; luckily, she did not understand Italian. She was our music teacher and walked with a waddle, feet splayed out, so when we were behind her coming to school we would copy her funny walk. Frances eventually became Head Girl. Not bad for a girl who spoke poor English!

It was our music teacher who sent my friend Morris – second from left in picture – and me, to receive the cane from Mr Honeyford. I suppose we had behaved badly in the classroom. As Frances, who was Head Girl in the school, was in Mr Honeyfords' class she witnessed the caning. We had to carry the book and cane with us. We knocked on the door and went in. Mr Honeyford said that I was to get two strokes across the backside, and told me to bend over. 'More,' he said, and while I was trying to do so he landed the first one. A cloud of dust arose from my trousers to a roar of laughter. Another one followed, with more dust and more laughter. I can't recall Morris' dust, as I was too busy trying not to cry! Once out of the room we both burst into tears. We walked into our class as if nothing had taken place. My sister was not happy with me, saying that I had showed her up!(After all, she was Head Girl!).

I was always in a rough and tumble. When I was fighting and I was getting the worst of it, I shouted, 'I'll tell my big brother!' as you would. Frances would interject, 'He hasn't got a big brother.' I remember that very clearly. She must have been getting her own back.

As I said, we did not go home for lunch but I would play

football with Mr Honeyford and the other boys. The girls would play among themselves. We were not the only ones who did not go home. Did we have a sandwich, I wonder?

When playing football an Italian lad, much older than me, showed me a 'Faccio' pin (a Fascist badge), which he had behind the lapel of his jacket. Very secret; I did not understand why he had it behind his lapel.

We enjoyed our school. In Swan Street I was getting to grips with my English. I was even getting a few algebra sums right, to everybody's surprise. My paintings were sometimes pinned up in the hall, and Frances had quite a few displayed. Just a few more years there, before moving on to Walthamstow, and I could have endured some more hidings for the sake of learning English, as they had more patience with a foreign pupil.

*Swan Street School – Ugo front right*

We were taken to the theatre at Christmas, to see the pantomime. All the kids who lived in the city centre were treated by the City of London every year. I'll always remember my first pantomime. Frances and I could not sleep, waiting for the day to arrive. It was Snow White, and another year it was Dick Whittington, then Blackbeard the Pirate, and so on. Every year we would sit on the windowsill of our uncle's barbershop and watch the Lord Mayor's show passing by. The sill was very wide and it was quite safe. We were very excited. We had front seats for the Jubilee of King George V and Queen Mary – just a mass of kids waving flags. The City was good to us. We had souvenirs from these events, which later in Walthamstow our father sold for his own gratification, either in the Ringwood pub, so that he could treat his clients, or a bit extra for the Walthamstow dog track.

The school had a big crowd of Jewish kids and they had their own religious class in the mornings. I had the job of punching holes in the top of the milk bottles for my class. I was caught hitting a boy over the head with the Bible; we all did – the more you hit him, the more he giggled. My punishment was to be sent to the Jewish class. I suppose that was because I was Catholic. On returning to my class, I was told that I had lost my job as milk monitor. After a while, I raised my hand to go to the toilet. On being released, I went on to the stage in the hall where the milk crates were stacked. I picked up the plunger that was kept always in the same spot. I proceeded to put holes in all the milk bottle tops; I did not leave one out! I can't remember whether I got the cane or not – maybe it was too painful to remember.

At the midday break, when not playing football with the boys who did not go home for lunch, I would be about on my own, strolling the narrow back streets. I remember walking around those streets, fascinated with the smell of the tea all packed in big boxes that had been loaded or unloaded, with their tops sealed with heavy silver foil. The place was a hive of activity and no one took any notice of you. The boxes were taken into the storage factories that were in abundance in the many back streets of the Minories. Morris's family had a laundry shop, and next to them a shop that sold hot food, which was displayed in the shop windows. What sticks in my mind is that a dollop of the pease pudding was put on white paper. It was yellow in colour and eaten by scooping it up with two fingers. I would watch with amusement. I can't remember if I ever had any. I wonder if they had washed their hands? It did them no harm; kids were tough those days.

Once a week the boys were taken to the swimming baths for lessons. On this occasion, Mr Honeyford took the class. He had a soft spot for me (after all, did he not give me the cane when needed? They were quite frequent). To encourage me, he said that he would give me sixpence – or was it three pence? Sixpence was a lot those days – if I swam the width. I swam with all my might, but could not do the distance. However, Morris did, and he asked Mr Honeyford for the money. I still remember how persistent he was. Eventually he got it, but it was given with a bad heart.

It was just before we left the City of London (Aldgate) for Walthamstow E17, that Olga and Gino our cousins arrived from Italy – Olga to stay with Aunty, Gino with his dad. Most likely, it was why we left. It was getting overcrowded. (I must be joking – it was bloody overcrowded!)

When we were leaving Swan Street School for pastures new, we were asked by our teachers where we were going. We got the word from our aunt who spoke English very badly, 'Woldemso,' – the teachers could not make it out, and neither could we.

On leaving, I can't remember the family saying goodbye to Ena and her mother. I hope they think of us, as we think of them, with affection. We made our way, each carrying a bundle of something or other, but not our parents, just us. They were too grand. We made our way down Houndsditch road. Liverpool Street Station was at the end on the left-hand side of the road. The station was busy with the noise of the trains relieving themselves of their steam, and shrilling with joy and relief. The steam train took us to St James station, E17. There was or is a door from the main road that that had a gang walk, which led you down into the station. As a younger lad, I would watch with fascination the steam billowing from below, with a smell of its own. The trains from this part of the station would set off to the continent. I wish we had stayed in Aldgate longer, as we were just about beginning to take things in, and understand what was happening around us. I was beginning to comprehend what was being taught.

I can't remember too much from leaving and the journey to Liverpool Street Station. But you can bet your life that I was carrying the biggest bundle of clothes, to my embarrassment! Frances did not get away with it, though she had the smallest. I was glad to get on the puffing train, with its smoke belching, and the whistle blowing. We were off to Walthamstow. It was all an adventure for us, pastures new. Wondering what lay ahead for us. I was soon to find out.

I liked to try and see what was in the houses, as we chuffed by. I'd try to look into the windows – maybe I'd see people eating or waving. Anything as we speed by the houses that were cheek-to-jowl! I let my imagination take its course. What I miss nowadays is the billowing smoke from the trains; and the clatter of the wheels when they hit the gaps that joined the railway lines.

In later years, returning to the streets I knew, I tried to find my old school, but I could not even find Swan Street or the school. Things vanish as if you were never there. (Mind you, I'm going back seventy-five years.) Times change – things then cost pennies; today you turn the pennies into pounds. Haircuts were sixpence; now they're £6–8!

# Walthamstow

We moved to Walthamstow in 1934. Whereas before I could not sleep because of the comings and goings of trams, now I could not sleep as it was so quiet, compared to the City of London's never-ending throb.

It was midday when we arrived at St James' Street Station. I remember walking from the station, Dad in front and the family behind, following like sheep. The sun was out and the day warm. We passed a cinema (now a dentist's), an alleyway beside an old stable, that in later years I would use for an arranged fight. A row of shops, containing an amusement arcade that took my pennies in later years, plus a butcher's that has a tale to tell, also the pub on the corner. The road opposite lead to the back of Markhouse Road School, where there was a sweet shop. In a mad moment once I looked in. There was no one about, so I ran in and pinched a bar of chocolate. I ran off as if my arse was on fire! I still remember it as if it were yesterday. I don't think I ever went down that road again.

I can't remember what shops there were on the other side of the road. Turning left, passing the Essex Brewery, Tolly-Macks. Opposite was the Brewery Tap Pub on the corner of Markhouse Road, where Frances held her wedding reception, after the war. We continued on to South Grove, lined with thin trees, a factory on the right and houses on both sides. At the T-junction under the bridge on the left led into Selbourne Road and the High Street, right into Gosport Road. Opposite the T-junction was a café/stall, which I would frequent later. It was next to an engineering business, whose yard adjoined the baker's at the corner, from the rear. The corner sold good bread and fancy cakes. The bread was baked behind the shop. The baker also had a sideline. The local women bought their Sunday joints to be cooked by the baker, who would place the joints in the big oven and have them ready for the women, to take home before the old man came back from the pub. In those days, nine times out of ten they would be pissed – I should know (my father) – staggering from the Ringwood Castle, or the Brewery Tap in Markhouse Road, helped by two of his cronies to the front door; halfway down the passage he'd spew up. The smell of gin lingered in the house for days! The cronies would turn for home, burping and farting along the way.

The joints would have been bought in the High Street late on Saturday night, when the butchers would auction the meat to get rid of it. I remember the crowd pushing and waving their coins in the air! Who had fridges in those days? Opposite the engineers' factory was a greengrocers, run in early days by a big man with a big family, who would never fail to tell me what he could get for a bar of soap during the war in Italy. We continued down the road, passing rows of houses where two families lived, one up and one down, sharing the outside toilet between them and no bath, as I was soon to find out. (Not that we had one in Aldgate.) The run of houses was broken by a parade of shops with a wide frontage. The trees continued down the road past the shops. Ours was the second one past the butchers.

(My friend Ray Whites' reminiscences.) 'Elmo the ★★★★★★! We all gave him our money, 1956 for the FA Cup semi-final tickets v Blackpool, never saw him again and Spurs lost 1–0! [Ray loves Spurs, is that a kick up the arse or not?] Bugger! You ask about memories, mine go back to 1949. Cycle speedway over the car park, now James Street clinic. Those days it was behind St James Street Church with a lot of space behind the old brewery. Opposite was the brewery pub. Going up South Grove, on the corner was Piene Elegant and the old cardboard factory. Our dads, Goodman, O'Leary, Hollingsworth, they used to go to the Little Artful pub, while we'd play football outside with a tennis ball until closing time, ten o' clock. Great days. I'd like to turn the clock back. The Ringwood pub has not changed a bit. Our dads also used the pub; we'd have to climb the windowsills with the green tiles. Still the same today! Chris, the governor of the pub has been there for nineteen years. Nice chap, very friendly.

'Saturday mornings we'd all go to the baths at the top of the High Street, and come out clean as a pin. At 10 a.m., we'd meet at the Willow cafe, for tea and corned beef sandwich all for one and three pence. We'd walk up the High Street, to Curly's stall opposite the Charlton Cinema. He sold ties, Realbrook and Ben Sherman shirts, and the false pocket handkerchiefs, that were attached to a square piece of card that fitted the top pocket of the jacket, with just the little bit of handkerchief showing over the pocket. We all had our suits made at Lew Rose or Arthur Sharps, opposite the Cock Tavern, next to the Green Stores – now known as BHS. Saturday afternoons we were over to Spurs.'

On my return to E17, Ray would be waiting outside the barbershop, every two weeks for his haircut without fail, for two bob (shillings). Inevitably having a battle with Ernie May, who always wanted to be first! Ernie came from Leyton, Ray just around the corner, both watching me come under the bridge on my scooter, (Lambretta), thinking, who would be first?

Since retirement to Norfolk, I meet Ray once or twice a year in Feltwell, Norfolk, where his brother Ron has retired. I remember Ron in E17, coming into the shop with his thumbs wrapped in surgical trappings. He had been reclining in the back garden on a wooden deckchair, and wrapped his thumbs around the back of the chair that promptly collapsed trapping his thumbs in the joint of the chair! He could not get up – the pain was too much – so he yelled for some time before his neighbour came to his rescue. He had a big job in Canvey Island decorating. It took a bit longer to finish the job! He's a very good decorator, so I'm told. It's all about recalling the old days; that is when Ron returns from Spain. One of these days, he will not return, as he loves it there. (I'd think twice about going, Ron.) Ray told me to mention that he was captain of his football team, with Brian Harvey and Dave Andrews. On the High Street songs were sung – Kay Star, 'The Wheel of Fortune'. That was from the music shop, next to Manzies Pie-Eels shop. I still miss them. On Saturday afternoons, it was over to Spurs; in the evenings over to the Eagle Pub in Tottenham near the police station. For twelve of us it was seventeen shillings and six pence for a round of beers! (That's eighty-seven pence, in today's money.) There was a jukebox in the corner; 1959 was the best year for records. November '59: Third – 'Oh Carol, second – What d'ya wanna make those eyes at me for, No. 1 – Dream Lover, Bobby Darin. Marvellous days, were they not?

## Silvio's Barbershop

A step led you into the recess to the door that opened to the tintinnabulation of a bell, fixed under a fanlight above the door and between two double windows. Two Brylcream display cards with Ted Dexter were displayed in the window, slightly obliquely. The display did not change much over the years. I can't remember a show of toiletries in the window. Maybe it was that the High Street was only a few minutes from the shop, and cheaper. The shop interior consisted of a large mirror that covered the front wall. Under the mirror were two Osborn sinks and a cupboard, with a worktop in between. The shop was clad in white-painted wood (tongue and grooved). There were two wooden barber chairs, with separate footrests covered with lino; a copper urn for heating water and the hot towels, suspended from the wall.

A gigantic jug stood under the tap, to catch the drips from the leaking tap. It continued to leak until it was thrown out thirty years later by me. Beside the half-glazed door, which led you into the house, a row of six chairs lined the back wall where you would find the *Daily Mirror* and the *Greyhound Express*, plus the pin-ball machine, where you put a penny in the slot, and tried to ping the balls in the holes that lit up on contact, sending flushing lights on the Head Boarder, to put the right numbers up and win a few pennies. The shop windows had cupboards under them, filled with nothing.

I would get up early, rake the ashes and lay the fire ready to be lit with a match, wash my hands, and there would be Ben Palmer at the door for his morning shave. I would already have the gas on, heating the water in the leaking urn. I would start lathering Benny Palmer, as I did every morning. After a good lathering, I'd shout up the stairs, 'Pa-Pa!' The old sod would be still in bed; he took his time to come down. After my coffee and toast, I'd go off to school. It was either Frances or me who raked the cinders and prepared the fire.

I was around nine years old when I started as a lather boy. Did I play with the boys in the street? No, I had to earn my keep, no time for boyish things. My father taught me well; I was fully able to cope with cutting hair and shaving before I had reached the age of fourteen. But I did not like my father, who took my childhood from me and gave me nothing in return.

Years later, when I came back to the shop, by the conniving of my family, and under duress, Ben was again my first early client. There was something going on between him and Elmo. Ben was a bookmaker, but I don't know for whom he worked. There was a fiddle going on with Elmo. I don't know who turned who over. He did not go back to Elmo when he reopened in Markhouse Road. Ben weighed roughly twenty stone. The last morning he came to me for his shave he seemed all right, – always smartly dressed for work. He caught the bus at the Bakers Arms, and just before Whips Cross Hospital, he had a heart attack. He was transported from the bus into the hospital by a trolley, and died that morning. Ben thought the sun shone out of my father's arse, as did quite a few more. I was to find out why a few years later.

Around the chairs, the lino was worn into a semicircle from the continuous shuffling of our feet. I did not like the trade that held me prisoner from after school until we closed at eight or nine o'clock at night, washing the clients' hair using the heavy jug. At the weekends, after they came out of the Ringwood pub, the clients would be pissed and on bending their heads over the sink, they would vomit into the bowl. I would have to clean it all up and try to push it down the sinkhole. No one would say a word.

The worktop between the sinks contained scissors, clippers, combs, powder puff, razors, Brylcream and oil for the hair, even gel. (Well, it was like Vaseline – it would leave your hair stiffer than the gel of today!) Plus the perpetual torn newspaper, which was used to wipe the lather off the razor when shaving. Two pieces of paper would be used to rub the burned ends of the hair, after having it singed with the taper (a six-inch long thin candle); it served no purpose at all. It was supposed to stop the hair from 'bleeding' – what a load of b—s! I would lather a client's face, while my father finished off another client in the next chair, then he would shave him. I'd call the next client, get him ready, and then return to the client that my father finished and wash the leftover soap from his face, and dress his hair. I would have a job getting the parting right; those days it would be in the centre of the head. I'd brush their coat and get a tip – a penny or two pence. One client would always give me sixpence: I thought he was a rich man. I swept the floor and kept things tidy. If a towel had slipped on the floor my father would never speak, only give me a dirty look. I would get my own back by putting a Billy Bunter comic in between the newspaper – that fooled him! Why? I don't know.

I resented working in the shop. Most of the boys were taller than me. They stood behind the barber's chair, and I would put a sheet around the neck, to prevent the cut hair sliding down their shirt. It never worked; they would go out scratching their backs. I'd start with the number four, hand clipper, and then my father would finish off and correct the mistakes I left behind. I would then brush the hair off the client and dress his hair, while my father finished off the boy. I would get the next client ready for him. If there were no boys waiting, I would have to follow him around the chair and watch what he was doing. I was soon using the number two clipper and the scissors; he would then straighten the hair up if it did not look right. After that, I was on my own at the end of the day. He would take all my tips; I would get nothing – except on Fridays. It was my secret! On one side of the shop was Mr Bergman the grocer, who never complained about my father's language. Mother used to say, 'Think of the neighbours.' He would shout, 'F— Bergman!' and throw things about. Next to Bergman's there was a laundry shop, a greengrocer, a sweet shop, and a fish and chip shop. On Friday, we had fish and chips. There was always a queue but it was worth the wait: the fish and chips were lovely. As I waited for my order, I would pop into the sweet shop next door, and eat as many as I dared and drink some pop. When I returned to E17, the shop was used as a carpet store. The upper was let and the fish shop had become a radio TV establishment. I always kept on my white coat with my tips in the pocket. I wonder if Dad knew that I was spending some of my tips?

My Judo mate, Barry, lived above the carpet shop; the carpet shop has a tale to tell. The owner, Arthur Western, fancied himself and would tell me what he'd get up to, among his carpets. I would see this woman pass by my shop; I knew where she was going. I also knew her husband, a very nice fellow. How can you say anything! He was also a good mate of the husband. Whom can you trust? Not your barber! Nor your friends! He would say that she did not like the foreplay. 'Just get on with it!' she would say. When her husband complained that she never showed her orgasms she said, 'You're never there!' He thought it was a joke. It makes you think, doesn't it? Who are we to laugh?

Next door to the fish, shop was another grocer's shop and a second-hand shop. The old man had two daughters: one was gay. She dressed like a man and used to drive a horse-drawn rag and bone cart. I'm sure she smoked a pipe. Next to them was a paper shop; while I was in Gosport Road the second time round, the proprietor was a Mr Shadbolt whose son, a big lad, would gain his brown belt in Judo at my club. All he wanted was to show his belt off! Barry Wilson was the top Judoka in my class, but was very aggressive; he would put me out if he could – that happened a few times! He became an instructor in his own right.

On the corner facing the Ringwood Castle pub, there was a coal shop that sold loose coal to suit the pockets of the locality. Their daughter was a big strong girl. She used a shovel that was four times the size of an ordinary one to fill the bags that the locals brought in for their weekly fuel. Her brother was a bit slow. One snowy night when he came in the shop, his flat cap had a good six inches of snow on top of it! My father told me to take it outside the shop and get rid of the snow. I could not take my eyes off his cap. As I said, I did not like hairdressing; the clients were all working class, drank beer and fought outside the Ringwood Castle pub every Friday and Saturday night. The womenfolk, waiting outside trying to get money from their husbands, would get into an argument among themselves and have a go at each other while their men pissed the week's takings up against the wall, including my dear father!

Opposite the paper shop was Mr Jacobs's shoe repair shop, which had his name painted upside down. The shop always fascinated me. You have to think of Mr Pickwick to imagine the interior of the shop. Steps led you down into a dingy dark room with all the paraphernalia of his trade. I can't remember an electric light bulb, so it must have been gas. Mr Jacobs fitted in with the small surroundings, he being small with a hunched back. I can't recall him having a haircut in the shop.

At that time, a lot of people would use Gosport Road as a short cut from the High Street to Markhouse Road. When night fell, the High Street came alive, with the kerosene lamps giving out a bluish glowing light; their hissing and popping added to the sounds and smells and the shouts of the vendors. The people also had their own sounds and smells: the shuffling of feet, rustling cloths, oaths were liberally given; there was lots of shoving; kids being cursed by the stallholders when caught stealing anything they could lay their hands on; and so on.

The lights of the barbershop would draw the kids like moths to a flame. They would cluster on the shop entrance and block it. I would be sent to tell them to sod off! I would linger for a while on the step. If anyone held my eye, I would shout, 'Who the f— are you looking at!' I spoke poor English, but I swore well. I was then ten or eleven years old. I must say that I've improved over the years and swear a lot better. You don't believe me? You must try me out.

The customers' favourite haircut was a trim with a Pashana friction shampoo, which would be rubbed in after the old man cut their hair. What I enjoyed the most was that after the old man shaved the clients, they usually had hot towels. It was me that got the very hot wet towels out from the urn with a big jug catching the drips. I would pass the towels from hand to hand, wring the steaming water out of them in the basin, then place the towels on the client's face; remove the first one, apply cream and work it in. I would slap the clients under their chin, slowly building up until I was going twenty-four slaps to the dozen that was the massage. Then I would apply the next hot towel. Their pores were well open from the heat of the towels. I asked them if they wanted Pashana on their face, as I liked to see their legs shoot up in the air when the spirit bit. Their hands would grip the arms of the chair and their knuckles would turn white. Naughty Ugo! My first proper customer was old Mr Ramsey. He was a tubby man and let me cut his hair. I would cut it all off with the clipper and just leave a tuft of hair on the front. He said it was so that his wife could grab hold of him. He would also let me shave him to get some practice. It was nice of him. His son, Alfred, would also have the same haircut.

Our house did not have the appearance of wealth! Just above the shop façade that needed painting was a big window that was in three parts, separated by two columns. The small panes were fixed; only the centre was able to move. I don't know if my father was too tight to have it mended or if it was a fixture. All my dear father had painted was his name above the shop. I can't remember the shop front ever being painted.

*Frances and Ugo with Mother in 1939*

From the side door of the shop, a passage led you to the stairs up to a small landing where there was a bedroom opposite, plus a smaller room, with a window that looked on to the back garden. On the right of the landing, two steps up there was a bedroom on the left, and in front was the main bedroom that overlooked the street. It was some time before we had lino to soften the sound of feet hitting the floorboards. I don't know which came first, the gas light with its continuing popping and hissing or electricity. It was a transformation that threw light into gloomy corners, that had never seen light before. I do not know why the shop had electricity, and not the rest of the house.

Back on the ground floor, off the passage and behind the shop was a small little-used dining room. The passage led to an eating room that had a coal cupboard under the stairs. A coal-fuelled iron stove heated the room, plus the kettle on top ready to be used to save the gas bill. Through a door that separated the room to the scullery, it contained a big sink under a window, on the left a gas cooker, and in a recess beside the cooker, a big boiler heated by a coal fire. Going through the door on the right of the scullery led out into the garden. The garden was small, but it had the main attraction: the path around the kitchen led to the loo! Icy cold in the winter, when hands were used to sit upon, the perpetual torn paper, threaded with string, hanging within reach. It took courage to do your business in the winter. I'd go in with my hat, scarf and coat, then sit on my hands. Did I wash my hands in the Butler sink? I'm sure I did.

My mother could make anything grow in that garden. She also kept chickens that she fattened up for Christmas. She was a fantastic cook and Christmas would be a busy time for her. Nothing of the chicken would be wasted. The intestines of the bird were slit and cleaned, then left to soak in salt water overnight. 'Ugh!' you might say, but they were lovely fried with herbs and put into an omelette. It was the same as salted cod, stiff with salt, soaked overnight, marvellous fried. There were many delicacies made from bits and pieces, such as dough in all shapes and cooked in olive oil. We had no toys but there was never a shortage of food. Offal was the food that my mother could turn it into a fantastic meal. It was so tasty! The food made up for the toys we did not have. Or did it? The offal was the cheapest bits of meat you could buy. Nothing would be wasted! If you come from farming stock you learn to be frugal.

## Markhouse Road School

I remember the first day at my new school: the chap who worked for my father was only there for a few weeks before my father got rid of him. He took me to school, and introduced me to the headmaster, Mr Wolf. I thought, that's a good start! The headmaster took me into the classroom and introduced me to the boys; stony silence reigned, and their eyes followed me as I took my seat. I was soon embroiled in a fight. It was a very tough and rough school. I was the only foreigner there. ( You can laugh now!)

I was picked on by a boy called, Fred (Penelva) who lived opposite the barbershop, next to Mrs Hall. All had one toilet in the garden for two families. I had learned to fight with the boys at my old school in the City of London. I hit him and slapped him more times than he did me; it was a normal fight – no one got really hurt – which made me be accepted by the rest of the boys. Their favourite game was to call me, 'You go where I go!' a pun on my name, 'Ugo'. It used to be a chase. I would catch them, put their arms in the railings that separated the girl's playground, and squeeze them together until they shouted, 'I won't say it again!' I would let them go, and it would start all over again. I used to enjoy it, as I'm sure they did also. It would be racial today and that would have stopped me integrating with the boys.

One fight I do remember was held in a part of the playground that had a corrugated roof over it, which we'd take cover under when it rained. The boys formed a circle, and the two went hammer and tongs at each other, and the boys shouting, 'Whoo! Whoo! Whoo!' like braying wolves. When either boy was knocked to the edge of the circle, they would push them back. It was only the school bell that stopped the fight. I always stood my ground at school. There was never any ill feeling after the fight! (Well, I never experienced any.) They had no fear of being overwhelmed by one Italian boy.

Markhouse Road School had no time to teach one foreign child, so they gave me a job of ringing the school bell, but I rang it too loud and too long. Then I had the job of making the tea for the teachers. That was also short-lived – the biscuits were disappearing too quickly. That at least was filling while it lasted. My sports teacher gave me a note to take to my father, asking if I could play football for the school on Saturdays. Dad tore the note up. You see, I was his worker and worked from 7.30 a.m. until 8 p.m. – or later! I had to earn my keep, always up before him while he lingered in bed. I can't recall him ever smiling at me.

I always looked forward going to school; if only I knew what they were trying to teach. I liked woodwork classes; they were held on the ground floor with Mr Chittle, a nice old man, but with an unruly class. He would take things to heart, and often burst into tears. One day he was showing how to do a tongue and groove, with us gathered around him. Being small, I thought I would climb on to the bench to get a better view. I lifted my knee and caught a chisel that was left in the vice and split my knee. There was plenty of blood and a big bandage around my knee – I still have the scar. That did not stop my father having me working in the shop until eight or later, limping around the chair. Today I would have had him hanged The thought makes me happy.

On the other hand, Mr Watson was a bugger! He was a big portly man, his belly well to the fore. He would creep up behind you and hit your fingers with the ruler. He caught me one day and hurt me. I leapt up and hit him in the belly. He kept me in after school and gave me a good talking-to. He made a mistake; he should have given me the cane. All my mates were waiting outside to see how many strokes I got. When I told them, cocky, that he did not cane me. I'm afraid they all had a pop at him in the weeks that followed. (There's a lesson to be learned there, surely?)

School was rough, but we had laughs. At certain times of the year, we would be pushing hoops along with a stick, whirling them around our bodies; then gobs, throwing four or five stones up in the air and trying to catch them on the back of your fingers; swapping picture cards that came out of cigarette packets of your favourite footballers, cricketers or cars for the ones you did not have, and flipping the cards to knock other cards down that would be propped up against the wall. We also played throwing halfpennies, trying to get them nearest to a line, when we had any. Throughout the year of course, there was cricket and football, for which rags were tied together with string to form a ball. This would lead to fights when other kids pinched your ball. You could never have a rubber ball – it would disappear. I must not forget the marbles, all in different colours. Yes, I loved my school. When term finished, the boys would all sing, marching out of the school gate into Markhouse road, 'No more pencils, no more books, no more teachers' ugly looks.' I never joined in as I knew what was awaiting me. I must not forget the conkers that the boys would pickle in vinegar, and cook in the oven. I tried all sorts of weird concoctions to make the conker hard, but I never succeeded.

The Welsh teacher had a hard time in our classroom. The class was divided into three: clever boys on the left facing the teacher; the not so clever in the centre; and the idiots on the right. I was near last in the exams – well, third from bottom! I did not know what it was all about. The Teachers did not care. However, I was not bad at geography – pictures, I suppose. The Welsh teacher walked out, leaving a hell of a noise; rubbers and pencils flying about. Mr Wolf, the headmaster, came in. Silence. 'Come to the front, those who were partaking in this fracas!' he yelled. No one moved. Again he shouted, 'Come to the front!' I thought I'd be clever and own up first, and I'd get away with it. I did not get away with it; half the class came to the front with me. I had to fight my way to the end of the line, waiting outside Mr Wolf's study in the corridor. I think I was fourth or fifth from the end. They were bigger than me! We each got two strokes of the cane – he did not spare the rod. If he caught your fingers, you knew all about it. He went over the top with one boy, whose father came to the school and punched Mr Wolf so hard that he fell to the floor. That was a laugh and the talk for weeks among the boys.

Often the smog would be very thick in the mornings on going to school. You could smell the smoke in the dark heavy folds that seemed to cling to you. When you got to the end of Ashford Road, running by Reeds stables, they smelled very strong from the horses' manure. (In the summer you would run past quicker, to dodge the host of flies that would be around your head.) You had to feel your way by hand along the alley to get to South Grove Road. It was not until well after the war that this smog slowly thinned out. On leaving school at fourteen years old, I knew I was behind in my education; in fact I could not write but could just about understand and read Billy Bunter. I would not miss a week of my comic paper. In fact I improved my reading with fat Billy. I asked my father if I could go to night school, as I was well behind the others in my class. He replied by asking me, 'If a haircut costs six pence and a pound is given, how much change is there?' I replied, 'Nineteen shillings and six pence,' to which he said, 'That's all you need to know.' Thanks Dad!

# Great Balls of Fire!

The old man would send me out to cut Tom's hair in Ashford Road, just round the corner from our shop. Tom was a cripple and not able to move about much. He lived in an upstairs flat and his mate, Charlie, was a bookies' runner. Although Charlie did not live with him, he lived in Gosport Road (not far from the shop). Charlie was usually in Tom's flat on my visits; it was not until later I found out that they were queers. It was all right at first, but then one day Tom said, 'Ugo, I'm losing the hairs around my balls; will you singe them for me?' I replied, 'I haven't got any tapers with me.' (A taper is a long thin candle.) He said, 'Bring them with you next time.' I thought of telling my father, but we hardly spoke to each other. Despite that, I knew what I had to do.

Two weeks later, I had a taper with me. While I was cutting Tom's hair he said, 'Charlie likes boys.' Charlie never said a word. He was always there. I said, 'Oh, yeah!' Tom asked, 'Have you got the taper, Ugo?' and pulled down his trousers. 'Yes,' I said, lit the taper, shifted his dick to one side with my comb and set fire to his hairs around his balls. For a cripple he moved very fast to the sink, shoving his balls under the tap! I moved faster, and was down the stairs, out on to Ashford Road!

It seems that I was the only one not to know what Charlie was. My old man had been sending me to cut the queer's hair every two weeks. I was not fourteen years old. After this episode I was never sent to cut his hair again. Nothing was ever said. Dad must have known. Bastard! When I left the shop to work in the High Street, my younger brother, Elmo, was sent out to cut his hair. I warned him about Tom. Elmo just laughed and said, 'Everyone knows all about Tom.' Except me! As barbers are father confessors to all their customers, why did Dad send me? Did he hate me as much as I hated him?

With the dog tips flying around the shop, every client had an infallible system. Elmo soon learned all about racing, dogs and betting; after all, he had a good teacher! On Saturdays the shop would be busy, and the old man could not get to the dog track in time. Dad would give Elmo the money and tell him what forecast he wanted – six and one, two and four, etc. Elmo soon got the bug. He became very good at maths, though writing was not his strong point. Elmo would use Dad's money and pick his own dogs. In the end, he thought that he knew more about the dogs than the old man – I think he was right! They would lose all, in the end. Elmo did well with the old man's money. If I only believed half of what he said. Now and then he would be found out, when Dad's forecast came up and no money was put on it! That did not stop the old man sending Elmo to the dogs to place his bets for him. As long as Elmo brought back a wad of tote tickets, it did not matter that they were losing. He would point them out to his clients saying, 'If number six had not had a bump on the last bend, I'd have won a fortune!' The old man was happy as a pig in s—t. Did my father remember what I said to him. When he was punching me around the room above the shop? I can't remember what I'd done as it happened frequently. I do remember saying to him, 'I will kill you, when I grow up!' War was looming and Italy had taken Abyssinia. Coming from school the boys would all sing this song, and I would sing it with them – to the tune of 'Covered Wagons':

> Roll-a-long, Mussolini, roll-a-long,
> As you won't be in Abyssinia very long
> You'll be sitting on the grass,
> With a bullet up your arse,
> Roll-a-long, Mussolini roll-a-long!

I can't recall having a fight in school for being Italian. (That would have been later!) You were picked on because you were new to the school and had to prove yourself! There was no one to turn to. If you were fighting and lost you were still accepted as long as you had stood your ground. I was all right as my old man was keeping me tuned up, in the room above the shop!

I can't remember if I ever got into the tin bath that hung outside the garden wall. Surely I must have washed somewhere along the line. I could step into the big Butler sink – or was I put into it? Vaguely at the back of my mind a picture appears of the tin bath and a fire. The time came when we used the public baths in the High Street. 'Hot number two, or cold,' we would shout. The attendant would let the water in your bath from the tap outside of the cubicle. It was a treat for us boys.

The flock mattress that formed itself to my body was so comfortable that when I had a real mattress, I could not get used to it. This was when the bedbugs were on the verge of disappearing. Sleep was hard to come by, as I slept with Elmo, and would have to tell him all about a film I had seen. He would prod me if I fell asleep during the telling. I soon learned to take him with me.

Was it that the populace were getting cleaner? I don't think so! In those days men's cuffs were shiny from wiping their noses. Looking back to the kids with running noses and not wiping them, just hanging like macaroni; dirty hands, torn trousers and patched socks that the mothers darned with a mushroom, as mine did. I was nearly like them; but I had to wipe my nose more often, because of working in the shop.

I was sent to the baths by the doctor, as I had a bad skin complaint. I must have been bad with it. It had to have been caused by the bedbugs. I was bitten more than the rest of the family. There was a large separate room with a pool in the centre, from which arose steam with a strong sulphurous smell. I slid in very slowly – it was bloody hot! Three visits it took for me to be cured of the rash I had.

Where did all the bedbugs go to? I would be bitten all night with them in those days. The bugs raised lumps all over me. I'd get up in the night and catch some, go downstairs into the kitchen, pull their legs off so they could not run, then burn them to death. Vengeance is mine! saith me. My blood did not smell nice, but they gave me hell. We would hunt them down, in the corners of the bedposts, under any loose wallpaper. In those days the paste was made with flour. Mum would take the beds to pieces in the garden, and pour boiling water into the iron joints. The treatment would keep them at bay for a while, but they would return in abundance. Somewhere along the line they disappeared! Did we get cleaner? I don't fink so!

*Walthamstow Baths, 1964*

War came, and Italy was on the verge of going in with Germany. Things were going to be a bit hard on the family. We did not know what would be in store for us; in fact, I was not concerned about it, not being fourteen years old yet. I never thought that we'd be involved. I can't recall any backchat from the boys. What did we know about war?

# Freedom

It was a Thursday morning in 1940 when two policemen came and searched the house and shop. Just before they arrived, my mother took down the photo of me dressed in the *ballili* uniform (young black shirts). As far as I can remember it was like the boy scouts. I think that was the only link with the black shirts. (Shame, I could have had some fun with it! I'd have hung it in my shop with Scargill and Ron Todd, whom I have great respect for! That would have got the boys going.) Italy had declared war on England and they took my father away. They took him to Forest Road Police Station E17. The police had no cars in those days, so we walked from the shop along Palmerston Road, with the police in front, Dad behind, and me behind him carrying his suitcase. Halfway down Palmerston Road, he took the suitcase from me and told me to go back and open the shop! I was fourteen years old and a qualified hairdresser. I will always remember that Thursday when I reclaimed my freedom, while he lost his. I can't recall any regret – maybe I just hoped that he would not come back. I don't know why the Government interned him; he was only interested in the Walthamstow dog track, Ringwood Castle pub and knocking me about!

They were happy days for me. The shop took just enough to pay the rent of one pound and ten shillings, with a little bit over. Elmo, and Ena, were still at school. Frances was working and bringing some money home. We managed, never had any hassle for being Italians, and I started to play football in the street with my mates, or a halfpenny nearest the line. Again, the ball was a bundle of rags, tied together. Elmo had a bit of trouble in school; two big lads were picking on him. I closed the shop and went to the school and waited for them to return from lunch. As they were taller than me, I placed two stones in my hands to give my fists more power. They did not want trouble when I approached them, and I left them alone. In retrospect, I realise that if I had hit them it would have done me more harm than them, as I would most likely have broken my fingers. Though times were hard, I never missed my father. I even got hold of a bike (did I pay for it?) and promptly knocked a kid down with it. I did not know it had no brakes! No harm done, though his mother got a bit excited and a bloke told me to sod off! I did not hang about.

Walking down the High Street, just past Vernon Road, my pal, Harry, gave me a nudge and a nod of his head at this girl, whom an older mate, Carter, had said that she was all right if you paid for it. Well, I had half a crown in my pocket – my weekly wage. (Mum also took my tips.) Harry had nothing. With Carter's tales of lovemaking, we would listen to him with mouth agape and a little stirring in our loins! We approached this girl; we will call her Molly (I've forgotten her name). I was cheeky, plenty of mouth – the price started at ten shillings. Still walking beside her I said it was too much. Still walking and talking she came down to five shillings. There was more talk; Harry did not say anything at all. I was taken aback when Molly said she would take the half crown. My bottle went! We walked along to the end of the High Street, turned left into St James Street and on to Lynmouth Road leading to the playing fields. Then it happened: I completely lost my nerve. I gave my two and six, my week's wage, to Harry! I said that I had to go home, I had forgotten to leave the key and no one could get in. Molly grabbed my arm; I shook it off. Harry stood there with his mouth open as I ran all the way up Grove Road, and did not stop till I got home, and made sure the door was shut behind me! In talking we knew everything; but when it came to two and six, I ran, and he was stuck. I can laugh now when I think back. He did not know what to do either. Later on, Harry joined the Navy and saw plenty of action on the motor torpedo boats in the Channel. I found no animosity among my friends.

## Air Raids

We had an Anderson shelter in the back garden. Why we had it, I don't know. We never used it, as it was damp and water lay on the bottom when it rained. However, when the bombing got heavier, we trudged to Lindon Road into the cellar that Fish Brothers, the jewellers in the High Street, opened up for public use. I had the job of carrying the bundle of clothes that served as our bedding in the shelter. I hated it, as did Frances. I'd lose the battle with carrying the bundle of clothes, and cringe on meeting people! Everyone was happy in the shelter. Once the family was in, I would be out with the boys, running like hell when the bombs were dropping, laughing it off afterwards. One of our mates, when the ack-ack opened up, would be down the road like a shot. We were down the alley, going to St James Street, and he had his girl up against the wall (that was the saying in those days). Then the guns opened up, he left her with her knickers down, and you could just about see his arse disappearing down the dark alley! We could see hers – we took our time in meandering off! He did it more than once. He joined the Navy. Coming home on leave, we would ask him where he ran to when the ship fired its guns. He was a nice boy though.

We really enjoyed ourselves. I know it sounds funny, but we did! Eventually you get used to the good and the bad. Quite a few of the boys joined the Navy – they reckoned that it would be a cleaner death. Butler's mother had a stall in the High Street, and the family would rent out other stalls along there. His brother also ran banana stalls, and supplied other stallholders after the war. The High Street was a mile long, the longest in London. Butler's aunt's at the bottom of the High Street and outside the post office sold rabbits. They would skin them at the stall by tying the head to a fixture, then cut around the neck and pull the skin off like a glove. They sold peanuts in the summer.

One night I was on my own down the bottom of the High Street when the bombs started to drop. The ack-ack was very heavy. I ran up towards the shelter. Passing a woman carrying a child, I stopped and took the child and told the woman to follow me. I soon left her behind – I don't think I told her where I was going! On reaching the shelter in Lindon Road, I ran up the Alley and there was a heavy length of wood across the door. By that time the lady had caught up with me, so I handed over the baby and moved the obstruction. It was a heavy length of a beam that had been blown from over the road by a bomb exploding in

Vernon Road. On opening the door, I could hear my mother calling. The dust was floating in the air and she was at the bottom of the stairs. The lady went quickly down the steps; it was a very close call. The bomb had fallen less than a hundred yards away.

*Vernon Road, 27 December 1940*

After the war, I read that the ack-ack was futile, as the shell bursts could never reach the enemy aircraft. It was just a gimmick to make the populace feel they were doing their bit, as with all the iron railings that were taken away but never used!

The shelter was always packed – the jocular sound of the people made it more like a club, especially when the bombing was heavy. I knew a boy called George who, with his mate, had a stall that sold vegetables, outside the jewellers. They were a rough tough pair, and had this young girl who was the daughter of the chap who sold newspapers outside the Palace Theatre. They were laughing and playing about. A bomb fell near by and the lights went out. The hurricane lamp came on, but it was a very dim light. My mate and I were watching them, straining our eyes to see what was going on. She then said, 'Tell him to stop it, George!' We looked harder, but all we could see was moving shadows. We heard short deep breaths, then George saying, 'Here it comes!', and a yelp. It was years before we knew what she had yelped about.

It was also in the shelter that this bloke tried to undo my

trouser buttons, while I was lying beside my mother. I punched him in the eye, and he moved away. No one said anything. He was a lay preacher from the church in Palmerston Road. Dirty bugger! It makes you think – whom can you trust? Did my mother not see? Or was she too frightened to say anything?

*Walthamstow Market in the Blitz*

One night, my mate and I were in the café in Willow Walk. It was a narrow place, table and chairs on each side a walkway dividing them, with a ceiling of glass. I was having a go at one of the boys at the other table, saying that if he did not shut up I would give him one, as I had his brother at the Buxton Boxing Club! I did a bit of boxing, but I was short for my weight. He had been having a go at my nationality, I think. Then the bomb dropped. I could not get under my table, as I was too near a big fridge. My mate was under with the rest of the boys. Not one pane was broken! We rushed out into the High Street. On the left, we could see that the Chequers pub was damaged. The bomb had dropped in the road, opposite the house of one of our mates, which had been damaged. Luckily his family were elsewhere. We went inside and the damage was quite extensive, but I don't think anyone was killed.

Anyway, next day there was a knock on the side door. Ena answered it, as I was not in. She relayed the message to me to meet the brother of the chap in the café for a fight. The fight was to take place in the old stables next to the cinema in James Street on Thursday afternoon. I can't remember his name, but he turned up with his mate Harry, who was older than us. Off we went, hammer and tongs. I tried to grapple with him as I was better at wrestling than boxing, but Harry would not have it. My pals urged me on. It seemed to go on for ever: it must have been boring. In the end, neither of us could lift our fists. My mates had all gone home. His mate, Harry, said he would fight me. (Not daft, was Harry!) I told him to give over; I was knackered! The three of us walked off up the alley beside the railway line that led into Gosport Road, home to dress our wounds (I don't remember any, but it sounds good).

At Lieberman's Café and snooker hall, opposite Erskine Road, I nearly clobbered a bloke with my snooker cue. He would not pay up when losing at skittles. It was during the blackout in 1941. After leaving Lieberman's, I left the boys and made my way down the High Street. Our favourite game during the blackout was to walk up softly behind people, then cough and see them jump, then do a runner. Anyway, on reaching Willow Walk, where there was a dim light on the corner, and a few people about, I heard this shouting right behind me. It was the old boy that had not wanted to pay up at the billiard hall. He drew people's attention, whipping the cap off his head and showing his white hair by lowering his head, then he shouted, 'Trying to hit an old man with a billiard cue, you sod!' I took my eyes off him to see who was watching. He punched me in the ear. I swung at him and a small crowd shouted, 'Don't you hit an old man!' He swung another punch and missed. I was ready to give him another one and again the crowd growled. I did no more and walked off. I was on a loser.

# Father's Return from the Isle of Man

My reflections are hazy of the barbershop at the time of my father's internment: it must have been very boring. I used to daydream a lot, as there were long gaps between clients. I'd use the arm of the barber chair by striding it, pretending that I was riding a horse. At that moment I was, Hop-along Cassidy, always dressed in black, wondering if I would kill my father as I had promised him I would. It all came to pass as usual – all would be sorrow on his release. Apparently, he volunteered to serve in the army, but was unfit. Bloody shame! I was not overwhelmed with clients, but still opened the shop from eight until six. Bored stiff.

One night in 1942, we were asleep in the shelter under Fish Bros, when I was awaked by Mr Bergman, our neighbour from Gosport Road. Although feeling sleepy, I was soon awake when he told me that my father had come back from the Isle of Man, and was waiting in his house. My heart sunk as I explained it to Mum. We gathered our clothes and trooped back to the shop. I cannot recall any feeling on seeing him, or any welcome from him. He started where he left off. My mother had saved forty pounds, which was money that we had gone without. I did not know then that my mother received some help from the government – was it a secret, in case she felt she would have to give me more than two and sixpence a week? That Saturday night he took the forty quid to the Walthamstow dog track, and blew it all away! It was the first time that my mother threw something at him – an iron. Shame it missed. The only good thing from his return was that we stopped going to the shelter, and did not have to carry that bloody bedding!

## Premier Plating Works

It did not take my father long to get me to work for his gambling mate, the governor of the Premier Plating Works, just a few minutes from the shop – the entrance to the factory was from an alley at the end of Ashford road. On going past Reeds horse stable I'd run as it stunk like hell, especially in the summer when you would be bombarded by the horse flies. At that time coal was delivered by cart. I would finish work on the buff, standing all day. The fluff would be floating in the air, along with an acrid smell from the acid that was used to nickel chrome the torches. We should have got half a pint of milk a day to quench our thirst from the dust, but it was not regular! On arriving home at five o'clock, my mother would ask me to go and help my father, as he had been busy. Did she not know what I was doing all day? But like a good boy I did as I was told and would work until eight o'clock or later, with nothing to eat or drink until the shop closed. I was working twelve hours a day – no wonder I ended up in hospital.

I did not tell the family what happened during my first week in the factory. There was this very tall cocky lad who had the habit of throwing a homemade knife and just missing your hand. More often than not it was me he tried it on. He had just missed my hand by an inch and I got fed up with his intimidating us. Although he was much taller than me, it ended in a fight. He did not attack but just circled around and would not close with me. The other workers intervened and called it off. A week later the governor's brother who worked there offered me a drink of lemonade. I took a swig but as it reached my mouth I realised it was piss! I spat it out at them and threw the bottle, shouting, 'bastards!' to a roar of laughter. In the end it all calmed down. I dare say if he had known, my father would have expected me to have drunk it. It was not that I was Italian, it was because I was the new bloke *and* Italian.

## Herman Hill Hospital, Wanstead

One day in 1940, I came home from the Premier Plating Works not feeling well at all; my head felt twice the normal size. I still did as my mother said and helped the old man, as he was busy. It was the weekend that Octavio came to visit. He was a well-off relation who made me an offer to live and work for him that I refused – what a fool I was! (He held his daughter's wedding in Hampton Court and we all attended. Very grand!) I did not eat much at the table and asked if I could go to bed. By this time I was really bad; my head felt as if it had swelled to double its size. I had not gone to work and still in bed, I was boiling and asked my brother Elmo to bring me some water, as my mother would not. He brought me a milk bottle filled with beautiful cold water. Down it went – lovely! A few hours later I was heaving up mucus and blood; I was in a mess. I banged on the floor with my shoe; Mother came up and went berserk. Frances went for the doctor. When he came he told my mother off, as the room was cold, no fire was lit. It was winter and a Thursday; half day for the shop. My father, bless him, was at the dogs, as usual. I could hear my mother having a go at him later. He did not come into the bedroom to see me.

I was taken by ambulance to Herman Hill Hospital in Wanstead, my chest sounding like a rusty gate. The ward was long, with beds on both sides – there must have been thirty or so. A lady, Dr Barsby, was nice to me and gave me a through examination. The funny thing is that I felt better as soon as I was in hospital. I did not know then what a bottle was, though I heard people calling for them. I was busting for a wee, and finally caught on. 'Bottle, nurse!' When one was eventually brought, I filled it and asked for another, which I also filled to the brim. The bedpan I could not use. When the curtains were drawn around the bed, I got out of bed and placed the pan on the floor, to the amusement of the chap in the opposite bed, who could see my feet under the drawn curtains.

A few days later the squeaking in my chest had gone. A lady doctor gave me a sweet to suck. It seemed to swell my tongue. I was wheeled from the ward to a side room, and placed on a tilted bed where the students gathered around me. Doctor Barsby started to oil a long steel tube while she spoke to the students, then told me not to cough and started to ease the tube down my throat. It started to irritate. 'Don't move!' she said. As the students took turns looking down my throat, I had to grip the sides of the table; I felt that if I coughed I would have broken my neck – it must have been a yard long! It seemed that the tube was never-ending, going down my throat.

They thought I had TB. I had my doubts, as they had tested me and the other patients for TB. I noticed that I was the only one whose injection on the arm did not rise into a bump. Mum would bring me food and also homemade wine, mixed with lemonade. I would share the drink with the rest of the patients. Lucky for me, I would have the first drink. (What did I know about TB?) In Herman Hill Hospital the TB patients were kept separate from the rest of the patients. We were kept in the corridors of the hospital, and during the day we were wheeled out on to a walkway that led to another part of the hospital, where we could breathe fresh air. We were wheeled in our beds between these locations. Obviously the hospital could not cope with all the TB patients and I was transferred to Bloomfield by ambulance. I don't recall any one else coming with me.

## Bloomfield Hospital

Bloomfield Hospital is near Chelmsford. All I can remember was that it was in the country and very quiet. We each had small single rooms. In the next room was a chap from Walthamstow, a perky lad. We would talk together when we were wheeled on to the balcony for fresh air. Real fresh air! On the second day the doctor examined me, and then started unwinding a coil of rubber hose! He said not to worry – just to swallow slowly. I thought, this is better than the tube! It was no trouble. The doctor then asked me if I was getting enough to eat at home. I must have been skinny. They looked after me well; the food was ample and I did not leave any on my plate. As far as I can remember, it was better than what we had at home.

The only activity we had was long walks around the gardens – that was when we were allowed to get out of bed. The chap next to me was a bit of a card; he came from E17. He'd play the comb with a piece of paper over the teeth, and knock out a tune with me banging the rhythm out on the side of a steel cabinet.

I had one surprise: my father and mother came to see me. It was the first time he had come while I was in hospital. One night, as I was asleep, I was half woken by a noise – it was the noise of love! I turned over, and saw a nurse in my room entangled with a patient, her skirt was way up. I always wanted to know what they did. What did I do? I turned over and went back to sleep. (Ho, you puritan, you!) Next morning the nurse said she was sorry; I said that I saw nothing. She was pretty. Later on this chap came and also apologised. I did not know him, but I hated him! Why him and not me? I would have known all about *cova*. You know what I mean!

While we were on the veranda, I saw an amazing thing. I was stung by a bee; I pulled it off and threw it on the floor. It was not dead, and I pulled the sting out which had its bum still attached to it. Another bee came, flew to it, clasped it with its legs and flew off with it. What was that about?

I am happy to say that I was out of there after two months, and even happier to be home. I did not have TB. I did have a weak chest, with all the fluff that had got into my lungs, plus the long working days.

(Years later my nephew, Mark, was in the same hospital – with a broken neck after diving in shallow water at Dovercourt. He too made a full recovery. Mad as a March hare!)

# Opportunity Lost

On returning to the shop, I did not go back on the buff! One of Dad's clients, who worked in an engineering factory in Billet Road, asked my father if I would like to work in the factory, as a barber. They were doing so much overtime for the war effort that they had no time for anything else. My dear father said, 'Yes.' I went for an interview and got on very well with the manager, who showed me the room set aside for hairdressing with a chair and basin, plus a phone to call the departments, to instruct them to make their way up at a spaced interval.

He asked me how I would like to be paid – a wage from the company, or to charge the men individually. After a little thought I said that I would charge them. It was all agreed for me to start. I told my dear father what had happened and that I was to start next week. Next day he said I was not going; it would be too much for me. He had not thought that I would get the job! I think he got jealous. He knew my ability as a worker. On the bright side, if I had taken the work on, I most likely would not have gone to work in the country, which was an experience I would have missed.

*Ugo's mates*

The photo above were clients, they were my brother's mates. Well, Ray thought he was a mate. I used to hang in and around the billiard hall above Burtons on the corner of the High Street and Hoe Street. I also used Burtons, when the boys above were younger and still in school. (It was hit by a flying bomb later in the war, when I was working in Surrey.) It was there, having a game of snooker, that I met Joe Modes, who was managing a barbershop, opposite the Palace Theatre. On chatting, he found that I cut hair and offered me a job on trial. I was fifteen years old. I went home and told my father and he promptly said, 'You're not good enough!' But this time I said I was going.

Joe's shop had two chairs, and at the back a ladies' salon, the owner of which was a Mr Morris, a nice man whom I gave the trial haircut. Joe was pleased with it and I was offered four pounds a week with tips. I was over the moon, and started the next Monday morning. My mother, bless her, said that she would take three pounds and buy all my needs. I never found out what my needs were, unless it was the woollen vest that drove me mad with the itch?

Later, I learned that my mates were giving their mothers one pound ten shillings a week. On coming home from work at 6 p.m., at my mother's pious request, I would assist the old bugger. This was as soon as I stepped in the house! No tea until the shop closed at 8 p.m. But eventually help was at hand. Elmo was now old enough to help the old man out. They made a good pair, and Elmo would become a good gambler under his guidance.

I was happy working with Joe. He was Yiddish, as was the shop and the majority of the clients. They gave good tips, but your work had to be good. I have an ear for languages and soon picked up some Yiddish. They called me the 'Yok with the Yiddisher Kop'. I had some belly laughs. I would stay out as long as I could – the atmosphere was always heavy at home – but I still had to be home by ten o'clock. I had Thursday afternoons off. I knew I was doing well, as I started to smoke Players instead of Woodbines, and also played snooker at the top of the High Street 'Burtons'. The wide boys would try to get me to play for money but I knew that I was not good enough and only played for the table. Was I beginning to live or not?

## Jerry de Lacy

Frances was in the ATS and had started to court Jerry de Lacy, a Scots Irish soldier. They married just before the end of the war, so that he could be demobbed earlier. When Jerry came home on leave he'd sleep at our home. My father let him sleep in my small bedroom, and I slept with Elmo. I can still hear the old man bemoaning, 'Sleeping and eating, and nothing in return?' If he had his own way, Jerry would have been sleeping in the smallest room, but that was in the garden! I invited Jerry for a drink – he was taken aback when he found himself in the café where the boys met. I bought him a hot chocolate! To his credit, he drank it, and came back to the house. I wonder what he said to Fran? For a man who drank pints, without the beer touching the sides of his throat, he did well drinking that hot chocolate, but never came with me again. After the war, he tried to make me a drinker at the Flower Pot pub on Wood Street, and a few others like the pub in Queens Road, but drinking was not my scene.

(I was surprised to learn that Jerry was the one who, on my enforced return to E17, nailed me to the shop. Frances had arranged the meeting with the solicitor in Hoe Street. I thought the lease was to be signed over to me. Instead, it was to bind me to the shop, stating that I could not sell the shop while my mother was alive. Frances said in later years, 'You always wanted the shop!' I could not reply, as she was very ill. I wanted the shop. Like a hole in my bloody head! The family don't want to know what it cost me, returning to Gosport Road! There is an old saying: 'What a tangled web we weave, when first we practice to deceive!' It was later in life that I found that I had paid a very heavy price through the conniving of my family.)

# E17 to Commercial Road (1941)

Joe left the shop in the High Street to take over another hair-dresser's shop off Commercial Road, near Hessel Street Market, a completely Jewish area. He asked me to go with him with extra wages as the pull. I said, 'Yes,' to get further away from Gosport Road. This time I did not tell my parents how much I was earning. I was yet to reach my sixteenth birthday. To get to my new employment, I had to take a train from James Street Station to Liverpool Street station, then a bus up Commercial Road. It was the road before Hessel Street Market that I walked down, passing a café on the right with the lovely smell of food coming from the open doors. At the bottom was a T-junction, and opposite was the two-chair barbershop that you stepped up two steps to enter. Obliquely to the barbershop was a bread shop. I have never tasted bread like they made there, before or since! If it were there today, I could still find it by following the aroma. Ben Cohen was the owner of the barbershop. Ben did not work in the shop at all; he left it to Joe Modes to run it for him. It had an old-fashioned Jewish clientele, where clients would meet for a chat and not always for a trim. It was all new to me as the atmosphere was so different from the Jewish people in Walthamstow. But I was pleased to be further away from the family.

Shaving was not my strong point, and Jewish men had the strongest of beards. My razor would jump all around their faces when it met the bristles that were like bits of steel. But they were good to me and stood for my rough shaving. I quickly settled in and Joe would leave me on my own in the shop.

On one morning, the first client to come into the barbershop had long hair. It covered the side of his ears, hanging down in ringlets. I was on my own; Joe had gone out. I thought to myself, 'What a schnorrer!' He sat in my chair, easing his thin black trousers from the cleft of his arse as I started to cut his hair. First I cut the long curl from the side of his ear – with a yell he leaped from the chair, picked up the lock of hair that I had cut off, shouted something to me in Jewish, and ran from the shop! I thought he had gone mad.

When Joe came back, I told him what had happened. He went very quiet and then left the shop in a hurry to sort things out. The Orthodox Jew had thought that I was Jewish. I had not seen an Orthodox Jew in Walthamstow; I saw the long hair, so I cut it off!

Another client would come into the shop three times a week for a shave. He had a very thin moustache. The razor used to jump on his beard. It was like a horse jumping over a hurdle. He must have liked it, because he still came in the shop. On this day, he came in and I lathered his face. I used to show his moustache by removing the lather with my finger. I don't know what happened that day, but I shaved it off! I did not say a word; after all, it was very thin. Two days later, he came in again. I lathered him and made my confession. 'Don't worry,' he said, 'I did not notice it had gone until this morning. I shan't bother with it any more.' He had had the moustache since he was a young man and he was well into his sixties. Another one whose life I had changed.

A lot of black Yanks used to hang around Hessel Street Market. I had never cut a coloured man's hair until that day, when three American soldiers came into the shop for haircuts. The first one sat in my chair; his hair was very tightly curled close to his head. I did not know where to start. I used the clippers on the sides and back: that was OK, but I was stumped with what to do with the top. I was trying to comb it through, getting into a right kettle of fish. One of the other soldiers said, 'You've never cut a coloured boy's hair before, have you?' I said, 'No, I haven't.' He then showed me how to do it. He used the clippers to cut the curls on top; just short enough to be able to comb them through. It turned out he was a hairdresser back home and I thanked him for the lesson.

Joe was a nice fellow to me, but he had bad habits. Joe would wait till I had put a hot towel on an American's face if he came on his own, and then quickly go down his jacket that was hanging at the back on a peg. I was taken aback, but what could I do? Later that day three more black Yanks came in to the shop with a Jewish girl, while Joe and I were working. They took their seats at the back of the shop. My eyes were all over the place! The Yanks were pawing the girl with their hands up her skirt; she was giggling away, enjoying it. The chap that I was attending to had the worst haircut that day – I don't think he noticed, as he was busy looking also. She came into the shop the following day and was, to my young eyes, very pretty. She was telling Joe how much she had earned from the Yanks, saying that after the war, she would be well off. It was the first prostitute I had met!

Frances came to see me where I worked when she came home on leave from the ATS – most likely to get away from the family. After a little chat she left. The black Yank whose hair I was cutting said, 'I'll take your sister out tonight.' I said, 'You bloody won't!' He gave a grin. I was not quite sixteen, and small with it. To me he looked like a giant.

At the weekend I had the job of lighting the fire at Ben's flat, just around the corner from the shop, switching on the lights and even taking the money; they were not allowed to touch *gelt* (money). It was a Jewish thing. There were a lot of black Yanks around that area.

I had got myself into a fight down the High Street in Walthamstow; my face was in a bit of a mess. The Jewish lads wanted to come down and turn over my assailants for me. They were not all soft as some people think. Some were very tough! They said that I was beaten with knuckledusters. I told them that it was my fault, it was only to look good in front of the girls, and it backfired. It happened like this. Being small I was cocky (have you noticed that many short people are cocky?). My mate and I – he was smaller then me – passed two blokes sitting on the edge of the wall near the corner of Willow Walk, talking to two girls. I tripped over a raised pavement stone and blamed one of the blokes for tripping me up. He stood up, head and shoulders above me, and said, 'You want some?' I said, 'You put your foot out, and tripped me up!' as I swallowed hard! I could never back down. We went into Linden Road, up the alley behind the jewellers. It was me who suggested going up the alley. We squared up, and he hit me so hard that I staggered down the alley into the road. It was a long alley! He followed me and started to punch me (I don't recall any knuckledusters). I could not get near to him at first, but when I did, I took him to the ground and had a go at him. He was too strong for me. I think he wore himself out punching me. That was how it ended.

I did ask a bloke who was passing by for help, but that was asking for too much. He wanted to give my mate one. I got between them – my mate was frozen to the spot. He lived on the right-hand side over the road next door to a family whose son was killed in Lea Bridge Road by a bomb coming home on a bus. I think he was a postman. Next day I met them just under the bridge in Willow Walk. I had a razor in my pocket and a knuckleduster loaned to me by my mate's brother who was home on leave from the Navy. All they wanted to do was talk. I can't remember what the talk was about. Maybe he was saying, 'If I see you again I'll give you another one.' I'm glad I did not use the razor, but I did note that win or lose, they never came back for more. (It was my father who gave me the razor.)

I left Joe Modes and my Yiddish clients with regrets. It was a different life that I would not have known had it not have been for the war! Now I was off to another phase of my life, away from London. Again I was happy in retrospect to be further away from the family. I missed my mates from Walthamstow, and wished that I were with them. Instead, they made me an enemy alien at the age of sixteen.

# Wartime in Surrey

In 1941, Frances and I had to go to Forest Road Police Station in Walthamstow. The officer behind the desk spoke and asked Frances if she wanted to stay British, as she was born in Scotland. She answered, 'Yes. I'm Scottish!' She was eventually called into the ATS, and posted to Dover. I was also asked and replied with arrogance, 'I'm Italian!' (I was always contrary to my sister.) I can't recall anything else said. Did they explain what it was all about with us? After all, I was only sixteen! It would have been a different book of memories that I would be writing, had they done so.

*Frances in ATS*

Before writing further, I would like to say I was sorry for not going into the Forces, as all my mates were English. If the interview at Forest Road had been handled better, saying that when I reached the age of sixteen I would have a choice that would have been my out from the family! Me being Italian did not bother my mates. On leave they used to tell me all that had happened, their ups and downs. I had some trouble with my nationality, but nothing I could not handle on my own (cocky sod).

On reaching the age of sixteen, I was summoned by the powers-that-be to Dean Street in the West End of London. I cannot remember clearly, but I do remember entering an office – it was quite spacious, filled with clerks. I had been there before. Something must have happened the first time. As I entered the office the second time around someone shouted, 'Look out! Here he comes!' and they all ducked behind their desks. I knew I was cheeky and had a chip on my shoulder but, for the life of me, I cannot remember what happened or what I had done to cause that reaction. They seemed to enjoy the situation.

When I reached the age of sixteen, I was given a choice: to work in a factory or in the country to do my bit for the war, or to be interned. I chose the country, to get away from home. I knew that I'd be working in the shop after coming home from the factory! Before I left, my mother gave me this advice, 'Look out for the English girls – they will make you *cova* [squat]. Wait until you get to Italy and pick a flower that's never been plucked.' I acquired an alien registration book with my photograph and particulars, and off I went to Victoria Station, wearing my itchy woollen vest, with no one to see me off, and looking forward to the squat. (I wondered if it was what I thought it was?) I was so slow – still I was looking to pluck the flower wherever it was, but where was it?

# Reigate, Surrey

I arrived at Redhill Railway Station, picked up a bus that had Reigate on the front and found the house. It was where the buses turned round for their return journey to Redhill. I had a letter of introduction for the lady. There were four Italians in this house; Gino, Joe, Cesere and me. We all arrived separately. The lady, Mrs King, also had one kid of her own. It was very slapdash and we all washed in the kitchen sink. This was no change from home! Cesere was the odd one out; he never used soap, only cold water. He said it kept the skin fresh. He thought himself a singer and a cut above us. Obviously, he did not come from E17. I can't remember too much about Reigate, as we did not stay there too long. It was too cramped for all of us, sleeping, eating – I can't remember sitting with the family to eat. I can't remember where and how we slept. I'll have to ask Gino. We still keep in touch. Gino tells me we were getting three pounds fifty pence per week. I thought it was two pounds fifty. I'm sure it was!

*Ugo's Alien Registration document*

# Redhill

On 1 July 1943 Gino, Joe and I went moaning to the ones in charge of us that we were living like sardines. Somehow thy found us new accommodation. Cesere did not come with us; he was happy where he was, with plenty of soap that he never used. We were moved to a fine house by the name of 'Ilsley' in London Road. Opposite the house, there was a large public park. The three ladies of the house were mature ladies; one was old and blind. The two sighted ladies were called Mrs Warren and Miss Stone. They looked after us par excellence. We were well fed and clean, as there was a bath in the house – well I never. The blind lady would run her fingers over our faces with a very light touch.

We were informed at what point in town to await the lorries taking us to work. The three of us were allotted different points to wait at. I was picked up in the centre of Redhill (ten minutes' walk from our house) by an army truck. It was filled with Land Army girls, all singing, 'Roll me over, lay me down and do it again.' They all looked me up and down; I looked straight ahead – I was not yet into girls. Anyway, they were sitting, not squatting. Sex; we could talk as if we knew it all, but you know – I knew nothing, yet was cocky with it (was that a joke?).

After the war, I took Marie to meet the ladies; Mrs Warren and Miss Stone made us very welcome. They had not changed at all. The blind lady had died while we were living there, a sad time for us all. I was told off by Miss Stone for calling Marie my girlfriend instead of my fiancée. They were very kind people, and we thought a lot of them. You become selfish and forget people who have been kind to you! It is only as you get older and start to regress that you realise how lucky you were to have met them.

We had a foreman called George in charge of us. He was old, but we liked him. He used to smoke his cigarette until the only thing left was the hole between his lips, holding the husk of the cigarette paper, plus a nicotine stain on the upper and lower lip. He came from Crawley. The group was supplied with an axe a piece, to clear a small wood, the trees no wider than a sapling. I swung my axe with force at a tree. The axe rebounded off it! I looked at the tree, no more than twelve inches in circumference; I had barely marked it. Eventually, I could cut a good-sized tree, nice and clean, instead of chewing at it. We paid one pound and fifty pence a week in rent to the old dears; there was not a lot left. None of us was a drinker; we never went to the pub, but made our own fun.

*Gino, Ugo and Joe*

Joe, Gino and I, on returning home to Ilsley from work, would always find our dinner waiting, after washing of course – the ladies made sure of that. They fed us well and packed our lunch to take to work. Who said that the English couldn't cook? They were great! We became a family. Gino played the accordion well, although he drove us mad with his practising. Gino and Joe were six-footers; I made it up with aggression.

After a few months, the ladies told us that they had believed we were French. We were taken aback at this, and thought the end had come for us. I spoke for the lads and said that we would leave, as we did not want to offend them. But they would not hear of it, which pleased us no end (I was never shy in coming forward!).

London Road at that time ran to the centre of Redhill past Ilsley and round the bend towards Crawley. Opposite our house, the park ran nearly to the town centre, passing a few shops on the way. From Ilsley there were nice houses; to the right a pub, and houses which led to the church on the top of an incline that led to the centre where there were offices, and a police station. After a few more shops, you came to the crossroads at the centre of town. A pub on the corner faced a barbershop; I could not muster courage to apply there for a weekend job but (no!) went home instead.

We worked around Surrey, especially on the Buckland Estate, a large area, sawing branches off the gigantic oak trees that overhung the fields to make it easy to harvest the wheat.

Being young, we did silly things. They were high trees on which we used to play Tarzan. I tied a rope that reached the ground on this high branch of an oak tree. From where I was perched, the boys looked small. I shouted to them to hold the rope for me. The rope was about five feet away from me. Instead of jumping straight at the rope, I dived at it (I was only young!). Luckily, I grabbed the rope with both hands and did not let go, but the weight of my body was too much for my hold on the rope. I shot down the rope, my body swinging everywhere because I was coming down headfirst! At that stage, I saw the boys who had been holding the rope scatter, leaving me to swing more violently! Somehow, I managed to land on my feet, sinking to my knees. My hands were burnt, but luckily, that was all. I never did Tarzan again!

*Ugo, Angelo and Ugenio*

I would cycle to work from Redhill. We were allotted to different farms, when no transport was available in the winter. My eyebrows accumulated a cover of frost, with the winter winds blowing against you and that bloody heavy bike! I'd always meet this Land Army girl just past Redhill Railway Bridge; we cycled part of the way together, and then it would turn into a race. She always beat me! In the winter it was sugar beet frozen in the ground. We'd gather in a shed with the Italian boys from Godstone, and get in among the straw, to keep warm. It was a hell of a job for the foreman to get us going. Pull them up, chop the top with your billhook, and throw them on a pile that was accumulating. When we started, your hands would be so cold that you could not hold the billhook. After five or ten minutes your hands would be warm as toast.

When we came to a prisoner-of-war camp, it was not hard to slip under the wire, and draw the attention of the Italians. We'd just talk with the prisoners and give them cigarettes, which we could ill afford. On this particular occasion, Gino and I (I can't remember Joe being involved) had crawled through the wire – it was not difficult and we were getting better at it! We'd draw the attention of the prisoners, who were on the periphery of the camp. They were always pleased to see us. As we were handing over the cigarettes, we heard a shout, 'I can see you!' The prisoners scattered. I was through the wire before Gino – he was six feet tall, while I was only five foot eight (and shrinking!). I ran up the lane as if my arse was on fire. Hearing feet pounding the ground, I thought I'd had it, when Gino came flying past me! I could not run any more, so I darted into a small hazel coppice. The trees were thin, but I hid behind one with three-quarters of my body showing. A voice behind me said, 'Come out of there.' It was a military policeman with a blue band around his cap.

Gino was stopped by a farmer further up the lane and detained. We were not put into a compound with guns pointing at us, just told to, 'stand there and keep quiet!' We were told, after a longish wait, that we were in trouble. We were led in front of officers who were sitting at a long table in a field, as if they knew what was about to happen, and were waiting for us. They looked high up – top brass? There were a few soldiers in the background.

I must say I was cocky, but Gino had more sense than me. The sergeant brought us forward to the table – they did look stern. I cannot recall what questions we were asked, but they soon realised that we were idiots, and let us off with a warning. We were warned if we did it again, we would find ourselves wearing the monkey suits, a term we used to refer to the uniform that was worn by the prisoners.

Another time, working on the Buckland Estate, George the foreman had told us that there had been a party in the big house lasting well into the night. We were clearing a hedge; I was using a billhook and cut my finger just below the nail. It bloody hurt! I was told to go to the farmhouse, and a lady tended to the wound for me. I remember asking for water, as it had made me feel queasy. Later that afternoon, a Spitfire started buzzing the house, swooping very low. The people of the house were coming out and waving to it. The last time he came down, he went too low and crashed! We all ran over, but there was not much of him left. Poor sod.

# Godstone

I left the comfort of Ilsley, and my two mates, Gino and Joe, to rough it in a hostel in Ivy Mill Lane, Godstone. Before I left, I was called to the unemployment office in Redhill where this chap, who was quite nice, had a good talk with me, and asked if I would like to join the British Army. If only they had asked me before I had got to know the Italian boys, as I had never known any before, I would have gone in. I did think hard, but I would have not been able to face the boys, so I declined the offer. I always wondered why they asked me and not the other lads – though some of the older Italians would disappear from time to time. I just thought that they were shifted around. (It was when my mate, Fred, sent me a book on the Isles of Man where my father was interned that I remembered that the old bugger was sent home because he volunteered to join up! He was rejected as not fit; shame!)

To go to London for the weekend, I would first have to report to the local police station in Redhill, and on arriving in

Walthamstow, I'd report to Leyton Police Station in Frances Road, and would reverse the procedure, on my return. Frances, who was in the ATS in the thick of it in Dover, came to the police station with me. She raged at the poor copper behind the desk, saying, 'Why is he an enemy alien and I'm in the ATS?' I felt sorry for the copper. I came home a few times without reporting, but got caught on returning to Redhill, and ended up in court. It was an experience. I had sat in the wrong place, and found myself in where the police sat. They sat around me when they took their places, as if I was under guard. The magistrate had me moved, to the laughter of the court. I was fined twenty-five shillings, my week's spending money, to be paid off at half-a-crown a week at the police station. On my next weekend home, I had to report to an army office outside Whipps Cross Hospital, Leytonstone. It was a more of a hut on the green. The officer took my alien book, looked me in the eye, opened it, took his rubber stamp and marked the page with a great thump and pleasure in red ink! Enemy Alien it read. I was only sixteen.

## Back to Surrey

I liked to be with the boys in the hostel. There was a mixture of nationalities. We slept in bunks in two long rooms, and there was a recreation area with table tennis. We went about in gangs (well, one gang, four of us). Godstone was a nice village, with a green on which cricket was played at the weekends. I used to lie on the green shaded by a tree; in the background would be the sound of ball hitting the bat and the buzzing of the bees; it was so peaceful that I would go to sleep. The hostel had a German prisoner who was the hostel's cook. We got on very well with him. One day we caught several pigeons, which had tags on their feet marked 'MOD' (what did we know?). We broke their legs to remove the tags, and plucked the feathers. This was all by the roadside. With the wind blowing, it looked as if it was snowing, with all the feathers flying about in all directions. We took the pigeons nice and clean, to the German cook, who proceeded to stuff them with bacon. We had them later with our tea. It caused some jealousy, with the 18 B's, (Englishmen who refused to go into the army) but we did not care. The cook taught us some German marching songs and we sang them with gusto. One of the Italian boys, older than us, was a good fighter. You did not mess about with him. He tried to teach me how to fight, as I was the youngest and the smallest there. He packed his girl up as by all accounts, she farted while on the job. He knew what *cova* was; why not tell me? Later he disappeared.

We would meet three Land Army girls whom we became friends with and muck about on the village green in Godstone – nothing serious. You know what boys are. My mates got fed up and broke away from the girls – except me. I made a date to meet my girl in Redhill the following day. Do you know what they did? They locked me in a shed for two hours! The rotten sods! That was the end of my first courtship and my chance of finding out what *cova* was. In the evening, we would gather at the edge of the green and sing Italian songs. When people started coming out of their houses, we thought that we had upset them, but no! They said they were enjoying the singing.

I got friendly with a nice-looking girl who lived in Purley. Being a gentleman, I would take her home by bus, to where I can't remember, but it was a very nice house. I think I got a kiss and was sent packing. I do remember walking all the way from Purley to Godstone! I had not reached the stage of *cova* yet – where is it? There was a curfew, and I should have been back in the hostel in Ivy Mill Lane by ten o'clock. I did not arrive back until midnight, and on the way did not meet a soul. Walking those lanes was scary, expecting to get shot, and every tree was someone coming to get me. After all, I was not yet seventeen years old. I did meet her again in Godstone, at a dance at the village hall. It was full of (young) sailors. I, inquisitive, poked my nose around the door and saw her the same time she saw me. She came to the door to speak to me. The young sailor whom she was dancing with came with her, and told me to bog off! As he pulled her back into the hall, I'd like to think she resisted a bit. (I don't know why we were not invited.) Would I ever find this squat?

Where we slept was like army barracks; it was built of wood, long and combined with the recreation hall that had a ping-pong table plus a room that accommodated all the inmates. There was a long table where we'd eat. The German was at the end cooking and dishing it out. I enjoyed the atmosphere – all hustle and bustle.

There was only one toilet between thirty or so people and it was situated at the furthest end of the dormitory. My bunk was near the entrance. One night I got up to do a wee, and had to pass through this room. In doing so, I saw my mate, called Ugenio, get up from his bunk and go to the toilet before I reached his bunk. Angelo, who slept on the lower one, was out for the count. I climbed into Ugenio's bunk and hid my face – just one eye peeking out. Ugenio came back, went to climb in and stopped dead. He took a good look and walked down the aisle; he looked around then came back, he did not know whether he was coming or going. He stood there looking at his bunk, never once did he look at Angelo. I could not control myself any longer. I leapt out of his bunk and did a runner. The names he called me; you would never believe it! I came from the Latina region of Italy and they came from the north; we got on well. There were English (18 Bs) who did not want to fight, some German Jews and Italians with English names like Nelson. There was a turnover of faces; new ones would appear, old faces would be missing.

Working in a desolate spot, we came across sheds that had military markings. We broke in, and found boxes of hand grenades! We took as many as the five of us could carry, although we had never handled such things before; did a little drop of pee tingle down the leg? At night, just outside Godstone, we pulled the pins and threw them in the water, not thinking about the noise of the explosion. Luckily, for us, they did not go off with a bang, more of a splash. They could not have been primed. We could have killed or maimed ourselves, or ended in prison – silly sods!

When we heard our first Doodlebug, we all rushed out of our digs, not knowing what it was. As the engine cut out the others all scattered! I was soon behind them, but I did not get far, as a hand grabbed me by the neck and my feet were treading air. It was Gerolemo, a big husky Italian built like a tank. He said, 'Let them run; we will not!' I would have done if he'd let me go! The bugs exploded in Croydon – quite a few landed there. Working on top of a hill overlooking Croydon on a lovely summer's day, clearing the ground for planting, we heard the drone of the doodle; it cut its engine right above us. We threw ourselves to the ground and saw it plunge down into Croydon. As we were about to get up, Angelo yelled, 'Another one!' It had already cut out and glided in behind us, again right into Croydon! I didn't then know how they did it. Apparently, the bug had just the right amount of fuel to reach any target, and when it ran out of fuel down it came – simple really. We were too far away to help or see the damage caused. I could not understand how they got through, as my sister was shooting them down at Dover! If the shells failed to bring them down, I'm sure she could have brought them down with her tongue.

We worked hard and liked it. We had fun. One afternoon I was asked to fetch a shovel from the barn. On doing so and picking up the shovel, I noticed a mattress and on it a lay a long snake. With my shovel raised, I crept up on the snake and gave it a nasty whack. It jumped up in the air. I hit again and again. The more I hit it the higher it jumped! There was a roar of laughter. The boys were all watching my battle with a dead snake, the springs of the mattress had made it jump up and down.

Pulling a tree root from a swampy area, we tied a strong rope around it, and six of the boys pulled. The knot had not been tied properly, and slipped off the stump and we all landed in the water. What did we know about knots? We all came from London! We were always laughing and chasing water rats – the rats on the farms were very clean and looked like rabbits. Digging a ditch, the farmer came with his little terrier. We came across a hole in the bank. The farmer and his dog stood at the other end of the hole, and we dug along the hole in the bank; as we got near the end the rat shot out of the hole. The terrier got it between his jaws, gave it a shake and it was dead.

What with snakes and beer, I did not miss London at all. I particularly liked harvest time. The sun shone on us stripped to the waist, showing off in front of the land girls, two sheaves on the pitchforks. What I was doing riding on the side of the tractor, I do not know. A nice-looking Land Army girl was driving, and every time she leaned over to change gears, she rested her chest on my hand that was holding on. The foreman got on the other side of the tractor and told me to get off. I held my corner for a while – after all, I was enjoying the moment. I think he got jealous.

Another silly episode involved Gino and me. We were working together clearing an area of brambles and a party of Italian prisoners of war marched by, a corporal in front and another at the rear with rifles on their shoulders. Of course, we tagged in behind them just for a talk with the prisoners. The corporal stopped the group and told us to bugger off. I replied in the same vein. He said, 'I told you to f— off!' The POWs had not moved. I told him where to go! He unslung his rifle and stuck it in my stomach (did I feel a drop of pee, down my leg?). I had a bag that held my lunch and also a bottle of drink. I took the bottle out and threatened the solder with it! The prisoners broke rank and had the solders in a circle. The corporal hung his rifle on his shoulder, shouting that he would report the incident at the camp. The Italian in charge ordered the POWs in line and off they marched. We never heard any more about it, but it was one of the silliest things I had ever done. In Germany, it might have had a different ending. I was told later on that the guards always had a bullet 'up the spout'. Was I lucky or what?

We played football against a team of German Jews who were also working on the land. Gino arranged the match; it was the worst thing he could have done! I had not kicked a ball for some time, and that was a bundle of rugs! I'm sure the boys had never seen one, as they all lived in London. We all ran out of steam; but I may say that I was the only one to get near the goal and then to shoot, only for the keeper to save my feeble shot. The score was nine to them and nil to us! Gino was not happy when he read this. 'I did not want to be reminded of it!' he said.

I became friendly with two Italian POWs, whom we saved from a punch-up with a couple of Canadian solders. On finding out that, I was a barber, they returned to the farm where they worked, and asked permission from the farmer for me to cut their hair. I can't remember the name of the farm, but will always remember the farmer and his wife, but again, to my shame, I can't recall their names, which upsets me, as I was really fond of them.

I would cut their hair as well as that of the Italians. Instead of going home at the weekends, I would go to the farm. The Italians would be back in their barracks. I learned to drive a tractor, and also a horse and cart, being quite a dab hand with the reins. I helped them as much as I could and had the run of the farm. They treated me as one of the family, having none of their own. I'd get among the cows and bullocks and twist their tails to get them to go where they should be! I loved it! To this day, I have always regretted going home.

One weekend, coming home from Godstone, Giovanne (John) Gerolemo said, 'Come and visit me in Islington.' I thought, Why not – it will get me away from Walthamstow.

I walked to the Bakers Arms to get a bus to Islington. I knew the address was near a well-known market. Eventually I found it. It was a tall building with two or three upper floors. John opened the door to my knocking and took me downstairs to the basement into a kitchen-cum-diner. John was a big lad, as were all the boys in the family. His father was even bigger, swearing in a northern accent, which was like a foreign language to me. More Germanic, he was holding a frying pan over an open fire and asked, 'Have you eaten?' Feeling somewhat nervous, I stuttered, 'No.' He broke two eggs into the pan, cut two slices of bread and handed me the frying pan, with the bread in it, saying, 'Eat!' I didn't hesitate. John later showed me around Islington – at that time it was a dump.

Two of John's brothers were blonde, big and strong. The eldest was Ernesto; he had brown hair, and was to join us for a short while in Godstone, but then disappeared. (He was the one who did not like his girls farting!) Nothing was said. Of others whom I met there was an Italian called Nelson – you can imagine what was said about him – and Zito, a Sicilian with arms like tree trunks.

Back in London, Ugenio, Gino, Johnny, Angelo and I would meet outside the church in Clerkenwell Road. We'd walk down the sloping road to the Italian club on the left, have a drink together and a chat. It always fascinated me, watching the Italians bashing their knuckles on the table playing More, like cut and thrust, very noisy. The chat would be about us going to

Argentina. We were adamant – there was nothing to stop us, but after a couple of months the boys got good jobs, Gino was into music, and I started to court Marie. Then we gradually drifted apart. Joe Fugacia is in Canada, and Ugenio in America. I still keep in touch, mostly by phone to Gino, and meet them now and then. Gino, who lives in London, is the one who keeps in touch with us all.

When Italy packed it in and it was time for me to go, I would have dinner with my friends the farmers. I used to eat there often at the weekends instead of going home. They asked me to stay with them and treated me like a son, but no; I wanted to go back to a family that had used me badly, from the time we arrived from Italy – what a fool I was! I was beginning to know the meaning of the word prat!

# Brighton

When the war was over, we still kept in touch with each other, and would meet nearly every Sunday morning outside the Catholic church in Farrington Road, Islington. We made arrangements to meet at Angelo's house and cycle to Brighton. The lads all had bikes except me. Angelo hired one for me, a heavy bike I still remember so well. Thanks Angelo!

I slept at Angelo's house in Camden. his mother gave me a jumper to wear (It seems that people were noticing that, where clothes were concerned, I was lacking). After breakfast, we set off early that Saturday morning before there was anybody about. It had been very hot the day previous, and on that morning it seemed hotter still. We were not more than ten minutes on the bikes before I came off, head over heels. In those days the roads in the city were laid with blocks of wood that were tarred. You could always smell the hot tar – it was said that it was good for you, but it killed you eventually. The heat of the sun had melted the tar and the blocks had risen. Not a good start – I wondered if I were doing the right thing. We met the rest of the boys at London Bridge, then cycled on to Croydon. Struggling with my heavy roadster past Croydon, I could not keep up with the boys and was holding them up. We stopped. I said, 'You go on and I'll meet you there!' I gave Angelo my money – why, I don't know. Off they went and I was left to my own resources.

I passed the house (Ilsley) in London road Redhill, but I could not stop, as I was too sweaty. I was getting hungry and thirsty. Cars had stopped on the green verge of the road; people were having a brew up and eating sandwiches with their families. I felt like jumping off my bike and pinching the food, but I would be too tired to sprint away. I stopped further on and picked dandelion leaves and ate them. My mother used to cook them like spinach (quite nice, with just a taste of bitterness).

Eventually my legs just made it to Brighton. With a long straight road under a big arch, to me it was like a Roman entering Brighton in triumph! I saw the sea! It led me to the beach where the boys were waiting for me. There was a resounding cheer from them, as they had nearly given me up. After all that hard work, the bloody beach had no sand! After resting and eating, in our swimming trunks we walked past the pier to the concrete fingers that stretched out into the sea. Gino plunged into the roughish sea and we all followed. As soon as I was in the water, I felt the current tugging at my legs. I did no more than swim back to the concrete. I'm not a good swimmer, and it took me some time just to swim back. At one time, struggling to get back, I thought of letting the current take me to the pier; then I'd be able to climb up the steel struts. That would have been bloody mad – I'd have been cut to pieces!

We were all back except Gino. We could see his head bobbing in the water far away. We were all shouting, 'Come back!' He took ages to do so, and was struggling all the way. It was only because he was a big strong boy and could swim well that he made it back. It was soon after that Gino went down with a chest complaint. I'm sure that day was the cause.

The day ended with no one wanting to admit that they did not want to cycle back to London. I said, 'If you think that I'm pushing that bloody bike back you can all *vafaculo*!' We were on that train to Victoria in record time, putting our bikes in the guard van. I often remind Gino of that episode and how lucky we were – especially Gino.

On coming to London for the weekend I'd go and visit Gino.

The train from Redhill finished its journey at Victoria. Gino's father had a café-cum-restaurant in Wilton Road opposite Victoria Station. Like me, Gino had to help his dad when he came home. When the war finished for the Italians, Gino was stuck in that café with his dad and hated it! (He had been studying Law when war broke out.) One day his father said that he was just off the see a friend up the road. He walked out of the restaurant with just a jacket, as he was not going far. After an hour Gino went to find him, but the friend had not seen him. He and the family searched high and low and eventually reported him missing. The police did nothing as they said there had to be a certain period of time before someone was regarded as missing. The family and friends continued their search in earnest, looking under bridges where the down-and-outs slept and along the nooks and crannies off Milbank Road, but of Gino's father, there was no sign. The Salvation Army did its best to trace him. To this day, Mr Lanzarote has not been seen. They put it down to sudden loss of memory. He was just over the road from Victoria Station, and could have gone anywhere.

But there is another sad tale to relate about Ugenio's family. During the Blitz a multitude of people sheltered in the underground Tube station. Ugenio's family were among them. During a heavy raid the Tube station was packed, though the trains were still running. Ugenio's dad had to go to the lavatory and on the way back found himself at the front of the platform. By all accounts it was the only way back. People were sleeping on bunks, on the floor, even sleeping leaning against the wall. The family say he was pushed, or did he fall? Who can tell? Not everyone was enamoured of the Italians at that time. There is always someone who hates that little bit more.

I really had no trouble as such – a little dig now and then, and the prat who tried to strangle me! The time comes to mind when the old man was 'on holiday' in the Isle of Man. There was a knock on the side door, and there in the gloom of the night stood Bloomfield's sister, a tall blonde girl. She looked me in the eye and said, 'My brother killed four Italians.' I think that I shrugged my shoulders and said 'So what?'

It was just before the war ended that I had racial trouble. I'm still looking for him! No one will tell me his name. (An army mate of Tom Giddins, the paratrooper?) Where are you? Give us a bell!

It was in Godstone that I caught mumps; I was told that it was catching. I think I had some medication, but was not separated from the rest. When the blokes found out that they would drink from my cup, they must have been sent home, as they disappeared. Yes they caught it – as you would! I did not know then that it made you infertile.

# Walthamstow Again

I returned to Walthamstow from Reigate, leaving leafy Surrey behind, on 5 November 1944. On arriving at Victoria Station I popped over the road to Lazarotes' restaurant for a cup of tea and a chat, then made my way to Liverpool Street Station, with the trains whistling and belching steam, with the smell that hung in the air that I remembered from my younger days. True to form, I was put to work in the barbershop as soon as I had arrived. My mother still said, 'Go and help your father,' and I would go like a lamb. No money was ever given to me by my father. My brother, Elmo, eventually took my place in the shop as a lather boy, and learned the trade as I did, shuffling around the chair. He learned how to handle Dad, by becoming like him!

I went to Morris, the hairdressers in the High Street, where I had worked before I went to Surrey. The barbershop was now managed by Ruby Cohen, who said he had no work for me. I was somewhat upset, thinking where to go. The following week, Ruby came into the shop where I was working for nothing, said that he had made inquires about me and had been told that I had worked in the shop previously, and that I was a good worker. It must have been Mr Morris, as he was still working in the ladies' salon at the rear of the gents' barbershop. Cohen offered me the job and I took it with both hands!

I got five pounds a week of which four had to go to the family. But the tips were all mine! It was the same wage as before I left. I did not care: I was out of Gosport Road. I was happy working in the High Street. We used to get all sorts of people in: actors from the Palace Theatre, the market traders and the Jewish shop owners. The old boy sold newspapers from outside the theatre. I wonder if one of my clients knew what his daughter had get up to in the shelter under Fish Brothers? It was not far from where he stood selling papers. Kid Berg, the ex-boxing champion of Great

Britain, appeared at the Palace (I think it was called The Red Barn). He came into the barbershop, and was a nice chap to talk to. He won more fights on disqualifications than any other fighter I've known! He had the habit of jumping up to land a punch. Therefore his opponent's counter-blow would land below the belt! He'd go down like a ton of bricks. He was called the Aldgate Tiger.

*Palace Music Hall, Walthamstow*

Jane with her dogs was a caricature from the daily paper – the *Daily Mirror* – strutting with the dogs, up and down the High Street. At night she posed on the stage, her feathers wrapped around her nude body. (They were not allowed to move in those days.) There were many plays; Murder at the Red Barn and so on. The lads and I would be up in the Gods waiting for Jane's fan to slip, it never bloody slipped. I can't recall the price, but I think it was three pennies. Not forgetting Sweeny Todd the barber (I'll soon polish them off!). 'Lilly of Laguna' was my favourite. I still sing it.

In the winter, (the weather seemed colder then), on coming out of the Palace, we'd stop at the baked potato man, an Italian, who had his pitch outside the Chequers pub. He'd break open the potato with his hands, and sprinkle on salt for a couple of coppers. They tasted great and warmed your hands also. Another Italian, who stood out in the same place in the summer, sold ice cream. (Or was it the same one?) At that time, it was kept cold by big blocks of ice, which were delivered to various shops, pubs and fish stalls in the High Street. The Iceman was very strong, and also Italian. He became a client of mine and acted as a minder for the West End Italians when they were being bothered by the Yanks during the war. His son took up boxing, but never had the punch that his father had, which would send them skidding along the cobbled street on their arse in the West End. This is true! Rocky Marciano became world Champion by doing the same thing in a pub in London.) He was well known down the High Street, with those big blocks of ice on his back. It's a shame he did not box!

I always enjoyed working with Jewish people; they had a good sense of humour, laughed all the time and trusted me. There was a client called 'Sailor', who would come in for a shave, and had Saint Vitus' Dance (a movement disorder). His head was always on the move, but I never cut him. I would lather his face, strop my razor, then, getting into motion, my body would do a little jig, up and down with my knees, following the motion of his head; that is, after a few dummy runs. He could play a good game of snooker in Lieberman's in the High Street (which was taken over by the Kray Twins later on).

I was on my own in the shop once and saw a client on his way, with the nickname of 'Duck', as he was so short, and very short-sighted. He was a street cleaner. Two white coats were hanging on the coat pegs at the back of the shop and I stood among them. He came in and did not see me, not even when I giggled. He shouted, 'I know you're there.' He turned his head left and right, but could not see me. I came out from among the coats and we had a good laugh. He was a nice man. It was looking out of the shop window that I saw Marie come out of the café next door to the Palace, after having her tea before starting work just a few shops down from the barbershop. Who knew what would be in store for us?

When finishing work, I'd take the long way round to get home and pass the butcher's next door to the Penny Arcade in Station Road E17. My friend, Peter Noble, worked there, and related what happened in the shop. At that time, he was renting the flat above my shop in Gosport Road. The butcher's had a walk-in freezer where the sides of meat were hung. A funny thing was happening: the tender part of the meat (the eye) was nearly always missing. No joy arguing with the delivery driver. This kept on happening for some weeks. One day Peter walked into the freezer and caught a movement with his eye. He looked closer, then ran out of the freezer shouting, 'There's a big animal in the freezer!' The manager took hold of the chopper, and running in saw a big bundle of fur. It was a rat! It had grown extra hair, and had been feeding itself from the best meat – the eye of the loin. God knows how long it had been there. It did not last long with the chopper! I hope they never sold it to get some of their losses back.

One of my clients' wives was very liberal, as was he. They lived not far from Elmo's barbershop, (his in-laws opened it for him when he came out of jail). Elmo told me that when the Krays came into his shop, she would come in and sit on their laps, allowing them to kiss and cuddle her, and she liked it. Then it started in Elmo's shop. Her husband knew what was going on but could do nothing about it. She was a good-looking girl, who worked at her brother's stall in the High Street selling dresses – I used to see a lot of ducking and diving, but never got involved; I was too young and had not found the *cova* yet! The owner's daughter, Rose, was a nice girl. I nearly took her out. I said I would take her to the Granada Cinema in Hoe Street. She turned up with her girlfriend; I was taken aback, as I had only enough money for two tickets. I said, 'I don't take two girls out together.' and they quickly walked away. I gave a sigh of relief. It would have been the first time that I took a girl out!

I was very happy working in Walthamstow in the High Street opposite the Palace Theatre. As I said, I had first seen Marie coming out of the café next door to the Palace Theatre, when I was looking out of Morris's shop window. She worked in a ladies' dress shop, just five shops down from the barbershop. I would look out for her in the mornings. I was invited to their shop Christmas bash, but went home early, as I was expected in by ten o'clock! I had not told Marie that I was going home. Marie came knocking on the door. My Father said, 'There's a girl asking for you.' I'm happy to say that the Giddins family brought me joy, from my late wife Marie, who brought me sorrow at the end, to my present wife, Norma, without whom I would be lost.

A year later Rose married. Morris, her father invited Ruby and me to his daughter's wedding, which was held opposite Aldgate Station in the City, where as a young boy I'd get the papers while my father would be reclining in his warm bed. I had never been to a Jewish wedding and it was an experience. I could not go into the synagogue, being a Catholic, so was told to sit on the boxes of whisky in the reception hall and not to move! When they returned, the buffet bar opened, and we all tucked in. I thought that was the meal, so I was getting it down. Then we were called to dinner! I was seated with some young girls who gave me a paper hat; I did not know what to do with it. One of the girls put it on my head – I did not know what was going on. Then the rabbi sang; he had a lovely voice. As far as I can remember I had a good time; the young girls did not want me to go. Marie had not been keen on me going to the wedding. I explained that I could not get out of it, as they employed me and had left as soon as I could. Though I must admit that, I would have loved to have stayed longer. On reflection, I should have – but who knew what lay waiting for me?

A shop came up for sale in Ealing Broadway, a newspaper stall, tobacconists and confectioner's at the front, with a door leading to a barbershop at the back. Marie and I went to see it, and it was ideal for Marie to manage the front shop, with me at the rear. We could have made a go at it, but when I asked my father for a deposit for it, as a loan, he said he did not have it. But he could always find money for his drinking mates and gambling. I had kept his shop open while he was away, earning enough to pay the rent and a little bit over for Mum, but he never gave me the drips off his nose. I would never ask him again for a penny!

My friend George Burgess, an artist, said that my father would be very embarrassing in the Ringwood pub. He would insist on buying drinks to whoever was in the pub, and would not take no for an answer. To top this, he gave money to Jerry's brother, James, when he was on leave from his unit. 'It was a small wad, Ugo!' James said to me later.

The owner of a café stall, near the Railway Bridge at the top end of Gosport Road was a client who loved his drink – Guinness – and would often be found on the floor behind the counter, paralytic. He used to describe the taste of Guinness to me as nectar – I could not even swallow it! One evening he came for his haircut and said he was going to sell the café-hut. Now, my father-in-law Tom used to help him out in the café. I was interested and asked him how much. The price seemed right and I said I'd see a solicitor in the morning.

Boyce, another client, also came in that evening for his haircut and I, big-mouth Ugo, told him all about the café that I was about to buy. I went to the solicitors next morning to talk it over. He said there was no problem, but did I want to seal it so that there could not be a change of mind. I said, 'No – it will be all right.' That was until I got back. In the afternoon, the Guinness man came round and was very low key. It turned out Boyce had paid him cash for the café that day! There you go.

Opposite the Standard pub was a newsagent, a client of mine; he told me a sad story. He went into the cobblers next to his shop to pick up his shoes that were being repaired. There was no one in the front, so he walked to the back of the shop, and stepped into sticky liquid. It was semi-dark and looking deeper into the gloom, he saw the chap on the floor. He had cut his throat with the shoe knife. He said, 'The blood nearly covered the whole floor!' He was quite ill. (No! Not the chap on the floor!)

On the other corner of Forest Road, at the Standard pub, was a factory (Rael Brooks). This will bring a smile on your face! A few of the higher-ups came to my shop, and told me about a lady who worked there. By all accounts, she was very sexy. She worked a system – when meeting one of them in the lift if she had her hair up, that meant a no, but if it were down to her shoulders, it was a yes! They told me it worked quite well. (The clients have to tell their conquests to someone! After all, I am a father confessor to my clients. Tell me all, no one will know. Trust me.)

A client whom I have known for ages told me about his escapades. On having a quiet drink in a pub, he got chatting with this girl. After a few drinks, they ended up in her flat. The foreplay ended on the floor. He always liked to chat, and in doing so, to their horror, they discovered that they were cousins! He, being what he was, said, 'Shall we finish?' He told me that he was out of the door *very* quick.

The burden on my shoulders was getting heavy. Two of my West Ham younger clients came and told me their harrowing experience that they had had in Amsterdam. They and two other mates went for the day, and made straight for the red light district (as you would!). They saw the girls displaying themselves in the windows, and felt a stirring in their loins. Then they found themselves a sex club – they had a choice of many to pick from – but chose the wrong one! Entering the dark club, the smoke hung like curtains. The cacophony of foreign tongues added to the atmosphere, and made it all very exciting for the lambs who did not know what it was all about – but would soon find out.

The show started with the girls fornicating together on the stage, to the shouting and braying of the crowd. Then there was the sex-act; the crowd were being worked up for the final act. The girls, still sweating and wet, faced the crowd, seeing that they were well worked up and hot for what was about to follow. One offered herself to the audience; 'Who's man enough for me?' One of the boys sprang from his chair and rushed on to the stage, making sure he would be first! She explained to him and the panting crowd that he could do whatever he liked with her, as long as she could do the same to him! He concurred.

After he spent his lust on her and was nodding to the applause of the lusting crowd, she stripped him, tied his hands together, bent him over a chair and secured his hands to the chair with a pink ribbon, leaving him with his head down and arse up! There was a roar from the crowd – he tried to see what was behind him, but could not. His mates saw and froze into their seats! A big black man, naked; he looked as if he had three legs. He had a tub of Vaseline in his hand; opening the lid, he put a dollop on the lad's backside, then with his spare leg in his hand entered him lustfully to the urging of the braying wolfs. The lad's eyes were popping out of his head, the crowd urging for more! The original girl cut the ribbon loose; he could not walk, his mates helped him off the stage, and staggered out of the club to the laughter of the crowd. They swore on oath never to tell anybody! But there is always me, the father confessor. (Tell me all, my son, it will be safe with me.)

They were not lucky like one of my other clients, who went on business to Amsterdam with a group from the firm, including the young lady secretary. The men went to the red quarter. He was not too keen in describing what happened. You've seen one you've seen them all. On regrouping at the hotel he was asked where he had been by the secretary – who by all accounts was a looker! He had had his eye on her for some time, and thought that he had no chance. He told her, and she said 'You don't need to go there, when I'm here.' There was no looking back for him after that. She'd tell him what was going on upstairs, and he would get the right answers when confronting the board on the men's rights, he being the union representative. Eventually she went abroad to marry. They kept their love affair going until the last night together! There was no hard feeling. He was a happily married man with a family, and still is. I knew him well. (Don't worry, I shan't tell.)

At the crossing at Highams Park is the undertaker. A client had a part-time job there – they all worked part-time. The corpse would be embalmed. The blood was drained off, dripping into a bucket. The face was made up to give it colour. If you were connected with the bearer of the bereaved, you would get a discount.

One of my clients managed to borrow twenty pounds from me! Two months went by and he came up with an offer; he could not pay back the twenty pounds, but would I take his watch in lieu? I thought, it's better then nothing. It seems like a good watch; I still have it! Did it fall from the back of a lorry?

I still can't forget when they wanted to fill my passage in Walthamstow with boxes of whisky for their Christmas orders. I held out by telling them that my mate was in the CID. It's true. I made sure that they all knew. You would be surprised how many of my clients told me off for not giving them a chance to buy the whisky. After all, are we not all greedy? When asked if I wanted any whisky I said, 'I'll have a couple,' not a couple of dozen. I suppose you would have refused? (I don't believe you!)

I was approached by another DI, whom I had known through my mate, to help him to compromise the massage parlours that were more than what they seemed. I did not want to be involved either way. I made that known. When I told my mate he said, 'Don't take notice of him, the only time he makes an arrest is when there is swag written on the sack!'

I've recommended some of my Judo students to the police; one has reached the top – is that right, Goodley? My nephew David is also getting there. I can't mention all – Robert and his wife Susan whom I'll always have good thoughts of. Jeff – do you remember the heavy throw I was teaching you, and were slow with your break-fall, knocking yourself out? It has not hampered your career – it has done you the world of good!

# Boxing

I took up boxing, at the Buxton Club in Buxton Road in 1945. My brother was a big boy, always fighting, he was roughly sixteen years old at the time. I persuaded Elmo to join the club. Elmo, much bigger than I, would not take to discipline. He eventually told them to stuff it and turned into a street fighter. His so-called mates would start a fight; Elmo would be standing apart from them, then would step in to help out! What a dickhead. He thought it was funny, not realising that he was been used. He was at the assembly town hall in Forest Road E17; a dance was held there every Saturday night. He was on his way to the toilets, which were below ground level. Long winding marble stairs, very plush, led him to the toilets to relieve himself, two blokes came to do their thing. As you would, you'd start speaking. 'We come from Tottenham-Hale, we are here to turn over a bloke called Elmo, do you know him?' 'Yes, he's in the dancehall,' says Elmo. 'Will you point him out to us?' 'Yes,' says Elmo. Then he turns, while they were still holding their fishing tackle in their hands, lashes into them and gives them a good hiding. That's what he told me! I must say, I've never seen his face marked!

I carried on with the boxing but I was too short for my weight, (middleweight) and lost more fights than I won. I once had a lad refuse to fight me, as he thought I was too good – he must have had me confused with someone else. My last fight was at Tottenham Municipal Baths in 1948. Young Jimmy Newman, who fought in later years for the Welterweight Championship against Malloy, was on the bill; he cried as his opponent did not turn up. I nearly cried when I saw mine!

My opponent, Nightingale, was very tall, and I was small for a middleweight. We were to fight for four rounds. It seemed like six! At the end of the second round, my corner man said, 'He does not like it in the belly; go for it.' Out I went, a roar, then another roar and I had him against the ropes, he was covering his head, the crowd shouting, 'Uppercut him!' They did not know that I had a ton weight on the end of my arms. If I'd tried to uppercut him, I'd have hit him in the balls! I lost the fight, but I can only remember the first round. From the first roar, I had fought for nearly two more rounds without knowing anything about it. I did not realise that they were trying to kill me. I was very sick in the dressing room and everything was spinning around. I think I did the right thing by giving up boxing for Judo. At least I only had my bones broken in Judo; they weren't trying to kill me... Wait a minute! I'll think about that.

I enjoyed Buxton Boxing Club, though on reflection, I think I was used by the trainer. 'Go easy,' he said to me as I started to spar with this ginger headed chap. I slowed down and glanced at the trainer. Then I was hit by a right-hander. I felt myself sinking down to my knees. I now know what they mean when they say 'he pulled himself up by his socks'. I gave him one, and the trainer stopped the sparring. This happened more than once. I was green, as I heard him describe me. It's a shame that Elmo did not continue with the boxing; he would have made a good heavyweight. I thought that I was tough, and would show off my bruises with pride. Will I ever grow up?

# Leytonstone

In Leytonstone, I found work in *The Hairdressers Journal*. I had applied for the job in Leytonstone High Road, at Falco's, not far from the Green Man pub and opposite the post office. Frank Falco was leasing the shop from the owner, who was in the army. He, by all accounts, was 'not fit', being born here of Italian parents. I started on 20 March 1947 and after a trial, I was accepted.

Before leaving for Leytonstone I was counting the cost of getting there and I thought of a bicycle. I was talking about it in the shop and this chap said he had one for sale. I should have known better, as I was aware that he was a thief. The following day he came with this nice bike; I forget how much it cost, but it served me well and off I went! (I pushed this bike through the back window of the College later.) After a couple of months of working in Leytonstone, a friend who worked in a cycle shop in E17 said he would take it to the shop and do it up for me. Next day – it must have been a Thursday afternoon, when the shops shut for half a day – I met him coming from Lyndon Road and asked, 'Where's my bike?' He looked left and right and said, 'I should not be speaking to you. There are cops waiting at home – the bike was pinched.' I knew that really. I walked to his home and there they were, two of them.

They took me to Frances Road Police Station in Leyton, and put me in a cell. The cell was bare except for a bed and a toilet, but it was nice and clean. I lay on the bed, not bad! They asked who was going to bail me out. I would not ask my father, as I asked nothing of him. So they got in touch with Frank, who came and bailed me out. It was very nice of Frank, as I had only worked for him a few weeks.

The day of my arrest was St Valentine's Day and I had a card for Marie. It was stuck up my jumper and no one saw it. I thanked Frank for bailing me out and off I ran, along Leyton High Street, passing the old Essex cricket ground to the Bakers Arms, into Hoe Street, passing the High Street on the left and then left into Greenleaf Road opposite the Rose and Crown pub where my future father-in-law Tom would take me in for a drink. Crossing Forest Road into Mersey Road I took the Valentine card from under my jumper and gave it to Marie. It had been a long jog! I had no money on me, having spent it on the card, and I had been too independent to ask Frank for the bus fare.

At work in Frank's, I was advised to secure a lawyer: Day Bell and Day Bell at Stratford was recommended. I went to see him and he said the charge was twenty pounds and I was to appear at Stratford Court. After a few days, I started to think, twenty pounds – that's over two and a half weeks' wages. I did no more than tell Day Bell that I could not afford twenty pounds and after a bit of waffling he said he would take ten pounds, which I paid.

At court he made me look a simpleton, then waffled on about how I had done my bit during the war, working in the country, etc. I was let off with a caution. I think it was because I said a soldier, on leave and going to France, sold me the bike. On going down the stairs to be signed off, there was this chap holding the bike. The sergeant discharged me; I took the bike from the chap and started to wheel it away as you would. I must have gone six yards before the copper said, 'Hold on, it's his bike, not yours!' It was a reflex, but the chap said naught when I took it – it was funny!

I cannot think of any outstanding moments in the shop, but one thing comes to mind. We had a wooden till with a gap on the top to write the amount you took from the client. The top was locked. I took change from a pound note and on trying to close the till found it would not close properly at the back. I was on my own and looked in the back and saw banknotes rammed in there. Well, no matter how I tried I could not remove them. I told Frank and he removed them.

On being demobbed from the army, the owner wanted his shop back. Frank opened a shop over the road and took some of the clients and me with him.

Frank looked after me, and made Marie and me very welcome

to his flat above the shop. We often went to dinner there, as we had nowhere else to go. They had one son who, although he was only four years old, could pick out from a pile of records the record of your choice. Frank's wife had a ladies' salon at the back. I'm afraid Frank had a bad habit – gambling on dogs and horses. Often on a Saturday, payday, I would get only two thirds of my wages, on account of his losing it at the dogs. He would send me to pay his other bills, and was always short of the right amount. My pet saying was, 'Will you take this on account, as the rest is at the dog track.' I was never refused, and he always paid in the end.

## Marriage to Marie

Frances had held her wedding reception on 7 November 1945 at the Brewery Tap, Markhouse Road, and got the old man to pay. She said that she was entitled to a dowry! I also took the moment to announce my engagement to Marie Giddins at the reception. We could not afford a party; we did not have two halfpennies to rub together. If I remember correctly, no fuss was made about my announcement! Marie found a flat at 19 Holloway Road, Harrow Green, Leytonstone, and we married when she turned twenty-one. We could not go away, as we had no money – it was spent on the wedding. We married on 28 March 1948 in the Church of Our Lady, Blackhorse Road, Walthamstow. My father, bless him, gave me a bottle of whisky, and his clients drank my health in the shop. He had wanted to invite all his cronies to our wedding – 'No!'

Never keep your tie on, in a fight! Tom, Marie's brother and a paratrooper, took a dislike to me for being Italian, and for courting his sister. He tried to throw me out when I went to pick Marie up. He did not succeed. I said to Marie that I'd see her the following night and walked out! It was not until I was in the road past the police station on the left – it was quite dark – that I knew someone was following me. I turned and it was Tom's mate. He had me by the tie and I started fighting back; though I was at a disadvantage, before long his feet would start kicking! Lucky for me a policeman saw the fighting and broke it up, and sent me packing. The tie was so tight around my neck I had to cut it off.

They would not tell me his name, but he will always be in my mind!

The reception was held in Carisbrooke Road. It was a nice turnout, with Frank Falco and his wife, and all my and Marie's families. Even Tommy the Para, who was turned down at first, but insisted on coming, and got on well with Uncle Vincent. In fact the wedding was jolly! I gave all the money I had to Jerry, to buy a drink here and there for the guests. I was expecting some change, but Jerry said he had had to put some in himself! The other Tom, my father-in-law, wanted us to go to his home for a knees-up. Instead we got to the Bell Corner and travelled to Leytonstone by bus to our flat!

We spent our honeymoon at home. Two days later Frank came round the flat saying, 'Ugo, I got a phone call from your uncle; will you phone him?' What had happened was that Uncle had fallen down the Tube stairs going home from the wedding, and was not able to work. Would I open the shop in Aldgate? I was supposed to be on my honeymoon! But I went like a good boy. I was there for longer than I expected. I was caught again by my family, they having always to come first. What can I say about myself? Not much! Again I let Marie down, plus Frank, who agreed to let me go for a few weeks.

While working at Uncle's the Aldgate shop door was always open. People came up the stairs for their haircuts and into the betting shop across the landing. Of course, betting shops were not illegal in those days, but there were always bookies' runners coming and going, and that was breaking the law! I'd see a constable knock on the bookmaker's door; it would open ajar, a few mumbled words, something passed between their hands, and off he went. No more than half an hour later, a police sergeant came up and knocked on the bookie's door, it opened just more than ajar, more mumbling, a little jig and off he went. Blimey! Soon after that jig, another officer of the law knocked on the door. The door opened and he went in: it just shows what a few pips on the shoulders will do? Ten minutes later he was out. I looked through the open door once to see what was going on – as if you couldn't guess! I was at my uncle's for two weeks!

Our first home, a flat in Holloway Road, off the Harrow

Green, was only ten minutes' walk to the barbershop in the High Street. The old girl, our landlady, was not a bad old stick; she loved her gin, and was often drunk. The flat had three rooms; the main room overlooking Holloway Road, was our bedroom. The room behind was our sitting room, and there was nothing in it. Down two steps from the landing led you into the kitchen-cum-dining room. French windows opened on to a flat roof with wooden steps leading down to the garden. The outside toilet was tucked away under the steps, of course with the perpetual torn pieces of paper on a string within the grasp of your hand. I don't think it was as cold as the loo in E17!

One morning, late for work – it had been raining all night – I hurried down the wooden steps. Two of them shot from under me and I was left suspended hanging on to the rails on each side of the stairs, my legs treading air twenty-four to the dozen. How I did not break my neck I shall never know!

## Marie's Work

Marie found work in a factory in Billet Road, as we needed the money. Well, two factories actually. The first job was poorly paid. The second factory was in Walthamstow towards the Billet, working on a drill, punching out discs by pulling a lever. It was all women working there. To earn bonuses, they had to turn over a certain amount. Marie noticed that no matter how quickly she pulled the lever, she could not get into the bonus amount. The drill could not keep up with her. She asked around to see who was earning the bonus: no one! Marie told the girls that she was going to complain. They did not want to know, as they were afraid of losing their jobs. To Marie, right was right and wrong was wrong. She called the foreman over and said it was impossible to earn a bonus. He did not believe her, so she showed him by keeping up with the drill. At the end of a certain time he checked and found that she was right. She told him to stick the job, and walked out of the factory. He tried to persuade her to stay, but she would not have it. In those days, women were put upon, and did not get a fair break!

Then she got work in a confectionery shop, next to St James

Street Station, working there until she left for Chingford Mount. Her manager of the tobacco sweet shop, a young lady, was having boyfriend trouble. Marie said that she was very upset. A week later when Marie arrived at the shop it was closed with the blinds still drawn. This was peculiar, as the manageress was always early. Marie waited outside the shop for half an hour then decided to phone Head Office. The chap arrived shortly afterwards. In putting the key in the lock he was surprised to find it was not locked. Marie had not tried to open the door as she had no reason to think it was not locked. They entered the shop to a smell of gas and went into the back room. There on the floor was the manageress, the gas ring on the floor and a coat over her head. There was nothing that they could do. Marie was very upset and blamed herself for not trying the door. It took her a long time to get over it.

At the inquest Marie wanted to talk about the boyfriend that had let her manager down, but they would not let her, as he physically had nothing to do with it. Marie left the firm and went to work for another confectionery shop in Forest Road near Wood Street. Marie worked for this firm until I was able to earn enough money for her to stop working.

# Frank Falco

Frank was easy-going. A certain client of his would always touch me up as I cut his hair, and he was persistent. I got fed up with it, so one time when he crept up my leg I shouted, 'He's at it again!' to draw the attention of the other clients. That stopped him, as he never returned to the shop! I think I had my fair share of gay people. I did not mind them, as long as they kept their hands to themselves. In all, I recall only two and one who was a persistent phone caller in Highams Park.

We had an advertising board in front of the shop, which I would bring in at the end of the day. One day I lifted the sign and on the floor between the boards was a wallet. I picked it up and in it was ten pounds – I kept it! I think about it to my shame, but then I have handed in handbags that were left in a telephone boxes on two different occasions, and heard no more about them.

(That's no excuse, Ugo!) But with savings of two and six a week, the temptation was too much.

I become friends with Fred Breyer, Dave Robinson and Ernie May (more about him later). Fred was a quiet chap, mates with Dave and his brother. At that time I had started Judo at the Tech in Forest Road, Walthamstow, and enticed them to join.

When Frank told me he was going to sell the shop, I was a bit taken aback. I had a thought, which I talked over with Marie, about me buying the shop. 'How can we? We have no money,' she said.

Looking back, I wonder what I was thinking of. I was so naïve and an idiot. I did have plans for the shop, in my mind. It was a big building with a massive cellar and I was going to turn the cellar into a gym, Judo centre and the like. In retrospect, I would have gone to the wall. The cellar had fungi that were as big as my head, if not bigger! I'd never before seen fungi in a house, but I did not think that it was anything serious. It's a wonder I never ate it as a mushroom.

I had no money to back me up, so I stayed with Stanley Brooks, who bought the shop from Frank. I cannot recall Stanley doing anything about the fungi; did he know what they were? Stanley moved the gents' hairdressers to the back, as he did not want to know about ladies' hairdressing and closed that section down. The front was turned into a handbag shop. Marie helped out for a little while. The clients came into the barber's via the side door. It turned out all right; I cannot recall any complaints from the clients.

Looking back at this episode, I do laugh at myself: I was immature. In some ways, I still am, living in a world of dreams, never taking things seriously. My favourite saying is 'That will be all right'.

Falco's brother was another hard nut; he came from Stratford in East London. They would fight over anything there, there was nothing else to do except drink – or fart; they seemed to get pleasure from that, looking round to see how the other chaps were enjoying it. I'm told that Falco's bother was never knocked out, but would take a lot of punishment while his opponent wore himself out. (This was street fighting.) To earn a few bob more he would have a sack with rats in it, take one out, put a cloth over the rat's head, and for two bob or half-a-crown, he'd bite off the live rat's head. Pre-war was hard in Stratford – I'm sorry to hear that it's getting that way again.

## Stanley Brooks

Stanley Brooks was a nice fellow, I always had a good laugh with him and the Jewish clients – we did have a mixture. I pick up languages and accents fairly easily. Jewish was no problem. They would tell me of their days in Russia. The weather would be so cold, with the wind and snow whipping your wrapped body from all angles. The Cossacks raided the Jewish settlements frequently (pogroms) and took all that the Jews had. They were left to starve. They would make do with a slice of bread, and garlic would be rubbed on the bread to give it flavour. They also made *locshon* – soup out of chicken bones, and things that would have been thrown away. One of the Jewish clients, a big man, had been a furrier in Russia. He would go into the vast empty space by horse-drawn sledge, to pick up the fox pelts that he bought from the trappers. He had such a lot to tell – if only I could remember all his reminiscing. He did tell me how they dried their washing in the winter. His wife would wring out as much water from the cloths as possible, then take it into the yard and hang it to freeze. When it had frozen hard, she would beat the hell out of it with a stick, shake the fragmentised ice out of the washing, then hang the washing in front of the fire. I admire the Jewish people for their tenacity.

Eve, Stanley's wife, was kind in her own way. She kept the Jewish traditions up; she had a whole set of plates that she would bring out use only once a year. I don't know what part of the Jewish religion that was! She would let you know that she was in charge, as Stanley was like a bull in a china shop. He liked his kosher bacon sandwich. He would creep round to our flat in Harrow Green, especially when he was on a religious fasting – a hungry wolf! If his wife, Eve, had ever found out, she would have had his kishkes!

Stanley was a good boss and we had many a good laugh, but

he would not loan me the deposit for two bicycles (lawful this time). However, the manager of the shop (a client) from the other side of the High Street stood as guarantor for me, and the bikes were well used. Marie and I would cycle to Southend from our flat in Holloway Road, Leytonstone. She had a terrible habit of not having anyone passing her on a bike, and I would cycle like mad to keep up with her. She nearly killed me one weekend: cycling behind me on the way back home, she caught my back wheel and over I went, the back of my head hitting the cemented path! I was very dizzy and had to rest for a while. We had to take it easy going back. If I moved quickly everything spun around. I still went to work next day, instead of going to hospital. I took things very slowly and took ages to lie down on the bed with out the room spinning around. Maybe it's because of the concussion, that I'm a bit thick. (A bit?)

## My Customers at Stanley Brooks

I loved working for Stanley Brooks. We had all sorts of characters at the shop. An air force pilot, with a typical moustache under his nose, would stand on the step and mow us all down with an imaginary machine gun. His name was Rose, and he had been shot down over the Channel. That made him a member of the Caterpillar Club. He had a photography shop in Leytonstone. Another client was torpedoed twice during the war while in the merchant navy. The first time, he was five days afloat! The second time he was much longer in the boat before they were rescued. He was a bit funny in the head, but a nice lad. My mate Fred – I got up his nose. I was bemoaning some thing about England. I shall quote what he wrote to me!

'1940 – aged twelve. Blitzed in East London – THREE times! 1942 aged thirteen – at work on a farm seven days a week for 12 shillings. 1945 – in Palestine, chasing Jews and Arabs. I was disgusted! You tell me you were made to come here? We (and that means you) British must be bloody mad!

Sorry Fred! Was I that bad? You know I have a go at anyone, even at the Italians! Anyway, you are English not British! Well, I always said the name was German.

George was another seaman for a short time – one voyage. The steward, a tough guy, was out drinking with the lads. Once drunk, he put his hand through a glass door, gashed his arm from the wrist to the elbow, and fainted. He would deal in anything. He had a dog and took him into Epping Forest. He had acquired an old hand gun, and tested it in the woods near the boating lake opposite Whipps Cross Hospital. On pulling the trigger, the gun exploded, nearly blowing his thumb off! The explosion frightened the dog, which took off with the lead wrapped around George's wrist. Luckily for him it ran into the entrance of Whipps Cross Hospital. George was in a daze from the pain, and the porter came out of his hut and helped him into the hospital. The doctors managed to save his thumb. He came into the shop the next day, showing off his bandage.

A couple of months later George came to the shop and said to me, 'I got it made!' I said, 'What is it?' He replied, 'I found a train truck that has been shunted to the side at Stratford Station. Looking through the window I saw sacks. I got the sliding door open and slit one of the sacks, and out flowed half crowns. I have already taken three sacks and there's plenty more!' I said I would help him. But he would not have it, the greedy sod! I know it was the truth, as later on he opened a taxi hire business. He did well, and attracted the attention of the taxman when he opened a minicab office. When asked by the Inspector of Taxes where he acquired the money from, he told them, 'My profession was a thief, and I have done my time for it!' Do you know – he got away with it.

Marie and I were invited to Stan's son's bar mitzvah. It was something new to us, but was spoilt by Stanley and his bloody top hat in a big black box that we had to take to the reception, and then bring the bloody thing back. The bar mitzvah was held in the City, not just around the corner. Marie was not too happy with it all, but it was the best champagne I've ever tasted – glasses with frosted rims and all. (When did I taste champagne last?)

One of my married clients would take a lady who worked for him to Whipps Cross and have it away in the woods. Then they would cross over the road to the stall next to the entrance of the hospital and have a pie. I said, 'You can afford better than that.' I think it's the thrill of getting caught that makes them do it. I knew her husband. The first client also used one of the flats opposite the shop in Walthamstow and would tell me, the father confessor, that he always had an ear open for the lift in case her old man was on his way up, so he could do a runner.

The Tower block opposite the shop has a lot to say for it's self! One of my clients, who is doing very well for himself, in the City went to see a lady friend. She was not in, so he turned to go, but a young lady living next door came out, informed him that the first lady was out for the day, and would he like to come in for a drink? He was not one to refuse. Of course he came into the shop as soon as he finished, to the father confessor, and told me all. (I'm listening my son!) The very pretty girl, after a few drinks, ended up in bed with him. 'But Ugo, she was kinky! She put long black shoes on that were up to her knees and with high heels. Then put on a big floppy hat. I was all for it! What will stick in my mind is the wide brim of her hat, flopping about like wings, with the up and down while I was giving it one!' I can assure you that not all my clients were that way inclined.

One chap (not a young man) fell out with his girlfriend. She would not let him in to the flat, which was opposite the shop on the second-floor. He told me that he pushed shit through her letterbox! On that subject, I was told by the caretaker that a well-dressed young woman who always greeted him with a good morning, had moved. When entering her flat, the smell hit him. It was a tip – it looked as if it had never been cleaned. They had to use shovels to scrape the floor, milk bottles stuck to the table with loose money, and so on! 'I can't believe it, she was so smart going to work.'

There was a suicide; this woman came out of her way to climb to the top floor – not a tenant. She threw herself off from the top. I'm told that she burst on contact! No, I did not rush over to see.

One of my mates was older than me, and randy as hell. During the war he was in the OSS – mad as a March hare. After the war he was working as a coalman and came to Leytonstone for a haircut. I cut his hair and he took me to Walthamstow for my lunch break in his coal lorry. We had lunch and while driving back to the shop he was cut up by a car. He went mad and chased that car all over Walthamstow! He never caught it, but it nearly cost me my job, as I was an hour late getting back.

Off Ashford Road one of my clients was courting a young lady. They were upstairs, and she was leaning out of the window talking to her mate below while he was making love from the rear – or so he told me. We still keep in touch with them; his wife is always full of life, writes to say that he still chases her around the bed, although at eighty he's a bit slower.

Stanley Brooks, who only came down from his flat when the shop was busy, employed Bill from Norfolk, who was much taller and older than me. I had a feeling about him by the way he would lift the young lads off the board that was across the chair for more height, and slowly slide them down his body. I told Stan, but he did nothing. He was there for some time. Christmas came, and I hung mistletoe over his chair. Nothing was said, but he left in the New Year.

I used to have four of the Leytonstone amateur football players as clients. Leon Joseph was very good, as were Brian and Dave. If I remember correctly, they would regularly find money in their shoes or top pockets, especially if they got to the final. Twenty-five pounds, someone said. They called it 'expenses', but then I was cutting hair for two bob (ten new pence) in those days. It was the same in boxing: you won your bout and received your trophy; then the trainer gave you money for it, ready for the next bout!

I learned a bit of Yiddish in the shop, topping up what I had picked up in E17. I was happy in the shop and turned down an offer to work in the West End where the wages were twelve pounds a week before tips! I was only taking home ten pounds with tips and I had the main clients. I was always the last one to finish. Marie was unhappy with the offer and did not want me to go. She said that I would not be better off, taking into account the fares I had to pay. I had missed the boat again!

I had a very Italian attitude about a wife going out to work. I become very selfish. If you can't support your wife you should not marry! It was all right for me to leave her on her own while I was enjoying my sports. Even when I worked for Frank, I'd go straight to the Tech Marshes and that was only up the road! From West Ham twice a week I would not see Marie until ten o'clock at night, and that became three times a week, looking back I was very selfish.

A client who became a good friend used to tell me about this Italian lady sales rep, very good-looking, with plenty of the other sales blokes after her. I had been told by him that, when attending a sale of motorbikes in north Italy, they were given an escort, a good-looking girl who spoke very good English, and you would be proud to have her hanging on your arm. Enticing you to buy, she would be yours for the stay. To cut it short, he came into the shop after with sunglasses. I told him to remove them. His eyes were bloodshot. I said, 'You did it then?' 'Yes,' he said, 'more than once!' He got very passionate with her, and of course he had to tell the father confessor of his conquest! He was going to get a flat and live with her. I think I talked him out of it! I would tell you his name, though he has passed away (with exhaustion?). His wife, God willing, may still be alive and enjoying the fruits of his money, in a pleasant climate. I wish you well, a very nice lady. He was a motorbike champion.

# Judo

Istarted Judo when I worked for Frank in Leytonstone High Road. The Technical College in Forest Road, Walthamstow, advertised the course. After getting a good hiding at boxing, I thought I'd try it. I found it very demanding but enjoyable.

*Walthamstow Technical college, 1960*

I'd cycle down Forest Road from Leytonstone, turning right at Bell Pub to the College on the left just past the Town hall. We would meet in the gym at the rear of the college, on the ground floor. Our first instructor was a Mr Frost, second dan. He was a glassblower, and wrote a book on the subject. We had the gym for free at the Tech, but we had to pay for the instruction. It cost two and six per person, twice a week. We also paid for the mats, and stuck them together with a rubbery substance to the canvas that was supplied by Vic Cocksedge. We laid them out, and put them back each evening. They were heavy! Many of today's kids would not do it; they are not as hard or keen as we were. After a few years, we came to the conclusion that we were masochists – the pain, stiffness, broken bones, and legs black and blue; why?

I got caught pushing my bike through a window at the rear of the Tech. 'I did not want it pinched!' I told the caretaker, but he had me take it out into the front of the Tech and, told me off in front of the class. I felt a tit.

I would use the lads (when I say 'lads', I mean men in their early twenties) that had the better of me in a *randori* (free practice) until I could hold my own with them; then move up one and get beaten, until I could reach their standards. That is the only way if you want to improve yourself. I was grappling (groundwork) with this strong lad (everyone was younger than me!), a wrestler from Stratford, and I was soon on my back, he between my legs. I swung my right knee to block him holding me down and caught his nose with my knee. He looked at me, a blob of blood appeared on one side of his nose, and he tilted to one side in slow motion. He did not hit the floor until he was more than halfway over, and then the blood spurted from his nose! He was out for the count. His nose was bent across his face. I told his mate to take him for first aid. When he came back he said, 'She said it's not broken.' The nurse would be fed up with us, as we were always at her door for some attention. I told his mate to take the Judoka to Whipps Cross Hospital – we did not see him again. My old governor, Falco, who had opened a barbershop in Stratford, told me that he was his client, and had said to him that I was a hard bastard. Not so! I was always giving away ten or more years in age.

Before we had a changing room, we would use an empty classroom, to change into our judoki. One time we were all in different stages of undress and, just as I took my trousers off, in comes this young girl who gave a shriek. And made a quick exit from the room. It was some time before she joined us – she was the girl friend of the chap who started the Judo group in the Technical College.

After Mr Frost we had Harold Hide, fourth dan, as our instructor. He was very good and by this time we were on the way up; I think most of the boys were green or blue belts. Those days you either won or lost; there was no points system. I was a brown belt. My mates, Cliff Baker-Brown and Dave, were first dans. I had no time to go in for my grading, as the shop took my time and when I did, I was not up to standard at that time. The order of coloured belts was white, yellow, orange, green, blue, brown and finally black (first dan).

*Shoulder throw*

Having achieved your black belt and progressed through these kyu grades, you moved on to the dan grades – from first dan on to second dan, etc. Your fighting dans went up to five or six. After that, it was for what you had done for Judo. You had to go to the British Judo Association in London – no soft touches there! When, eventually, I got my first dan, I went to the budokai more to keep my mates company, as I had not trained as hard as they, but I joined for my second dan?

Later, I was offered honorary second and third dans for my work in Judo, but I declined – I wanted to earn them the hard way. I'd been recommended by Cliff Baker-Brown and supported by the Judo Association. Mind you, you had to sweat to earn your black belt the hard way.

Cliff had been a prison officer. The first day on starting the job he had strutted in, noticing the webbing strung across between floors to stop prisoners committing suicide or throwing things on top of them. He had not been told that every new officer having his first walk would be peed on by inmates from the upper floors – it was an ongoing ritual. He did not last long in that job and became a bus driver at the Bakers Arms garage. Cliff reached sixth dan. Before he became sixth dan, we all worked hard at *randori*. At the start of a new term at the Technical College, we'd have new recruits. Students came to the gym and took up Judo. Most only lasted a few months, if that!

Picture, if you will, a large changing room with, showers down both sides at the end, accommodating roughly twenty students. Cliff and I were nearly always last to leave the mat, sweating like pigs; he thirteen or fourteen stone, I twelve. If he got on top of you, there was no way could you move him; he would try to suffocate you by spreading his hairy sweaty belly over your face. I could do no more than to bite it hard – it was all in the game. He and I were awaiting our turn in the showers – there were nearly twenty or more students showering, laughing and chattering. One looked up, saw Cliff and said, 'What turns him over – a crane?' Cliff, who could put on a nice sweet voice, looked at them and said to me, 'Ugo, whom shall we initiate tonight?' As one man, they turned with their bums to the wall – a sight to see.

Steven, Cliff's cousin, was a big chap and mad, and gave me many kicks to my legs. He was on the mat, charging like a mad bull, and on stepping back from his opponent he caught my left toe with his heel and broke it. I swore in Italian (I did plenty of that) as we watched the toe swell like a sausage. First aid was no good – I think she was fed up with us – and I cycled home painfully. I never let injuries stop me working. Marie would say, 'Serves you right, self-inflicted!' I strapped the toes together and that had to suffice. It is now well and truly locked solid.

On my way home from Judo, I would stop by the entrance to the Whipps Cross Hospital, near the entrance, at a roadside stall that sold hot pies and tea. The pie would be turned upside down and sauce poured over it – very nice. One night, while I was getting on my bike to continue my journey home after my pie, I was stopped by the police who enquired what I had on the back of the bike. Or would I like to go to the police station in Forest Road? I said, 'No, you can look,' and, undoing the holdall that was strapped to the back of my bike, out came the sweaty Judo jacket and trousers, somewhat high! If you threw the jacket down, it would have stood up on its own! I was soon on my way home.

Fred was not too keen on Judo. I think with the hard work he did, it was sometimes too much to do both. Also he worked away from home. One incident I remember concerning Fred was when this chap had a stranglehold from the rear and Fred could not get out of it. He got to his feet with his opponent still trying to put on the stranglehold and dived to the ground, head over heels. The chap, a scoutmaster, was frightened and shook up. I said to Fred, 'You could have done him serious damage!' Fred replied, 'It would have been his fault: he should have let go.' Fred was a good boxer. I wished I had known him before he packed it in. He is a gritty man, tenacious and never gives in. But he made the right decision and concentrated on his business.

Dave Robinson got his brown belt first, the rest – myself included – failed. He took over as instructor at the Tech when Harold Hide retired. I was the next one to get the brown belt. When I got to the gym at the Tech, all the class were on their knees facing the door, and as I entered they bowed their foreheads touching the mat – a very nice gesture, not forgotten. Thanks Dave. A nice-looking girl joined the club – Muriel. She was well educated, not rough like us! She could not get over hearing an Italian with a cockney accent. Dave kept an eye on us when having a *randori* with Muriel (greedy devil, kept her to himself!).

They have married, and have a nice family, and she's still laughing! Cliff was next, then Len Strommer who died young of cancer, followed by Terry Fields. But Cliff got his first dan before us.

Cliff started teaching Judo at the Bakers Arms Bus Garage, E17. He brought his lads to the Tech. He had been getting the better of me for a few weeks and asked me for a *randori* (free practice). I thought, Bloody cheek; he wants to show off. He rushed me and I went for a *tomoe-nage* (stomach throw) and over he went. To see a thirteen- or fourteen-stone chap flying through the air is something to behold! That shook Cliff and I did the same thing again and again. I saw he was getting worse and I said that I had hurt my toe. In fact his confidence had broken. Once it's gone, you put it down as a bad and painful night.

Cliff came to the shop the following week and said that he was thinking of packing it in. I told him not to be a silly sod. He got over it. I went with him for his black belt. He got it, but had to fight hard. I did not even get to the line for my black belt. 'You must come to practice where I go, Ugo,' said Cliff. It was in London and the instructor's name was Sekini. 'Why?' said I. 'When you take your shower it's mixed!' he said, 'you must come.' Every week he would bash my ears. I eventually went. After a good *randori* we went to the shower – to find only men. 'What happened?' said I. 'One of the chaps had complained,' he answered. I laughed my head off.

George, a butcher from Katherine Road, Upton Park, arranged a Judo match with the West Ham police. Unfortunately on the evening itself, I agreed to George's suggestion to go round his house prior to the bout. His wife had prepared a heavy meal of steak and all that went with it! I never normally eat before a bout, but I could not refuse and offend, so I ate this scrumptious meal, and we drove straight round to the police station, where six of them were waiting. Well, you can guess what happened: I was so heavy and sluggish that I was thrown everywhere. To say the least, I was embarrassed. George was up to it though, and finished them off. You should never go to the gym on a full stomach! He would give me a lift from West Ham to the Tech. We once turned into Forest Road and saw this chap with hair down to his shoulders. George wanted to stop and give him a good hiding! (He must be very frustrated nowadays.)

# West Ham - My Friends

My best move was to West Ham E6.

When Stanley was selling the shop to a Mr Green, an offer came from Frank Falco, to take over the barbershop in Barking Road, West Ham that he was running for his in-laws. I leapt at the chance, as I could not see myself going any further where I was. My earnings were eight to ten pounds per week, with tips. What other chance would I have of a shop? I never had a pot to pee in! I told Stanley Brooks. He was a bit taken back and said, 'Don't go yet; wait until it's all signed and sealed with Mr Green. I'll see you are all right.' When the paraphernalia was finished two weeks later, Frank said he could not wait any longer. So I gave Mr Green my notice. He was very upset, and said that he had bought the shop because I was the main man. I told him it was not my fault, as I had given Stanley Brooks my notice. I got nothing from Stan, despite all his talk that he'd see me all right. The story of my life!

## West Ham

I met the shop's owner, Mrs Fusco, who by all accounts came from the same part of Italy as my mother. She was a fat old cow, and her husband (her second) was not a desirable person. I don't think he ever worked, and I never trusted them. My solicitor, from Grays Inn Road, drew up the contract (it cost me a bomb!). One of my mates had recommended him. It was worth the money as it made me more secure. The shop was mine for five years and was filthy. My father-in-law, Tom Giddins, was good to me. When the shop closed Saturday night, we started to wash down and paint the shop. We worked throughout the night, finishing at ten o'clock Sunday morning. Elmo, my brother, came to help, too late. But he would never be too late in turning me over for money. Tom would always ask if Marie or me if we needed money, but we never borrowed. I do not believe in it. I always lived up to what I had in my pocket.

The shop was not far from West Ham football ground. On Saturdays the fans would pass the shop and keep going; no one likes going into an empty shop. I always had a broom in my hand, pushing the last clients' hair about, giving the impression that I'd just finished a client, with all the lights on. Along Barking Road and crossing Boleyn Road was Rossi's café, (the owner was a nice man) and next to him an antique shop, run by a single lady. She had wonderful things in there. She was nice but never looked clean – her hair was always greasy. Everyone thought that she had pots of money. One day she fell downstairs and broke her neck! No one ever found any money. Her brother would come for a haircut. He too looked unkempt, as if he never had a pot to pee in. In winter he would stuff newspaper down his trouser legs to keep warm.

Barking Road was very busy with plenty of shops, plus the public spilling over from Green Street Market. Next to the antique shop was Nash's pie, eels and mash shop, adjoining a sweet and cigarette shop. The shop, Fusco's, run by mother and daughter, had two bay windows displaying a gents' and ladies' hairdressing sign. The door of the shop led straight into the gents' salon. The gents' had two basins, six wooden waiting chairs, a hot radiator and, over the connecting door leading to the ladies' salon, was a loudspeaker that leaked music. The rent of the shop was four pounds per week, including rates, electric and gas. On the corner of Green Street stood the Boleyn pub, named after Anne Boleyn. It was on the site of a castle. A tunnel is believed to lead from under the pub to the entrance of the football club. The tunnel is sealed off now. But they say that Anne Boleyn still walks there. (Whom were they kidding?)

Three shops down from the pub was an Italian café, Casatari's, where the West Ham players ate in their own room at the back. The pram shop just past the café had everything for a child. The owner came for a haircut and seemed to have pleasure in telling me that I had bought a white elephant. Six months later, when he found that I was doing well, he did not come into the shop again.

Sod him! The wife of one of my clients would bring their son for a haircut. She was a nice-looking woman, blonde and flirty, and tried her best for me to go to her flat and cut her boy's hair there. She would hand me the money and hang on to my hand. When I was about to leave West Ham, she told me that I was the only one not to take advantage of her. There you go, I have always been silly. No! I do not like to cheat, as I saw too much of it in the shop, with families being broken up!

My price for a haircut was two shillings, which today equals ten pence. The first week I took three pounds including tips. Marie practically had kittens, and said I should never have left Leytonstone and a good job.

We had pamphlets printed and, with a friend, pushed them through the letterboxes of as many houses around the streets of the shop as possible. Week by week the trade improved to the consternation of the pram shop's proprietor. In six months the shop was taking twenty-six pounds with tips per week (at two shillings per head!). My clients were mostly dockers. I really got on well with them. They were the best people I had ever met! I loved West Ham and will always have a place for it in my heart. We continued to live at Harrow Green, Leytonstone, in the upstairs flat. I would cycle to work along Wanstead Flats (where I'd referee in later years) to Forest Gate and then into Green Street, a long, cold ride in the winter. The wind would always be against me! I tried the buses, but they were always late. Eventually, I bought myself a Lambretta scooter. Was I coming up in the world, or not?

The greengrocer in Barking Road was a funny bloke (not funny ha-ha). I had girly magazines in the shop, very tame compared with today. He would come into the shop, sit down and wait his turn. I had a feeling that it was him who tore the pages of the girls in the nude out of the magazines. So I laid a trap. In those days the clients came every two weeks on the dot. I stuck on loose hairs around the private parts of the nudes. I had already told my waiting clients what I was doing. In he came, dead on time with his bottle bottom glasses. I had two barber chairs in the shop; clients would always sit in the spare barber's chair to wait their turn. He sat down on the chair at the back of the shop and looked around him. The chap I was attending to peeped from under his eyebrows, the other one looked over the paper he was reading, looking into the mirror in front of him, keeping an eye on the groper. I carried on cutting and watching. He would hold the magazine close to his eyes. Then I heard, and so did the two clients, a very gentle tearing of paper. He was feeling the photos with his fingers as he slowly tore the pages out and put them into his inside jacket pocket. I had tampered with four nudes and he had the lot. I doubt if he could see us looking. I think I wasted my time showing him the haircut from the back with the mirror.

His son came into the shop; I did not say anything to him. I told his mate though. His mate told me that five of them would go to the shop late at night to have a game of cards. The old man would play a few hands, and then go up to bed. I'm told he was not a nice man. He would demand sex from his wife, very roughly and violently. She would plead with him, cry and yell, but he would have his way. The others would carry on playing cards as if they could not hear what was going on, as would his son. I would not trust his father alone with my cat!

Brian Harvey, Leon Josephs and Dave Andrews, the Leytonstone footballers, followed me to West Ham, but not many other clients did: they were not loyal as my new customers from East-West Ham, who wanted to open up a shop for me when I had to leave them, and who followed me to Walthamstow until I got going. I have the greatest respect for East and West Ham, as they took to me with open arms. I got in touch with Dave, whose photo I saw recently (2001) in the local papers, and learned that he is now coach for Dagenham and Redbridge, and was unlucky not to go up into the next league. He promised to look me up when around this way. They made the league in 2007. Well done!

But West Ham of today is very different from when I knew it. New culture has moved in and it will be no more. Still I had seen the best of its people, whom I'll never forget. In real life, nothing is for ever.

Two clients, who had a clothing factory in Boleyn Road, offered to open a ladies' salon in Barking Road for me to run for them. One was called Charley and the other was Bill; to my shame, I can only remember their first names. I must say a few words on Bill. Bill was a gambler and had a few dogs. He ran them at Hackney Wick Stadium. He would give me tips on his dogs, and once told me to back his dog at ten to one. I did not; it won. He told me to back it again at eight to one; I did not, and it won again. Again, he said to back it in a forecast with the favourite to come second; the forecast came in! He did not bother to give me tips any more. The clients did well, as I passed on the tips, but I did not like gambling, as I had seen what it did to my family. I was doing well enough on my own, a small person, small-minded, with small money. If I had betted, I might have got the bug and lived just for gambling.

I used Rossi's café for lunch and closed the shop for half an hour. But I had to give my lunchtime up, as my clients would come and sit around the table and watch me eat! In the end Rossi would bring my lunch to the shop and put it on the radiator to keep warm. I gave that up in the end and settled for a sandwich. If I were too busy, my clients would buy a jug of tea from Rossi's, and eat my sandwich. Whatever shop I had, the clients always ate my food and made the tea. It's true! Mind you, they would sweep the cut hair to one side, and these were Dockers.

One Thursday morning I accused Mr Fusco of pinching my razor blades. The connecting door to the ladies' salon was never usually closed, but I was very angry and closed the door. There was a banging on the closed door; it was Vera the daughter, a nice-looking girl. She shouted, 'Ugo, open this door, I have to go to the window!' I told her to use the side passage door and come through the front. 'No, I will not! I'm phoning my sister Olga!' she shouted. Now Olga was a big girl, solid and a bit cross-eyed, but always nice to me. She had a ladies' salon in Bow. While this banter was going on my clients carried on reading the *Boxing News* or the *Mirror*. Roughly an hour later Olga drove up with her husband, same build but also a very nice chap. In she marched down the side passage. I was still busy in the shop when there was a loud banging on the connecting door. Olga shouts, 'Ugo open this door!' 'No,' says I. 'I shall break it down!' says she. It was a hot day and the front door of the shop was open wide to Barking Road. 'I should care,' I said. Two clients were waiting their turn. They looked up at the sound of pounding feet, and the sight of the connecting door flying open with a bang, the momentum carrying Olga through the shop, out on to Barking Road. She looked at me with triumph and marched down the side entrance. My clients looked at me, I raised my eyebrows and they carried on reading. The shop was full of life!

Olga's brother, Romano, turned up in his army uniform a week later. Before he joined up he had courted Vera Lynn, the singer, who was a West Ham girl. But now there were no clients in the shop. He was six feet tall, and I five foot seven. He grabbed hold of me by the lapels of my white coat, dragged me through the ladies' salon and into the passage. 'You little weasel, I'll give you some for giving my family trouble!' he snarled. I thought that I'd better do something, but if I hit him in the house I'd be in trouble. So, to his surprise, I dragged him up the side passage towards Barking Road, saying, 'You'll give me one? You long string of piss – I'll give you two!' As I got him near the front door of the passage, he started to back-pedal, saying, 'Are we not both Italians?' Your mum comes from same town as mine.' Sad, really; I'd rather have got a good hiding than have backed down.

Marie and I had moved to a flat in 21 Badlis Road, E17. Once a fortnight, I'd pick up Dave Robinson, my mate from Judo, who lived off Lea Bridge Road, on the back of my scooter on my way to work at roughly seven in the morning for his haircut. I would drive up Forest Gate into Green Street, turning into Barking Road to reach the barbershop. The shop opened at eight o'clock but no matter what time I got there, there was always someone waiting. Poor Dave would do his nut, as he had a long journey back to Leyton. If I threw him once or twice at Judo he would make an excuse not to come and have his haircut, forgetting that he'd thrown me all over the place! As I write Dave has been to my home with Muriel, with Fred and Hilda; they are always good company. Dave is always smiling and a good friend. Dave was good at Judo as he had Muriel to practise with. I forgive her for laughing at me for being an Italian with a cockney accent. She has not got over it yet! Every time I phone her, she starts laughing. Did I ever have a *randori* with Muriel or did Dave keep her to himself?

Another client would come every two weeks for his haircut; in those days, men wore their hair tidy. He would always come after the shop had closed and bang on the glass door. I could never get home early, and my dinner would always be spoilt. Marie was always upset. He banged on the door one time too many. I lost my temper and on opening the door I told him I could not attend to him. Unfortunately he said, 'You won't refuse two and six.' I grabbed hold of him, turned him round and threw him out into Barking Road, whereupon he shouted, 'You're not the only bloody barber around here!' 'No I'm not!' I cried, and threw coppers at him to get a bus to where he was going.

His son came in the following week. I told him what had happened. He said, 'Take no notice of the silly old bastard.' Roughly six weeks later the old bastard came back, waited his turn, had his haircut, paid, tipped and said nothing. That's how it stayed until I left East Ham.

Some of the West Ham football team came to my shop for their haircuts: Eddie Lewes, Cyril Lee, M. Musgrove and a few others whose names escape me. I saw them play once, on a free ticket. I loved East Ham. I loved the people; there was always laughter in the shop.

One Friday I had a severe cold; two wipes, a snip and a sniff. My nose was red raw. The shop was always busy and by the afternoon my nose had started to bleed heavily. I said I would have to go home. The clients would not have it. I had put a piece of cotton wool up each nostril and the weight of the blood would slowly bring them down. I looked like a walrus, with two red soggy tusks of wool hanging down! A client got up and in a few minutes brought this young lady in from the pharmacy past Nash's pie and eel shop. She gave me quinine, which I took immediately. Next day my nose had stopped running. You can't get quinine now.

The shop became too busy so I employed a hairdresser to help me. My clients did not like it and gave me a choice. They said that they had come from a long way, past many other barbershops. If they had to go to my assistant they might as well go local. I got rid of my help and they were happy to wait, sometimes more than two hours! They were the salt of the earth. Now you know why I liked my clients, or governors. I enjoyed their company and often think back to the good days. (Maybe it was the tea that drew them in and my sandwiches that they would eat with relish.)

# Fred

Fred was a good friend, whom I had known since I was twenty-three years old, and he twenty. Dave was roughly about the same age but bigger built. I asked them to join the Judo class at the Tech, as they were interested in what I was up to, and would also enjoy the sweat and pain! They both followed me to East-West Ham when I left Leytonstone. Fred, who saw that I was doing well in the shop, had the urge that he had been nurturing for some time to start up on his own. I encouraged him. 'You have no commitments, have you?' He was an asphalter by trade. In July 1956, he started on his own, with one worker. Fred was finding plenty of work taking any jobs that came his way. Growing more confident in himself Fred came to the shop. Things had gone slow for him and he had only a few weeks' wages left for his father. (He told me on reading this book, that the worker was his stepfather, and that he had left a good job to help him.) Fred had a bad accident – he burnt his hand with the hot asphalt! When working for yourself, there is no such thing as having time off. He had put in a tender to asphalt a school playground, but had heard nothing as yet. I offered to go into partnership with him. I had been trying to get away from hairdressing; all the long hours I was putting in got me down. I had no love for it!

I had £2,000 in the bank, which was a lot of money those days. Fred said he wanted to be his own boss, and I said that was OK with me; he would always be the top man and teach me the trade. He said he would wait a week or so, to think about it. Within that time, the tender he had put in to asphalt the school playground came in. From that start, he never looked back. (Fred does not recall all that I've written. But this is what I remember! There is no offence intended.)

We could have made a good team; if nothing else, I am trustworthy, worked hard, never took time off, never let anybody down and asked for no favours. He was let down by so many people – he was too trustworthy. He was turned over by his assessor whom he trusted. It did him a lot of harm. He confided in me, and I told him that he was young enough to take it! He learned from it and got to the top. I'm glad I did not take the offer he put to me.

Despite Fred's highs and lows, he did well and overcame all his troubles, which were many. Fred tried to help me in many ways, but Marie was happy as we were. From saving two and six per week we were now saving notes! Fred had something to aim for: Hilda, a lovely looking girl whom he wanted to impress. Eventually they were married, and are still happily wedded. They have a nice family – three boys and a girl, and I'm very fond of them. His favourite saying to me was, 'Ugo! You will never make money sitting on your arse, watching TV. I only used to work ten to eleven hours a day! Fred tried to push me into buying a house in Matching Green in Harlow; just on the other side of the square to him, for £12,000, or it could have been less. Why? Because I worked late as it was, and from East Ham to Matching Green was a good journey. Marie was on her own far too long as it was. When I moved back to Waltham Forest into the old shop, Fred was selling his beautiful house at Matching Green and tried again to sell it to me, for a pittance. I hummed and hawed and did not buy. Within a few months it was valued at treble that amount. So there you are: it's no secret that I'm an idiot. Fred also wanted me to buy a truck to remove his hard core, as he could have given me all the work I wanted! I would have done well. (Small man, small thoughts and small money.) Fred, I'm happy to say, is enjoying the fruits of his labours.

I visited Fred and Hilda in Cliftonville; they had a nice house on the cliffs overlooking the sea. They made Marie and me very welcome. All the boys were there. Did I referee when they were playing football? Fred took his two-berthed boat out to catch fish for tea. Russell and me were in our swimming trunks, ready for a swim. We were quite some distance from the bay, and Russ was in the water. I climbed on top of the cabin, braced myself against the metal piping, then pushed off, removing some of the piping as I plunged into the sea, butting Russell in the mouth and taking him down with me! I had my eyes open and Russ had his closed. I got hold of him and pushed him upwards, going up with him.

Fred pulled Russ in, who was bleeding from his mouth. I was trying to climb the ladder that was hanging from the side of the boat but it felt like the sea was trying to pull me back in. None of us was very happy about this episode. When I meet Russell, grown up and a family man, he points his finger at me, and it's saying, 'You nearly drowned me!' I was told that the currents were very strong lower down, as we were near the sandbanks. I'm not a strong swimmer – were we lucky or not? (By the way Russ, she never got over it, remember?)

Tim, Russ' brother was a good lad with high ambitions; he could see the future. He would fall out with his dad now and then, as so many do, and tell me about it! At one time he was about to leave Fred, as his dad would not listen to his ideas. I suggested that when Tim had an idea, he should discuss it with Fred, and ask his opinion on it, so that it became a mutual idea. They did well together. Fred told me that when Tim went to a business meeting in the West End, the drinks were six pounds each! He was taken aback at the price. So was I, when I went to Qualingos' in St Martin's Lane. But then, that's another story! Tim was only paying two and six for his haircut (did you tip me enough Tim?). Alison, their sister, always had a wild streak, rushing here and there as a young girl, her cloak around her shoulders, flapping like wings. She turned into a good mum. Chris, shy at first, grew into a happy-go-lucky strong lad. ('Go on Ugo, tell me about Dad, he'd say.)

Fred and Stanley Brooks had both been in the Green-Jackets. Stan was in the last push of the war and told me his reaction on seeing the first dead German, which resulted in having to change his trousers! Fred was at the end of the war, and was very proud of his regiment. He finished his time, in the troubles in Palestine. Hairy moments! (I asked Fred on rewriting this book, if he wanted me to change anything – he said, 'Yes, all of it.) So I've left it all in.

## My Other West Ham Clients

I used to practise Judo in the shop when there was a gap between clients. The butcher lad who worked in the shop next to the Boleyn pub was also a Judo man. I was in the shop when he was serving a lady client wanting a leg of lamb; he opened the two legs apart, looked at her in the eyes and brought the copper down separating the two legs. He told me that they always flinched! (The butchers that I know are all the same – randy!) I would wrap a long towel under his armpits and grip the ends, as he did to me. He was twenty-two years old and I was twenty-four. He would do his best to up-end me, but I was going for my first dan and he was only a green belt. I think he helped a lot; I had to keep on my toes. If he had thrown me he would have done me a lot of damage. There was not a lot of room in the shop to sod about in. He did try!

I did hurt myself at the Budokai at 16 Upper Woburn Place going for my second dan. I was thrown heavily on my left side, and I thought that I'd had broken my collarbone. I indicated that I was injured, but they did not pull me out of the line! Judo was hard those days. At work I could just about lift my right arm up, to cut the hair. I'd sit the client low in the chair, to save me lifting my arm high, and dreaded when the client asked for a shampoo. I can assure you it was bloody painful. My clients would take the mickey out of me, but they did sweep the floor and tidy up for me – and kept eating my sandwiches and drinking my tea. That they would buy from Rossi's Café on the corner of Boleyn Road.

The shop was full, and this scruffy seaman off the boat came for a shave – I hated shaving. I lathered him, and did my usual rhythm on the strop with my open razor. He started to talk gibberish. I asked, 'What's that?' He said, 'Italian!' I gave him the quickest shave ever; my razor flew over his face and he froze! I'm sure he wet himself. Never saw him again – funny?

A client, Nash by name and a bus driver, had a haircut and shampoo, then put his hand into his pocket and found he had no money. He was very embarrassed. I told him not to worry and to have it on me. The bill was three and six. He would not have it, and brought the money the next day. By me trusting him, I had all his family in as clients.

He had a younger brother, Billy Nash, over six feet tall, a lorry driver and a nice chap, who found that I participated in Judo and ribbed me about it. I said that I could put him out within ten seconds! He was with a friend, who pushed us into it. I knew

Billy was strong, so I reversed my hands around his neck, knowing he would pull them apart. I applied *akuri-eri-jime* (a reversed strangle hold) – he six feet, me five feet eight inches. With my thumbs I put pressure on his jugular vein, and he did the rest, slipping to the floor – he was out for the count. His mate exclaimed, 'F— me! I don't believe it!' I brought Billy round and he was saying, 'I can hear bagpipes.' The radio was playing Scottish music from the ladies' salon, and it was leaking into my shop from the loudspeaker above the connecting door. This story soon got around and brought me younger clients. Billy Nash delivered scaffold up and down the country. When I left East Ham, he followed me to E17. He told me he had a job up north, to bring back a lorry loaded with poles. Driving at speed to get back to West Ham, he had to pull up sharply. The scaffolding poles crashed through the cab and drove through his back, killing him. I felt very bad about it. I don't know whose fault it was that the poles were not secured, but what a waste!

Five West Ham football players were outside the shop talking. I left my client in the chair, took a large empty Durex box, and ran over to them. Eddie Lewes saw the box and started to run away; Cyril Lee and Bobby Moore (not a client) started to run as well. I ran after them shouting, 'You've left these behind.' I threw the box at them (they obviously thought it was full) – well, it was funny at the time.

I would always brush a client's coat when it was needed. When cheeky, if they did not give me a tip, I would continue to brush the jacket, following them outside the shop into Barking Road, where they would always run off and I'd run after them, still brushing the jacket. Potty really! I did not like hairdressing for its own sake, so I made my own fun to break the monotony of cutting hair. Also I bonded with my clients; they thought that I was mad! (Whatever gave them that thought?)

One day I asked a young client George, if he would take my Lambretta and fill it with petrol, as I was running low. He assured me he could ride it. He was six feet tall. He sat astride my bike and took off like a rocket from the wrong side of the road, narrowly missing a bus coming head on, his long legs akimbo, and disappeared into the sunset! The clients in the shop all thought he would kill himself. Half an hour later, he turned up as if nothing had happened. God knows where he'd been. The garage was only a few minutes' ride. My clients were mad, but then, so was I! We liked it that way!

George was courting a girl whose dad did not take a shine to him. When she took him to her home, her dad threw him out bodily! George had a reputation with the ladies; her father must have heard about him. George did not give up. The girl was a shop worker and had Thursday afternoons off. He would go around to her home and have it away. On this particular Thursday, George was upstairs with his girlfriend, venting his lust and afterwards telling me all about it, leaving no detail out. After all, I was the father confessor. When he heard a car pull up outside, he looked through the glass of the window and saw the girl's father getting out. Panic! She tried to hide him in the bedroom, but he ran down the stairs, clutching his trousers that he had no time to put on. He ran along the passage, through the kitchen's back door, down the garden path, and then clambered over the fence, still clutching his trousers. He got into his car that was parked on the street behind the house, and made his escape with no trousers on! I never did find out what happened to the poor girl. One of George's sayings was, 'I always get my handful of sprats.' (I did not know that he knew anything about fish.) He also followed me to E17 for quite a while, until I found my feet.

Opposite the East Ham barbershop was a co-op store. Every Friday afternoon, it was pointed out to me, the manager would take the earnings to the bank in a carrier bag. While I was there he was never turned over – unlikely today!

I was offered a job in the docks by a ganger who was a good client. He said I'd never be short of work. It was the ganger who would pick the blokes for the jobs of the day. The money was out of this world, but I was doing well in my shop and liked to be my own boss. The dockers liked a drink and had a favourite pub. On the next corner to the barbershop stood a workingmen's club, opposite the co-op. The pub was near the docks. The ganger told me that he carried the stripper high above his head, naked, across the crowded floor of the pub they frequented. Nobody dared touch her, as he carried her aloft to the stage. If you saw the size of him, you would not have attempted to slap her.

In the docks much gear would go missing as boxes 'accidentally' broke. One of the dockers walked out with hams stuffed down his trouser legs, timing his exit with a friend who was on gate duty. There would always be some work left over for the weekend, at double or treble time. It was still a hard life, especially if you did not get on with the ganger. My friend Terry Lawless had a job in the docks, before taking up boxing with Al Philips, a former champion, as a corner-man. He was happy to leave. In retrospect, I think I would have enjoyed working in the docks.

I loved East Ham and my clients who put me on my feet. I loved them as real Englishmen; you knew where you stood with them. After some banter on foreigners that I started to keep the clients occupied, a docker lifted me up by my lapels and said, 'You are not a bloody foreigner!' I was not going to argue with him! I was always being ribbed about not having British nationality. A few weeks later, the shop was full, with a lot of banter around. I said, 'I'm going to apply to become a British citizen!' As one voice they all shouted, 'No you're bloody not! We'll all sign a petition to stop you!' I expected no more from them than that answer. The saddest day of my life was when I had to leave. East-West Ham was beginning to change as I left. Now you would not recognise it: people have moved out, different cultures have moved in, and the character has gone. I shall always remember them, as they were real English east-enders! Where are you now and where is the young lady who, when paying for her boys' haircut, would grab my hand and not let go?

# Referee

The talk in the East Ham barbershop in the late forties was nearly all football. With West Ham FC so near to the barbershop a few of the West Ham players were clients. On speaking to Eddie Lewes about the laws of the game (as I was contemplating on taking up refereeing), I was amazed when he said, 'I don't know the laws of refereeing. It's the ref's job, not mine; I'm there to put the ball in the net!' He was a burly man, strong and imposing, who would intimidate the opposition with threats to their limbs, if they did not release the ball to him – so he told me. Eventually Eddie went to South Africa to coach football. In 2002, he was still there. I asked a few of the other players, and received the same reply.

A Scottish player, whose surname has escaped me – I think his name was Dick – told me of an incident while on a visit to his parents in Scotland. Having a drink in a bar outside Glasgow (at that time no women were allowed into pubs. They even separated the cockerels from the chickens, at the weekend), he was being ribbed about his football ability. He drank his beer and walked out of the pub. Three men followed him and began to jostle him, so he did a runner! They ran after him but he kept just in front of them, to make them think that they were catching up on him. He kept going until they started to flag – then he turned around and gave the three breathless chaps a good hiding. (Learn your lesson – it pays to be fit!)

I must say a few lines on incidents that occurred while I was refereeing. It was in 1950 when I started, and I was sent all over East London. I soon found out that if you showed any weakness you would be punished. I started with the boys and worked my way up. One match that comes to my mind is the one I refereed in St James' Park, E17. It was Armistice Day and the kick off was at eleven o'clock in the morning. I had the two teams on the pitch all in their place of play. The boys were roughly fourteen years old. I said, 'On the first sound of the shot we will be at attention, and on the second shot, we will commence play when I blow the whistle.' It was a very nice moment to see them at attention, one that I shall remember. The parents and passers-by all joined in. The changing rooms were non-existent; I have changed in some weird places: toilets, sheds, grounds mans' huts and even behind bushes until I realised that I should change before I got to the ground. Slow learner!

1960-61  W.W.   30-12-60

**LONDON SUNDAY FOOTBALL ASSOCIATION**

**REFEREE'S CERTIFICATE**

THIS IS TO CERTIFY THAT

MR. H. PATRIAREA

OF 21 BADLIS RD

WALTHAMSTOW E.17

is a duly qualified referee with this Association.

Regn. No. N.14

*Chairman.*

THIS IS TO CERTIFY THAT THIS REFEREE HAS BEEN AFFILIATED TO THIS ASSOCIATION FOR THE SEASON

1961 - 62

1962 - 63

1963 - 64

1964 - 65

1965 - 66

*Hon. Secretary.*

I had a match at Lloyd Park, E17, off the Forest Road. It was handy for me, as I lived in Badlis Road, only five minutes from the ground. During the match on that Sunday morning, I was getting stick from some of the watching parents. They persisted right to the bitter end! I blew the final whistle and, as I had had enough, ran over to them and said, 'Now then; what have you to say to me?' They looked at me as if I was mad, and replied, 'Give over ref, the game is finished!' I watched them walk off and felt sad for them. I suppose they could not say much at home, so they came to the game to give the ref some 'verbal'.

At the same ground, I had a bad match, with kids around

sixteen years old. There were a lot of fouls, swearing and a few names were taken. I was told that their coach gave them money if they won. I reported this to the AFA but heard nothing more of it. I did note that the young players were copying the professionals – the diving, arguing with the ref – they picked it all up from television. The adults were worse, as I was to find out. For refereeing a match I was paid one pound, and for that I closed my shop on Saturday afternoon. Otherwise I would not have been able to get to the matches. I opened the shop all day on Thursday instead of closing at one o'clock. After a few weeks I made up the Saturdays losses and I would enjoy the banter with the players who would always try to intimidate me. I was taught the laws of football by a Mr Bird. The eye test was peculiar; four chequered cards were shown in quick succession and I made them all the same number. I was never told if it was correct. At that time I had acquired a blue belt in Judo. One of the other refs-to-be told Mr Bird and he was impressed, so I started being given more adult matches.

I refereed a match in Woodford Green. I had stopped smoking at that time for two months, to increase my lung power. I also bought myself new boots. It had been raining and the ground was very muddy. By half time my feet had become very sore from the new boots. Before starting the second half, I called the captains and said that I would have to remove my boots and continue in my bare feet. They did not mind. My feet were black as the ace of spades, with the mud being squeezed between my toes. To be fair to myself, I did not slip once. After a good shower I was knackered, and in the canteen I said, 'Sod it!' and had a fag – I had started smoking again!

# Wanstead Flats

It was a good game on Wanstead Flats, until I disallowed a goal and the players could not believe it! The goalkeeper did a good save, but he could not hold the ball, and it ran forward. The player who fired the shot could not stop running, and it carried him into the back of the opponents' net, behind the keeper. The ball going forward went to the opponents' captain, who drove it into the back of the net next to his team mate, who was hanging on to the net and not moving. I disallowed the goal! Their coach went mad and pulled up the corner flags. The players sat on the ground and I was standing like a lemon in the centre of the playing field. I told the coach to put the flags back and get his players ready to play. He said, 'I'm going to report you, and you are not getting paid!' I told him to please himself, and stuff the money where the monkey stuffs its nuts. The match finished with a lot of mutterings and looks that would kill you. I was reported to the AFA, but they supported my decision.

Opposite the City of London Cemetery were the Wanstead Flats playing fields. I always changed in the dressing room with the players as I always enjoyed the expression on their faces when I entered the changing room and sat among them. I noted just one space left at the end of the bench, and out of the corner of my eye, I saw the players looking at each other with smirks on their lips. I went to the space allotted to me, threw my bag on the floor and sat heavily but stopping just before my bum touched the bench. All the players stood up, thinking that I would slip off the end – I carried on as if nothing happened. The game starts in the dressing room.

## Lea Bridge Road

It was raining cats and dogs, with poor light. No ref would give the OK. I was getting harassed by the teams that had come a long way for their match. I had another look – it was muddy, but just about playable. I weakened and gave in. They agreed when I said the time would be cut to thirty minutes each way. It was a deplorable match, with me taking a couple of names and of course, it was my entirely my fault, the players muttered. I only did it for the money and we should not have played, and so on. By me saying we'd play, the other referees played also. It did not go down too well with them. The changing rooms had superb showers on both sides. I stripped off and walked into the showers next to six of the team that I had refereed. The water was nice and hot. I noted one of the players nudge his mate, then with his eyes indicate me. They walked to the other side of the room where more showers were situated. The others, seeing them leave, were also giving the eye, and crossed to the other side. I was left on my own, while they were all bunched together on the other side! I loved those incidents, and would relate them to my clients in the shop the following week. They would always enjoy my episodes.

## Deaf and I'm Dumb

I refereed a deaf and dumb side versus a hearing side on Leytonstone Football Ground. I was not given any guidance prior to the match. I blew the whistle and started as usual. I kept blowing the whistle until the captain of the deaf side stopped me, pulled out his handkerchief and, pointing to my whistle, waved his hanky. I got it! Bloody fool! Sometimes I'm as thick as two planks of wood. They may have been deaf and dumb, but they all knew the 'F' word. I'd shout, 'No swearing!'

## Barking

At this match the players all towered over me, except for their coach who, besides being small, was unfortunate in carrying an extra burden, a biggish hump. When I dismissed a throw-in from the sideline, he went berserk and actually foamed from the mouth. I was fascinated by it all. After some time, one of his players came over, and stood over me with his arms crossed. I looked up at him and said, 'Well?' He gave a look as if I stank, grunted and joined his team mates. Another two minutes and he could have been right.

## Hackney Marsh

This match was the nearest I came to a punch-up. I was given the match with a warning that the two teams were on probation, and this was their last chance before being thrown out of the league. It all went well, and I kept them under control until the last ten minutes. Then I gave a free kick and it was taken before I was ready. I told the player to take it again; he looked at me, placed the ball on the ground and kicked it straight at me, missing my head by inches. I showed him the card, but he would not give me his name as he was busy circling me shouting, 'I'm going to knock your f—ing head off!' But he did not decrease the circle. I looked at my watch – there were ten minutes left – and said, 'Get off the field, and I'll see you when the game is finished.' He went off uttering nonsensical rubbish. After the match I went into the players' dressing room. He was not there. He had lost his bottle and did a runner.

His captain asked me not to report them; it was their sport and the team would be split up. If I had had my pants down he would have kissed my arse. Even the opponents stood up for them. In my younger days I was also headstrong. So what do you think happened? They reported me! I had to appear in front of the Committee in Gants Hill, Ilford. I admitted I had been weak and I explained the circumstances, saying it would never happen again. I was reprimanded. I never understood why they reported me. It was just malice against the weak referee. Will I never learn? I had to close my shop for three hours to get a rollicking! Was it worth it?

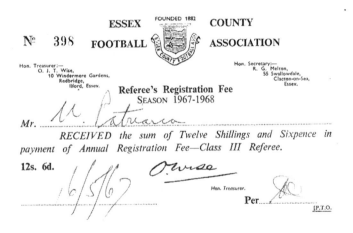

## Chingford

On the Chingford Plains, the match I was about to referee had ominous signs, as I knew the blokes on one side. All lived around me and some were clients. Again, the weather was bad but playable. One of the refs did not want to officiate, and the lads got on to me, saying, 'Go and tell that silly old bugger that we want to play.' It was a double match as they were all behind with their fixtures. I could understand their feelings, so I approached this ref and I got him to change his mind. The game started with everybody tense – and these were not boys. It was a hard first half and I was biased, and did not referee well. At half time one of the opposition players (not the ones I knew) said to me, 'Ref, I have been threatened by two blokes of the opposing side, who said they were going to break my legs!' Knowing them, I took it seriously and called them together. I warned them that if there was any more rough play I would abandon the match. I also reminded them that they had to work on Monday. I then refereed as it should have been, and it turned into a good hard match. Sometimes it's hard not to be biased. I knew the players and, if I had known beforehand, I would not have refereed the match, but at this level of football, you have to take things as they come.

# Highams Park

Just over the crossing at Highams Park, going towards Chingford, you turned left at the bend on to a small lane that led you to the biggest football pitch on which I ever officiated. My changing room was next to the players' dressing room and I could hear everything that was said. These were workers from a paint factory in Stratford, East London, who were playing a local team, the name of which I can't remember. I had no linesmen and could not get any from their sides to help me spot the offsides. I told them that my decision was final, and I would not take derision from any of them.

It was very hard trying to stay with them, and I was repeatedly reminded by the players to keep up with the play. I disallowed a goal, as there was a lot of pushing and tugging of shirts in front of the goal. I pointed a direct kick against the attacking side. I'd run to the halfway line when someone shouted behind me, 'Give me your whistle; I can do a better job than you!' I said, 'Oh yes! I know just where you will put it!' As I have said, you will always get people watching, and there was this chap leaning on his bike with his chin on his arms, on the sidelines. The game was hard and reasonably fair. One player was chasing his opponent with the ball, and roughly in line with the bike, he shoulder-charged his opponent, and sent him staggering into the spectator's bike. The chap had been mesmerised and did not move until he was sent flying. It finished with the player on top of the bike and the spectator under it, just like a sandwich. I thought that I had had a good game until when changing in my room, I heard one of the two captains say, 'How many points shall we give the ref?' The other replied, 'F— all!' That says it all!

## Hackney Marshes

It's usual for the players to unwind on the pitch before starting the game. Hackney always drew crowds of watchers and supporters, who would start on me and the other refs – jeering, and hyping the players up. I blew my whistle for them to get rid of the balls they were kicking about, but one end continued to kick the ball to his goalkeeper. I blew again, ran to him and took the ball and also his name. 'You can't do that! The match has not started,' he said. They play football and know nothing about the laws of the game. Once you are on the pitch, you are under the jurisdiction of the referee. That started the crowd off: the names I was called. The politest one was, 'Just because he's dressed in black, he thinks he's bloody Hitler!' Again, I had no linesmen, and no goal nets. I had to watch the reaction of the goalkeeper to see if it were a goal. If a good shot at the goal goes to the corner of the goalpost, you can't tell if it's under or over the bar. I would be slow in blowing my whistle, to see whether the goalkeeper placed the ball for a goal kick or threw it to the centre of the field. My clients all thought I was mad, but it was the aggro that stopped me going mad. As with Judo, it helped me work out my frustrations.

## Wanstead Flats Again

The weekend after a holiday in Italy, I was suntanned brown as a nut. The match started well until nearing the end of the game, then the losing side start getting ratty – one bastard and you're fighting for control. I took two names and just about held it together. On leaving the field of play, a voice shouted, 'F—ing Paki bastard!' I turned round, but no one admitted to shouting at me. I knew I was well tanned, but not that much. At another match, I was called a Jewish bastard. I wonder what would have been said if they had known that I was an Italian bastard? They must have known as they had seen my name. Maybe they could not pronounce it, and made wrong assumptions. After all it's a good English name!

[Just had a phone call – Angelo has died. His daughter said that he had the old photo of him, Gino and me on a bike from during the war, on his pillow. Are we getting old?]

# Walthamstow

Not only football went on down Sandy Lane, especially at night where the boys would take their girlfriends for a little cuddle and whatever! The football pitches were cheek by jowl, with only room for a linesman to run along – if you had one. On the next pitch the ref was having a bad time. He eventually lost control completely and was being manhandled. I had to step in, as it usually spreads. I stopped my watch and crossed over. I gave them a rollicking – I do that very well – and also said I would report them for abusing the referee. This brought a protest from the opposing side, who said they had nothing to do with it! I said that I would leave it with their ref, and had a few words with him. We both blew our whistles, started and finished with no further trouble. I heard no more about it. You can't be weak!

On the same ground a few weeks later I refereed a good match. In the second half it peed with rain, and we were soaked in no time. I put it to the teams that by the time we made it to the dressing rooms we would be gaining nothing, as they were some distance away, and that as we had only ten minutes left, we should carry on. To this they agreed. With only minutes left, a goal kick was given, the goalkeeper took his shot and the ball hit a player on the head, or perhaps the player was heading it. Remember that in those days (fifty years ago) the footballs were all leather, and a good strong leather lace to finish with. In all that wet, the ball weighed a ton! He went down like a stone, in slow motion. It took over five minutes for him to come round. He was helped off the field. He was taken to hospital, but was not kept in. Today the pros could not live with those leather balls; one retired professional is said to have died from injuries sustained from heading the leather ball! I can believe that.

## Tate and Lyle, Silver Town

I had a hell of a job finding the Tate and Lyle sports ground. I eventually found the pitch, covered in snow. I told the waiting home team that the pitch was unplayable, as I could not see the markings on the field of play, and would call the match off. The visiting team had not yet arrived and the home captain asked, 'If we clear the lines of snow, could you referee?' I had come a long way and they were eager to play. I said that I would if the visitors agreed. They did a good job clearing the lines. We waited half an hour, but the away team did not turn up. The home team were disappointed, and so was I! I enjoyed my refereeing; one man against two teams – I loved it! I was sorry to pack it in, but everything has an ending. All the incidents, I'd relate to my clients the following week. They would laugh with me.

# Gosport Road

## Turned Over by Elmo

My family would not leave me alone. Always demanding! Elmo was the only one of the family to come to the East Ham shop, but that was only to get money from me. The shop was doing very well. Marie and I wished to move from the flat in Leytonstone. Flats were available in Walthamstow – for a price. Elmo said that Fred from the market could get me one, but he had to have a hundred pound up front. The flats were going up on the corner of Markhouse Road and Lea Bridge Road. We saw them go up and also saw them become occupied. He had turned me over, and kept us on a string for a year! He had no connection whatsoever with the flats. What a bastard! Trying to get my money back, I went to my father with my troubles. He gave me fifty pounds, but would not give me the hundred. I said that he could stop it out of Elmo's wages – after all, you're the boss. I bet he never even asked. Two of a kind. With all the hustle that my brother gave me, we never came to blows. I think that he would have killed me if we had, being bigger and stronger than me.

When Elmo married Sylvia, he rented Selbourne Road Function Rooms. Food was included in the price. Again I was conned by my mother to be his best man. (He owed me so much money!) I must be a very weak person – I gave in. I put twenty pounds (a week's wages, in those days) in my top pocket, just in case.

At the reception, Elmo kept telling me how lucky I was, as I should be paying for the wedding, being the best man. I walked away. I could see that he was trying to corner me – it became catch me if you can. Eventually he did. 'I'll let you off; just pay for the band,' he said. 'Bollocks!' I replied, but he had gone. I looked at the bandleader, who in turn was looking at me. He knew he was on a sticky wicket. Elmo had already told him that I would pay him. I'm sure it was twenty pounds. I went over to him, told him I had been conned into paying and gave him his money. I said he was lucky, for which he was very thankful. Marie never did find out: I'm sure she would have left me. A few years later my sister, Ena, rented the same hall for her wedding. She had to pay in full before she even stepped into the hall, as Elmo had not paid a penny for his wedding. What a family!

My father had died, and Elmo took over running the shop. I was told that as I had a shop, it was right for Elmo to take over our father's shop. That was fine by me. I think my sisters thought I was getting too big for my boots. After all, was I not the family prat?

My mother moved down to the ground floor, and Elmo and Sylvia moved in the top. Just a few months after, my sister Frances was on the phone, telling me that Elmo was not giving any money to Mum and also not paying the bills! Elmo's clients loved him; he certainly had charisma, and a lot of bodyweight that would intimidate his friends. However, his self-assurance and attitude landed him in jail. One of his clients had loaned him money and saw Elmo at the Walthamstow dog track. The client said, 'If you can afford to bet, give me the money you owe me.' Unfortunately, when Elmo started to walk away, he grabbed him and Elmo, who had a very short fuse, got stuck in and hurt the chap badly. The chap had him for assault, and that started all my troubles.

Elmo phoned me at my East Ham shop, telling me that he was about to go to prison for assault, and that I would have to take the Gosport Road shop on to look after Mum. I was shocked at being told what to do with my life. I tried to find a way out, but at a meeting with the family, it was made clear that as I was the oldest, it was my duty to take over the shop. Why did they all of a sudden remember that I was the oldest male? After all, I was not asked when the old man died to do my duty. No! I had a shop, I was all right. The family put my marriage on the line: to choose between my mother and Marie. To my shame, to this day, I cannot forgive myself for the decision that I took. I was made to pay for that decision. It was years later that I found out how I had paid, not only in money. (I don't forgive or forget!).

I left a shop that had earned me £2,000 in the bank on 15 September 1958. Marie and I had been contemplating buying a house in Hornchurch and the price was £2,400. Within two years I had nothing! E17 took me a long time to build back. When Sylvia's family opened a barbershop nearby in Markhouse Road for Elmo, his old clients went to him as they would. Why Marie didn't leave me, I'll never know, but she stuck by me. The family had played on my guilt complex. After a couple of months in Gosport Road, I went to see Frances in Wood Street, and cried on her doorstep on realising what I had done to Marie. She did not sink to her knees as she had when she learned Elmo was in prison. That was because she was off the hook and the prat was standing there in front of her!

Elmo came out of jail and his in-laws, the Mead family, (they stood up for him as well!) opened a hairdressing shop, ten minutes' walk from Gosport Road. Half the clients I had left me and went to Elmo. They thought that I had done the dirty on him by taking the shop over while he was in jail. I persevered and the trade built up again, but slowly. His shop went down quickly as he did not believe in paying bills. He took money from our mother. I was giving Mother support, renting a couple of rooms for her, and she was helping Elmo. I was paying the bills!

One of Elmo's friends, who had left me when Elmo returned to the fold and who I knew slightly came into my shop and said, 'Ugo, your brother owes me twenty pounds. I went into Elmo's shop – no one was there – I looked in the backroom and there was this Radiogram. 'I'm going to take it for what he owes me!' I said, 'Do what you bloody like.' He and his wife carried it from Markhouse Road, along St James Street, crossing the bottom of the High Street and into Black Horse Road. It's a long walk to where they lived, near the Standard pub. When Elmo's shop failed, Sylvia was pregnant with twins and they went to Lincolnshire, near her dad. One of his clients came to me saying that Elmo owed him money. I said, 'Whom does he not owe?' I told him to f— off! He expected me to pay what was owed by my brother. I found new clients, plus my own clients that followed me from West Ham. The majority of my clients were not local. Those who had left me were not welcomed back, as I told them politely to take their money elsewhere, and put it where the monkey puts his nuts!

*29 Gosport Road, Walthamstow*

I did not know that Elmo had been living with my mother in Gosport Road. She never said a word to me; I was keeping them both! I only found out after my shoes were missing. One morning I opened the shop – the stinking oil heater had gone. My mother had given it to Elmo for his shop! He would be out of the house before I got there in the morning, but ate and slept at my expense. I told my mother off for taking me for a fool! She said, 'He was in need,' and that I was no angel. No – just the family prat!

I have a feeling that the family thought that Mum had the freehold of the shop a long lease. It was a fallacy. On a Monday morning, Mum said we had to see a solicitor about the shop, to sort things out. I never found out who told Mum to do this. We went to the solicitors in Hoe Street, just past the railway station. The 'sorting out' was that I could not sell the shop while Mum was alive. It was not freehold, and the lease had only a few years left to run (in fact, two years). My family had got rid of Mum, and put her on my back! When the grocer's shop next door was closing down they offered me the shop. The building was in a better shape than the barbershop. It also had a bath and toilet inside. At that time I still had some money. I told my mother that I was about to buy it. She said, 'I'm not moving! I have been here all the time and it suits me.' I pointed to her the comforts it had. She had me by the B— (this was the mother who loved me?). I found out later that Jerry had had his hand in my affairs. It was he who suggested the solicitor! Why? So he would not be lumbered with my mother? (I told you that I was a prat!)

I bought the head lease from the landlady whose solicitor came to see me and made me an offer that I took. Later we bought the freehold. In fact, it was Norma who gave me the money to buy the freehold. So in the end the family gave me nothing, but took everything. I had not realised how little money we had left, until Marie had died. She had kept it from me. After the expenses of the funeral, I was nearly skint. As my present wife, Norma, said, 'I don't want you to worry. You have a card to play: I can always work.' No, I did not like my wife working! It must be the Italian in me.

I had a taste of earning quick money! Working in Gosport Road one Friday, a client asked for a packet of Sword Edge Blades. These were new shaving blades that kept their edge, and lasted a long time. They were like gold dust! My wholesaler only gave me three packets at a time. I said I could not get them. A young lad took his turn and said confidently, 'Do you want some blades? How many?' I said, 'A box.' There were usually a dozen packets in a box. Two days later he turns up with a box of blades – a very big box! I think I had to change my trousers. First he wanted nearly a week's wages. I said, 'I haven't the money to pay you, as I only wanted a dozen packets. He said, 'I can't take them back; I'll be in trouble!' I said, 'Give me a week.' I closed the shop for a couple of hours and went around a few shops I knew. I sold them off cheap, very cheap, and still made a good profit – in fact, a week's wages. I kept it from Marie, but was nervous. I made up my mind not to buy any more.

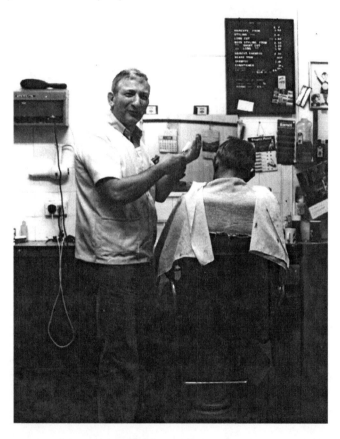

*Gosport Road shop in the 1970s*

I was speaking to a stallholder who the previous night had emptied scent bottles down the pan, because on the TV (*Police 5*) the presenter was asking the public to inform the police if anybody tried to sell them the scent (see later). I told him about the blades and told him I did not want to know! He got excited. 'I'll pay you. All you have to do is, when he delivers, give me a bell; I'll come round straight away!' I was getting more then working all week just by picking the phone up. What would you have done? The only trouble was that I was neither a gambler nor a drinker; therefore, I was loaded as the saying goes. When I gave Marie this bundle of money, she went mad. 'What will happen when you go inside? Do you think so little of me?' I phoned the stall chap; he was annoyed but said, 'I'll tell you what I'll do, Ugo, I'll give you half every time he delivers to me. You arrange the meeting.' I did, and still earned quite a few bob. It just shows you that sometimes it pays. (Cast a stone. If you can?)

I was lucky, as a few weeks later the police staked out the bookmakers' in Gosport Road, five shops down from me. They would have seen this chap delivering this big box. Temptation is a terrible thing. I have kept straight since – but it just shows that every man has a price! Now, what have you got for me? Well it was two weeks from Christmas, and my client asked if I wanted any whisky. 'Well,' I said, 'I'll have two.' The following week he came in with a pen and notebook, and said, 'You're sure you only want two?' He was taking orders and was not talking of bottles, but cases! He wanted to stack them in the side passage. I lost a client for refusing. It just shows how you can drop a clanger!

When my mother died, she left a little over a thousand pounds. I'm sure that even Elmo got a share. Funny, as my mother had nothing when I took over the shop – what a family. Mum had the rent from the letting, and had no rent of her own to pay. I paid the bills. Do I really protest too much? Elmo did get a share of Mum's money, thanks to my sister! (There was and is animosity from my family towards me. Why? Is it because my mother loved me? That's a laugh!)

I was only a few weeks back in Gosport Road when one of my old mates' mums came into the shop. 'How are you doing, Ugo?' she asked, knowing very well how I was doing as she always swung on her garden gate and saw everything. 'You were always good mates with my son,' she continued. He had left E17 and gone to Southend. 'Could you see your way and lend me four pounds for the rent till he comes next week? He's a good boy to me.' I did – but unfortunately, this kept on for weeks and months. I would lend her the money on Saturday, she would give it back on Thursday, and then I would lend it again Saturday. I had to put a stop to it, and then she would not speak to me; it was a shame. One of my clients became too old to come to the shop, so I'd go and cut his hair at home. Well into his eighties, he'd tell me of the days he would not go to the City by train, so he could save his sixpence fare. He would walk from Gosport Road, Walthamstow, on to Leyton and Hackney Marshes and on to the City. After he finished work he would return the same way – six days a week, saving a shilling a day. It went a long way those days. He lived to a ripe old age.

I was a soft touch for old people. One client asked me to cut his father-in-law's hair. It was winter, cold and very dark. His house was the last one in Corbet Road, a dead end off Wood Street. I was ushered down a passage into the scullery. The old boy was already sitting in a chair and the table was laid for tea with cups and saucers. The family were all watching me cutting his hair. Halfway through the haircut – SWOOSH! That put me on my toes, ready for anything. The cups were dancing vigorously in their saucers; everything moveable in that scullery danced along with the vibration. All except the family, who didn't turn a hair. The railway line to Liverpool Street, ran along the back of their house – they didn't even notice it. It's funny what you become accustomed to.

# Robert Barltrop

Robert Barltrop, author and journalist, wrote a nice article on me on 7 August 1981, entitled 'A Cut Above the Rest'. He became a friend of mine. He wrote on Jack London and the ways of Londoners in speech and mannerisms. He was a very heavy smoker and a strong left-winger.

One day he was invited to give a talk on the rights and wrongs of the government. He was given a rousing welcome as he took his seat on the platform. It was an audience of ladies. On seating himself, out came his cigarettes and he promptly lit one. He was quickly pulled up by the chairwoman and told there was no smoking allowed! He removed the cigarette with his nicotine-stained fingers, arose from his chair and walked out. He told me he was quite upset on not being allowed to smoke.

I was so pleased to be in touch with Robert, especially when he phoned me. He has had a rough time health-wise, but being a tough old bird, St Peter would not let him in! All is well and Robert has stopped smoking; I did not think it was possible. But after kissing death on the cheek, Robert saw the light! Leaving that all behind, Robert still writes articles and other news in the Recorder group of newspapers this side of London in 'Robert Barltrop – Reflections of the Past'. Robert mentioned me in 'Stolen Away in Italian Job' and how I was keeping a barbershop open at the age of fourteen years old when they interned my old man. He also reflected on other Italians he knew. I liked the ending when in 1970, I'd shout from the doorway of the shop, 'Italy for the World Cup!' Was that when Italy lost to Korea? My clients would come out of their way in their cars, honking the car horns to draw my attention and pull their eyes into slits. It was all in good fun. Just think, today I could have sued them. Mind you, they would have wanted half. Thank you Robert, you are always a good read. One day when I was thinking about my mates dying off Robert said, 'You get to that stage and wonder if you will get past your dinner.'

# Father Confessor

More tales from my clients in Walthamstow. Harry, an old friend of mine, told me about the time he and his two mates were finding their feet and a stirring in their loins. His family had moved south at the end of the war, then returned to E17. He and four of his mates made their minds to go to the West End, for a good night out. Two had never been there before. They set off from the Bakers Arms by bus, off for a good night out. They went to a well-known club, with just about enough money for couple of drinks each. They were making the drink last by just sipping now and then. One of the lads had a young girl hanging on to him; maybe he bought her a drink. He said, 'Don't wait for me,

I'll be all right,' with a wink and a nod to his mates. Off he went with the girl on his arm. After the boys drained the last drops from the glass, they meandered around until it was time to pick up the bus back home. 'I'll be all right' was not there. They saw the bus leave, and much later another bus went off. They started to search for him, but were lost – where to look?

Eventually to the police station they went. They explained the situation to the officer behind the desk, who said, arising from his chair, 'Come with me.' They walked down the corridor and he opened a door on his left. There was their mate wrapped in a big blanket; he was in the nude. The girl had taken him to Hyde Park where her mates were waiting, and they jumped him. Finding no money, only the drips of the beer on his shirt, they stripped him, tied his hands around a tree and left him. He shouted at passers-by for help, but all he got were laughs and blokes coming up to slap his bare arse! Eventually the police had come and taken him to the station.

Quite weird stories I'd be told. After all, I am father confessor. What about this one? Three mates went to a friend's party and got drunk. There is always one who will have more than the others. They took him to the upstairs bedroom to sleep it off. For fun, they found a jar of Vaseline in the bathroom and rubbed a little around his arse and left him on the bed snoring. They rejoined the party and left him sleeping it off. When he awoke, by all accounts he rushed down the stairs and out of the front door! They have not seen him to this day. I hope somehow he reads this, and knows that he is still a virgin. ROTTEN SODS.

The clients would come into the shop, eager to tell me their secrets. After all, whom else could they tell that instead of being at home with their wife, they were giving some blonde girl a good rogering! She thought it was the first time you had a bit. As you could not get off the nest, the pills your mate from the chemist gave you worked! Trust me not to tell a soul. Was it you that held my arm to stop me working, to make sure I had all your attention? Not even peeved that the clients were only pretending to read the *Boxing News* or the newspaper. Or were you telling the shop for your own gratification? A conquest is a conquest; it must be told!

One of my worst moments, on returning to the shop in E17, was when the wife of Mr Rossi, who had had the ice cream shop in the High Street and had died, had been trying to get the money that was owed to him by my brother. It must have been substantial. She'd come every Friday night when I was busy, and follow me as I worked around the chair, asking for the money that Elmo owed her! I knew how she felt, but I could not pay what he owed her. He owed me much more then her! She was not the only one who expected me to pay his debts! Word got around that I was a prat, as my family knew all along. Did you not? I don't believe you!

## Noisy Neighbours

The house was two doors from my shop. Two families – one up the other down – shared the toilet in the garden. No opulent bath, just the old tin bath hanging on a nail on the wall, beside the outside toilet. The blokes were both clients, with nice families. The one who lived below would always moan to me about the lack of sleep they were getting. He and his wife slept under the upstairs bedroom. The upper couple being young and frisky had regular sex. 'Nothing wrong with that,' he'd say, 'but the bed has one foot shorter than the others, and we have to wait through the slow bonking until the machinegun stage is reached; it's a long time getting there!'

The carpet shop four doors from me would have a lot to say, if only his carpets could talk! The owner also had a big vanload of carpets pinched while it was parked in Queens Road, while he was getting his hair cut in Elmo's shop; I think it was all arranged. Arthur Western knew more than was said. His friend served in the Navy during the war, in the submarines. He was in the Adriatic at the beginning of hostilities; it was depth-charged and it popped up. They were taken prisoners by the Italians, with no loss of life. At the beginning, it was very comfortable in the camp; they had sheets on their beds. Some time later, they lost the sheets, as the Italians got to know that their prisoners had no sheets. (How did they know?) He told me that they were treated well.

# Ernie M

Another friend was Ernie M, a long-standing client from Leytonstone, who followed me to East Ham and then to Walthamstow. Ernie came into Stanley's and started on the subject of the Jews, telling me about the trouble in Palestine. He had a bee in his bonnet about it. I knew what it was all about, and he thought I was a Jew. That did not worry me! This kept up for months until one day I said, 'I'm not a bloody Jew, I'm a bloody Italian!' He looked at me and said, 'I chased you lot up the mountains [Mount Kerren].' I replied something like, 'Bollocks!' and we started a long friendship.

I knew all his family from when they were children, and we still keep in touch. He was a decorator and came from East London. Ernie and his lads followed me to East Ham for their haircuts. It was there that he told me of this young girl, under sixteen, but a big girl for her age. She would always stop to speak to him, and he was beginning to like her. I told him not to be a fool and said, 'You're about forty with a nice family.' He had three boys and two girls. By all accounts, his wife had hip trouble, walked with sticks and had 'gone off the boil' whereas he was very virile.

He told the young girl to leave him alone, as she would get him into trouble, but she would not. Eventually he took her to dinner saying to me that he would behave himself – until she reached the age of sixteen. It was awkward for me, knowing all the family. Though it was not my affair, later on he would involve me. This affair went on for over three years and he had had a few narrow escapes, one of which comes to mind. He would pop around to her home in Loughton while her family were away. He always went in the house with tools, to give the impression that he had work to do, then have it away in her bedroom. One day, while doing what they did, there was a ring at the front door – panic! He ran halfway down the stairs, then ran up again, and hid under the bed. It was her auntie, who kept her talking for a considerable time.

When her auntie finally left, Ernie came downstairs and noticed a gun over the fireplace. His bum tightened up. On his next visit he brought along a file; with it he proceeded to file the pin off the gun. He said that he felt better after that.

Ernie's story is long and sad. His three boys grew up into good lads. The youngest lad, David, married in Leytonstone. Alan, the middle one, was to pick up the bride from her home in Chingford, but forgot! She eventually came, in her bridal outfit with her bridesmaids, by bus to the Green Man, Leytonstone. There were ructions, but all was well in the end.

Alan was a big strong boy at boxing and wanted me to manage him as a boxer. I said that I never had the time, and got him to box under my friend, Terry Lawless. I said that he should box as an amateur first, as did Terry. Alan won his first match in Southend by a KO in the first round, then could not get another fight. Terry took him on. Unfortunately, Alan had to go into the army for eighteen months. On being demobbed, he received his pro papers, but he never had the ability to overcome the crowd, and would go into a trance. But in the gym he'd fight like a champion.

Ernie would use me as an excuse for coming in late at his home. That was not nice! Dave, his son, would work for his dad to help him out when busy. He would say to me, 'Why does Dad keep a nice suit in the shed at work?' I said, 'Dave, does your dad look after your mum?' He said, 'Yes.' I then said, 'Mind your own business.' He took the hint.

Cancer took hold of Ernie; he had lumps everywhere, but still saw his girlfriend. I visited him in hospital and felt very sad for him. He came out of hospital and his wife looked after him well, she was a nice lady. Ernie told me that his girlfriend wanted to look after him, and he was going with her. I did my best to stop him, but could not. They went to Godstone, in Surrey where I had been during the war. A week later Dave came to see me at Highams Park and said, 'Come on, Ugo, you must help us. Where is he? And who is she?' I had a photo that Ernie had given me to show off his girlfriend. Dave was shocked. He knew her; she was younger than him, and had plenty of money and a big house. He could not believe it.

I gave him the address, and they brought him home; he was in a bad way. Ernie ended up in Hackney Hospice. It had bad memories for me, as Marie, my late wife, had also died there. I went to see him; his wife and daughter were there. They said, 'He can't hear you; he has only a few hours left.' I stood beside his bed, took hold of his hand and said, 'Ernie!' He opened his eyes and gave my hand a squeeze and then the grip loosened. I had told him that I would be there. I said I was sorry. I turned and walked away, leaving his wife and daughter to their grief. They had stood by him, what more can you say? Being father confessor is not all honey.

I asked Dave if he wanted anything altered on his dad. He said, 'Leave it as it is.'

There was another client, whom I will call 'Jack', with a family I had known for years. Jack, who had served in the Royal Navy during the war, had a few tales to tell. He was a good-looking man, with a tic in his eye, and lived in Ashford Road – not far from the man who wanted the hairs singed from around his fishing tackle. He did a stint in America, where he and the rest of the sailors were well looked after with frequent parties, and the girls were very friendly! A big fat girl was playing the piano, and he thought he would be safe going with her. He soon struck up a friendship with her, as he was also a good piano player. After all, who would fancy her? he thought. Obviously quite a few had the same thoughts as he ended up with syphilis, or was it gonorrhoea? In those days the treatment was a tube inserted into your penis; then an instrument was pushed into the tube that opened into a claw at the end of the tube. When the claw opened and was pulled up it made grooves on the inside, to release the pus. My legs are crossed as I'm writing this! The Navy always informed the wives. She forgave him, or so I'm told.

## The Bear

Tommy, known as 'the Bear' was also a client of mine with a few others from the Krays. He came into the shop and said, 'Ugo, I need twenty-five pounds, as the rates people are after me. I have until this afternoon to pay.' I had a feeling I had been set up, but he was a good payer every two weeks for a haircut and shave, and much more if he had a Pashana Friction, so I said, 'I don't have that money' (haircuts were only two and six) 'but let me see.' I gave him nine pounds in notes and eleven pounds in silver and nearly cleared my till. He demurred: 'No, boy, I'll not take the silver.' But I scooped it all into his big hands. He had a shop in Tottenham Hale and was back with the money within two weeks, when he had his next haircut. He always gave me a fiver. I've never had trouble with the boys. In fact they kept me straight. I was quite fond of Reg and George, whom my wife thought were gentlemen, and so they were to us.

Tommy Brown told me that when he was in his shop at Tottenham Hale, four blokes came in and started to give him a good hiding. There was a pole supporting the ceiling in the centre of the shop, and he hung on to that pole for dear life, as he said, 'If I was knocked down to the floor, they would have kicked my head in!' 'Didn't you fight back?' I asked. 'No, it was payback, you just took your punishment!' I was told that a relation of his from the Hale had killed a constable, and shoved him down a drain. This was told to me by Jerry who worked in a garage at the Hale. Jerry was also looking for a place to live, as he and my sister were living in a couple of rooms at that time. Telling his woes to one of the Browns, Jerry was told to find a house around the Hale and he'd get it! 'There are no empty houses around here,' said Jerry. 'Don't worry about that, I'll empty it for you!' said he. Jerry did not take the offer.

Tom would go into a shop, any shop, and bully the owner into buying whatever he had at hand. It was a roll of lino that fell off the back of a lorry – cheap? Greed will eventually take over, and you buy! That's a big mistake! Tom will come back a few weeks later and sell you more. You might say, 'I've still got the last lot!' but he will say, 'I need the money, if you don't buy, the police will know what you have at the back!'

Another thing he said to me was that he always had on him a stiff sheet of silver foil. If he were in a tight corner he would pull it out, and on doing a runner it would glint in the sun like a knife. They would stop chasing.

You're not even safe in the country, with fields around you. (Tell me all my son, I'm listening – I shan't tell.) 'I'd pick a big house, and I'd suss it out for a week. See what time they go shopping and return, how many live in the house, what time they go to bed, what type of alarm they have. It's hard work, and I sleep rough! I've got a good pair of binoculars and I see everything. I take food with me, but I still lose a few pounds in weight. When I'm satisfied, I get in touch with the boys in London. The large van goes straight towards the house, passing the people on their way for the day. We don't take long to load up, after neutralising the alarm. We would be well on the road to London before they are back home. That day would be picked as it had been noted that they did not return until late evening.' I did not realise how much detail they took in everything.

I've had some funny offers from my clients, who were very mixed in culture. These are some of the offers. (Offers?)

I was asked to partake in a boxing match up the West End. A dinner show and 'bow ties' – a posh club? We would fake the fight – pull the punches, stagger, cling on, grunt and groan. Even fake blood was used. I turned it down. I did not think that I was that good an actor, but they paid well.

# Porn!

I was also approached by a client in Leytonstone to partake in a film. 'What?' said I. 'Everybody would recognise me!' 'No,' he said, 'you wear a mask!' No thank you! When it came to sex I was too naïve, or too frightened.

# Decoy

I have a high regard for the police, and have recommended some of my Judoka students to the force. One is quite high; is that right Geoff?

I was asked if I'd take part in a scam, to catch out a massage parlour that was giving extras. I would have to go the whole way. I thought it was a bit over the top, and there was no money attached to the job. I said 'No thank you!' There's a limit in doing your duty.

The one offer I really thought about was in Soho. This client whom I've known for some time and who was never short of a few bob told me that he has to leave his job in Soho. He was running a bookshop selling porn films and photos. He had been fined quite a few times, and was told by the judge that the next time he appeared before him it would be a jail sentence! It came hard for him, as the judge was his best customer. Not only he, but many more in good positions were this man's best clients!

He was looking for the right bloke, and it was me! I really gave it thought, as I could never get near to such a sum as he earned. It was my wife who kept me on the straight and narrow. The chap who took over, whom I knew slightly, not long after he took the job, moved from his flat into a very big house. Who says that being straight pays? But there is always a price to pay somewhere along the line.

## George Burgess - Orologist-Artist

I'll tell you about George Burgess, an artist who lived further along in Gosport Road past the Ringwood pub. He started the art of orology, in which he made pictures from pieces of old watches – fantastic. George had a marvellous sense of humour. He used to hang his pictures on the railings in Green Park in the West End where there was a great variety of art on display. One Sunday morning Norma and I had a walk around there, and saw George was busy, with the tourists queuing for him. I joined the line. He was drawing their silhouettes. Eventually I reached him, without changing expression. He looked at me and said, 'Sod off, I'm not drawing Italians today!' I said nothing. The tourists stood open-mouthed. He drew my shadow and I walked off without paying. We gave the tourists some thing to talk about that day.

George came into my shop for his haircut, and told me that he and his lady assistant were having nightmares and could not sleep after the weekends. They had eventually worked it out – the pub in which they had a drink after work was filled with cigarette smoke, and it was the 'in' thing for artists of that time to smoke dope. They had been inhaling the smoke. Another artist, a photographer, would frighten the tourists by placing his big parrot on their shoulder and saying, 'It's all right; it won't hurt you!' apparently oblivious of his shoulder pad, that had been torn to shreds by the parrot's claws. George Burgess moved to Cornwall and is doing very well. He still comes up at weekends to hang out in Green Park, in the West End of London. Phoning George, conversing on the change in E17, I'd say, 'Do you remember when I was the only foreigner in Gosport Road?' He said, 'You were all right; you used to walk with your hands up!' (I'll have him, one of these days!)

I have many orological pictures of his hanging on the wall of my bungalow. He did a special picture of a galleon for Marie and me. George is not well at this time of writing, on reading my book of many mistakes. We speak over the phone.

George let me have his house in St Ives, Cornwall, to give Marie and me a break, when she was very ill. It never cost us a penny, only the petrol I used. The house was on the edge of the cliff, the balcony overlooked the sea, and far below were the waves hitting the cliff's side. It was beautiful, but unfortunately, Marie became worse and we had to cut it short. We had a horrendous journey home. She passed away in St Joseph's Hospice, Hackney, on 20 October 1975. May she rest in peace. I hope she will forgive my selfishness.

# Mafia

While living in Beresford Road, E17, on arriving home from work. Marie told me that she had had a phone call from a cousin of mine, who was in the American Navy and was on his way to see us. I did not know him and did not know our family in America only that my Uncle Donato Romano – Mum's eldest brother – had left for the USA before we came to live in England. Therefore I was somewhat surprised that he knew where we lived.

Around eight o'clock that evening this American officer turns up, in uniform. Unfortunately the dining room floorboards were up, as I had dry rot and it was being treated. I apologised as he stepped in between the gaps, and we made him at home in the kitchen. He would not have anything to eat, saying he had eaten on his way from Liverpool, where his ship was docked.

I asked him how he had found us. He said he had found us from the telephone directory; after all there are not many by the name of Patriarca in the phone book. Marie was bemused by it all. He said that this was his last trip, as he was leaving the Navy. He had a good job waiting for him, as the family always looked after its own. I did not grasp the significance of his meaning. He told me that the family had some business in London and he had been told to look me up to see if I was interested in working for them. Then the penny dropped. This was at the time when George Raft was trying to open gambling casinos in London, but would I been able to get a license?

Marie was trying to make sense of the conversation, as I was – I think they wanted me as a front man. I said that I was not into gambling, and knew nothing about it. Also I was up to my neck with repairing the house. He did not push it at all. All he said was that the family would look after me. He never mentioned the Mafia once. He could see that I was a pillock. I took him to Gosport Road, where Mum was living behind the shop. She had once met him in Italy when she was there for a holiday. I left him there with Mum.

It did not stop there. It was not long after Marie had died that I came home late one night to find a note on the mat. I had been at my Judo club. The note was from an aunt in America, who had come to see me, asking me to phone the number given. It was the number of a hotel in the West End; I can't remember which one. I got through and this lady answered the phone. To make sure it was me I had to answer some questions: what was my mother's maiden name; where was she born; whom did she marry; and what was my full name? After all that palaver I said I would come to see her. She said, 'You're too late, as we are about to leave for the airport early in the morning.'

That was the last time I had any connection with the family. Capiche?

A cousin from Italy came and stayed with us. He had just left university. He was a very nice chap, but spoke no English. He stayed with us for about a month or so. He would set off with a map of London each morning and we would not see him again until late in the evening. In that short time he learned to speak understandable English. He was very good with figures (he became an accountant) and knew London inside out. On returning to Italy and keeping in touch with the family he said he was offered a job in America, which he took. Within two years Mum's family wrote to say that he had died on the boat bringing him back to Italy from America. He had worked for our family, or should it be The Family. I never did find out how he died.

# Clients

The lads looked on what they were doing as a job and would tell me things that would not tell anyone else. After doing a job for his governor, the Krays (the gay one), my client finished late, as you would, and was told not to worry as he could sleep there in Stoke Newington. He said, 'My bottle went! As you know the reputation that he had but what could I do? I fretted and sweated somewhat, then made up my mind to take what was coming! Thank God he told me to sleep on the couch.

My mate Reg was a gentle yet tough guy; I liked him, and he always made me laugh. At Ilford one morning walking down the street, there was a fracas! People were running out of the bank, and two of them came running towards him. He shouted, 'I'm one of yous!' as they were giving him the eye – he did not know what else to shout! (I shan't recall Wood Street, Reg.) They took it as a job. They did not harm anybody unless they were opposition. I can't say they were saints, but who can cast a stone, I can't – we all have our weak moments, don't we?

Tom was a big chap, and told me of an incident in the Turkish baths. Entering the steamy room with a towel wrapped around the lower part of his body, a man and a lady were sitting there. After ten or so minutes the chap left the room. Tom let his towel slip, and gave her the eye. She responded and he gave her one! Tell me all, I shan't tell! Tom was also a sparring partner to Tommy Farr. (You must be old if you can remember.) He was good, I'm told, but would not train and ran out of steam.

# Higham Hill Judo Club

I received my black belt (first dan) on 5 November 1972 but I was already teaching at the Tech when Dave Robinson (the instructor) or Len were not able to make it. I started teaching the young ladies at the Girls' Life Brigade in Greenleaf Road, Walthamstow, with the help of Vic Cocksedge. In 1967 Roy Reynolds, manager of the Whittingham Youth Centre in Higham Hill, E17, asked me to start up a club from scratch. Originally it was for the youth club there, but it gradually became a mainly adult club. The centre was under the Walthamstow council (I knew the Mayor, Mr O'Brien – a client).

To form a Judo class in a youth centre is not all that easy. The youngsters, fifteen to sixteen years old, all want to be champions in the first week of instruction. They do not like discipline but like to inflict pain on others, not on themselves.

After two weeks you are lucky if you have more then half a dozen left in your class. You start by treating them softly and find out who's keen – and those who want to be killers! You encourage them to bring friends and start with groundwork. The grappling techniques – *kata-gatame* (shoulder hold), *waza-ari* (floor hold), *kesa-gatame* (scarf hold), *ogoshi* (hip throw or roll), *kata-juji-jime* (single cross strangle), *juji-jime* – makes them feel good.

The club members below were the hard core always turned up twice a week. As in any club, there are floating members who come when they like. The youngsters belonged to the youth centre, and all left as they did not fit in. I did not teach youngsters, as their parents would interfere, and hung around the hall throughout the evening. The dojo was on the first floor of a building containing two halls and was separated from the main hall. You entered the hall by a flight of stone steps on the side. On the floor of the hall mats were laid into a square (the mats are called *tatami*). These were donated by the Mayor of Walthamstow, Mr O'Brien. *Juji-jime* is dangerous and you had to watch the students all the time, as they liked nothing better than to render their opponent unconscious. You could cut off the supply of blood to the brain within five seconds, less at higher grades. The three youngsters below were the last and were gone the following week.

*Ugo's Judo class*

In a mixed class you have to be very careful, as there is a lot of body contact and accidents do happen. Once a young girl, Janet, eighteen years old, came off the Judo mat and said that John had grabbed her breast. I said, 'Look at John.' He was on the mat with an opponent, but happened to look up at that moment and saw me talking to Janet. He showed no sign of guilt. Janet was a very strong girl, holder of a blue belt, and you had to attack her strongly to get an *ippon* – a throw that was heavy and clean – from her. It's very awkward when you have to hold the jacket when your opponent is moving into you or away from you. I talked her out of it and it all settled down.

In the end I had to let in adults to the Judo class, as youngsters, though keen as mustard to begin with, if they find it a bit painful they lose heart. Reynolds was given the go-ahead from the council and the class built up. I had a very strong class in the end. The average weight of the class was twelve to thirteen stone. Three of them were at the sixteen stone mark. I would arrive home with sunken eyes, battered and bruised. I could not teach from the edge of the mat: I had to be involved. You had to show that you could do what you were teaching! Also it made me feel good. The class respected me. When in contest with other clubs who did not know me, I would be among the heavyweights, and the instructor of the opposition would always go to one of the big lads, who pointed to me. It was just my little pleasure on seeing the expression on their face.

I had a few injuries in my time, showing the class how to break-fall over four Judokas bending down. You run towards them, dive head first over them, and finish into a roll. It does not always work and once on demonstrating the technique I landed heavily on the base of my spine. I rose up, forced myself to speak, and pretended that all was well! For the rest of the class I could only defend myself; every movement was painful. I got home and lay on the hard floor for around an hour.

Another time, having a *randori* (free practice), I caught this tall Judoka as he came for me just right! I caught him with a sweeping ankle throw. He went as high as my head, if not more, and instead of break falling, he hung on to my jacket, pulled himself on to me, landing on my chest and knocking me down, with his weight across my legs. There was a crack that resounded around the room, I gave a yelp, swore in Italian, Jewish and gibberish! The class as one all shouted, 'That's nothing!' It was my saying when someone was hurt, as I pulled them to their feet. The man was upset, as I gave him a rollicking, and never returned to the class. It was then that I discovered bliss, hobbling over to the sink we had in the corner of the hall and putting my foot in cold water. It was such a relief. Robert, one of the top boys, carried me down the stairs on his back. I drove home – I was back in E17 then. I had worked two days before I had it seen to in Whipps Cross hospital (silly sod). I had my saddle bone in my foot broken. It was very comfortable when the plaster was applied and did not affect my work. Marie said, 'I have no pity for you. Self-inflicted.' It was a few weeks later, and I was still instructing with my leg in plaster, when Arthur Mapp came to see how I was getting on. He had a club in Chingford and ran it with his brother. He brought a few of his lads as well. Arthur had won a bronze medal at Judo in the Olympics. I asked him to take the class for a while, as I was leaving chalk marks with my plaster on the mat.

All was going well until Arthur took John Green for a *randori* and swept both feet from behind him in a very heavy throw. Unfortunately, John landed on his neck and went into convulsions. He was breathing out with a hissing sound and bubbles were seeping from his mouth; there was no intake of breath. I asked Arthur to do something, but he said he could not, as it was not his club. By this time, John was still shaking and the hissing was getting fainter. I knelt down and punched him in the diaphragm, and it worked: he sucked in and lost consciousness but he was breathing. By the time, the ambulance came John had been in and out quite a few times. I could not leave the class, especially when there was trouble. I sent one of the boys to follow the ambulance. He returned and told me the ward they had taken him to.

The worst part was on my return from seeing John in Whipps Cross hospital, as I had to go to his home and tell his mother. His house was in Carisbrooke Road near the bottom of the High Street. It was late at night – midnight – when I knocked on the door. His mother opened it. As soon as she saw me she fainted! I explained it all to his father as we attended to his wife. I told him that they were keeping John in for a couple of days but not to worry as he would be all right, and what ward he was in. John was on the mat the following week! Same as when he had his knee set. Hard man! He eventually married Janet, then they emigrated to Australia. They came to see us in Highams Park, on a visit to show their little girl to his parents. Norma saw that Janet still had a soft spot for me? But then, who had not? The club all liked me. Though they were trying to kill me!

One of my lads, Barry, was a sod, but very good in the art of Judo. I had to bully him to go for his grading. He had been parading in his green belt for some time. I held a grading at my club and other clubs were also there. My mate, Cliff, was taking the grading and I had told him not to let Barry off the mat and to squeeze the best out of him. He finished with a brown belt (first kyu) and next one a black belt. He accused me of not being satisfied until he was taken to hospital on a stretcher.

In one Judo session he had me in a chokehold; anyone else I would have tapped and given him satisfaction, but not Barry. It was a good hold and my tongue fell out of my mouth – you would be surprised how long your tongue is! I got out of it and was giving him the same medicine, with the same choke he gave me, but he tapped too early so I told him off for not putting up a fight! They liked to give pain, but were not keen to receive it. I had to watch them like a hawk.

My sister, Ena, and her husband, Roger, visited the club while I was demonstrating how to get out of a stranglehold and as usual I had Barry as my opponent. He was astride me and applied the stranglehold. I tilted my head to take the pressure from my throat and I saw Roger. That slight hesitation was enough for Barry, who put me out for the count!

When Marie passed away, you can imagine that I was very distressed. I lost the fervour for Judo.

At my club in Higham Hill Road, we held a seminar and the surrounding clubs attended. Our speaker was Sir Charles Palmer, sixth dan, one of the main players of Judo in England. I had my say. 'Why was the system changed to points which made the game negative, when before it was an *ippon* [point = score 10], *waza-ari* [a hold down] or *hikki-waki* [a draw], and it was attacking Judo? You either won or you started all over again.' He replied it was he who introduced the points system to improve it. I said that it made it too easy to get the higher grades, as the points would soon tally up. I knew what it was: Karate was on its way, and was becoming a strong rival. If the points system had started before, my mates would have become sixth dans. We would not have earned it the hard way. I was offered a second dan and also a third dan, recommended by Baker Brown (sixth dan). I refused them, as they would have been honorary.

Sir Charles's predecessor as head of the British Judo Association was TP Leggett, who had been captured by the Japanese, spoke fluent Japanese (as did Sir Charles) and practised Judo with his Japanese prison guards. He was a tall man, not my cup of tea. Palmer had been knighted when he took over from Leggett after supervising Judo at the Olympics. I think it was at that Olympics that Arthur Mapp won his bronze medal.

When my wife became very ill, I could not give the time to the club. I should have made Barry the instructor – but he was too vicious! (Though he became one in his own right.) I picked Roy Canham, a big fellow with a good temperament. On my wife's demise, I was somewhat lost. I took over the club from Roy. In retrospect it was a selfish and nasty thing to do – sorry Roy! – but I had a void to fill!

# The Fight Game

## Terry Lawless

Terry became a client while he was working at the docks in 1953. He lived with his parents, off Barking Road. He did not like working at the docks and became interested in boxing, as his friend George Dormer was amateur champion bantamweight. George turned professional under Al Phillips, the Aldgate Tiger, and Terry joined the boxing stable to become a corner man. George had his first professional fight at the Roundhouse, Dagenham Football Club and won by a knockout. I think that was the time Terry left the docks for good.

Terry Lawless opened two shops in Leytonstone and he enjoyed the experience. He and his wife, Sylvia, did well. When he progressed into boxing, it got too much for them. So they sold the shops. Terry started to work for Al Phillips as a corner man, becoming friends with Sammy McCarthy who was also in Phillips' stable. I went out with them a few times, boxing and up the West End. I could not keep up with them money-wise, so I did not socialise too often.

Terry was going up in the boxing world. He got backing from a millionaire businessman and jealousy reared its ugly head. Terry had some trouble – phone calls at all times of the day and night, plus gear being delivered that Terry had not ordered. This is what happens when people you think you know start looking at you in a different light! Sylvia phoned and invited us to Terry's 'This is your life'. I was asked a few questions on Terry, by the BBC. What was Terry in the army? Did he do any boxing? They could not ask Terry! We had a good time there, and it went very well.

I was their daughter Loraine' godfather, but I was not a good godfather to Loraine. I never had the money to give; even at my godchild's wedding things were tight. When I was better off, Terry had shot way ahead of me. When selling his house in Romford he asked me if I would like to buy it. It was a beautiful house that he had extended. I thought that I would have too long a journey from Walthamstow, and Marie would be too much on her own, so I declined. I always make the wrong choice. When I moved to Norfolk and Terry moved to Spain, we only kept in touch by Christmas cards. But I'm happy to say he has phoned – it was as if we had never parted!

George Dormer married, and invited Marie and me to his wedding. Marie did not want to go and was very apprehensive, but we went, as she knew Terry and Sylvia. All the boxers were there and it became a nice do. George's cousin was a tough bloke (more about him later). Later, Terry left Phillips to start a stable of his own. He rented a gym off Green Street, in Kathryn Road above the Royal Oak pub, and a number of Al Philips's stable went with him. Least to say, Philips was none too pleased, but they remained friends, although I recently learned from Terry that the 'Tiger' has passed away.

Terry had a good fighter in a man called Stracy and built around him, with the help of Jarvis Astaire. I went to the fights, at Shoreditch, York Hall, Streatham, Albert Hall and a few others. Terry would mouth words for me to shout, at the top of my voice: 'Use your left!' 'Go forward!' 'Uppercut him, you silly bastard!' Yes, it was hairy, but I enjoyed it! The trouble with some fighters is that they get greedy, as Terry would find out. (I told Terry that I was writing this book and that he was in it. He did not care and laughed.)

Finsbury Park many good fights were held there. A local lad unfortunately fought with his head and too many punches took their toll. He lasted longer than I thought he would. When he retired from boxing he opened a pub. His wife was a 'looker' and also quite lustful, enticing men to her bed, so I'm told. The man she chose, would not be her choice, but her husband's! He would hide in the bedroom cupboard and watch all that went on. This was well known to everybody. He would have fights in and outside the pub. That's how it was!

A relation of a friend of mine was getting married. The same week he was in the shop getting his haircut for the wedding day. While he was waiting his turn, the young lady apprentice from the ladies' salon, on hearing young voices, came in through the connecting door to borrow the broom, whereupon he grabbed hold of her, saying nice things and making suggestive motions while bending her over the basin! She liked it, but the shop was full and I pulled him off, saying that he would get me into trouble. He let go of her, but not before he said what he would like to do to her. Very explicit, it was! He took my big tea jug, came back from Rossi's café, poured half a bottle of whisky into the tea, and we all drank his health. But there is always someone who does not fit in. After drinking the tea with the whisky, this old boy said, 'I didn't come here for a bloody party, just a bloody haircut!' My friend replied, 'Shut up, you miserable bastard!' I think he knew him – it could have been his father-in-law. Everyone took things in their stride. It was rough and hairy in those days. Why did I seem to fit in?

I was invited to the wedding, but it was mid-week and I was working. Thank God – as the wedding ended in a farce. He floored his father in law at the registry office, and there was a free-for-all at the wedding reception, plus the bride was three months up the duff! I did not see him any more and heard he was in jail for a couple of months – assault, would you believe! While he was inside, I'm afraid he was involved in a fight with another prisoner – I did not get all the facts. His father was a different kettle of fish (a very nice man). Mind you, so was the son in the shop.

## Shoreditch Town Hall

One time I went with my mate Fred; we were late and there were only seats in the upper tier. There we were shouting as usual and I was abusive to one of the boxers when Fred said, 'Take it easy; we'll be run over by the caravans when we're out of here!' There were gypsies all around us cheering their man on. I stayed schtum! That gypsy boxer now lives in Norfolk, not too far from me.

Fred asked if he could bring his solicitor to the boxing show, as he had never been to one. I said, 'Why not.' Then, after we were introduced, Fred asked if it was possible to take him to the dressing rooms, as he wanted to experience the atmosphere. I asked Terry and he said, 'Yes, but he must not get in the way, and he has to stand against the wall.' I took them in and two boxers were on the table being attended to. There was some blood and gore, plus it stank, as it would! I looked at the solicitor and he was sweating, eyes wide open, muttering, 'This is the real thing!' What was that all about? Just the other side of life!

## York Hall, Bethnal Green

York Hall was my favourite boxing hall, the Turkish Baths were next door to it. I made use of that. The hall pulled plenty of fans, East End characters, with plenty of shouting and always the unexpected. The hall had a bar, always overworked and over-crowded, with two toilets that in the interval would also be more overworked and overcrowded. You would push your way in the toilet. Five of you would be around the bowl well, four of you would – this old chap was always there! He would say with a wet grin, 'Take no notice of me,' holding his limp dick and passing nothing, 'I've got troubles and take a long time to pass water.' From my time at York Hall I cannot ever recall him passing any water. Yes, he wore a raincoat!

I took Norma once; well, she condescended in the end to come and did a few shows with me. Not many females were there. The fights started, the shouting was getting louder, and the bloke behind kept swearing and then saying 'sorry' to Norma. This kept on for some time. I turned and said, 'Pretend that she is not here,' whereupon he said, 'Thanks, mate!' and let himself go – no harm done and we all enjoyed the fights.

Another time I was at York Hall with Norma and top of the bill was a black boxer and a white boxer. I knew there would be trouble, as there were few more black ladies than usual. We had front row seats, the BBC was broadcasting the fight and Harry Carpenter was commentating just in front of us. Norma was wearing glasses. I said to her that I could not always keep my eye on her and at the first sign of trouble to take her glasses off. She gave me a look as if to say, 'I know you are having me on.' The top of the bill came on and true enough a glass was hurled into the ring (it was plastic) and Norma got splashed. Out of the corner of my eye I saw Norma look at me. I looked ahead, as she slowly removed her glasses. Then this big black woman climbed into the ring and hit the ref. It was a great night out. Norma said she was not frightened, but I wonder…

# Jim Watt

I first met Jim Watt at York Hall, where I was watching Maurice Hope boxing. Terry came to where I was sitting and asked if I would mind looking after another of his boxers who had just arrived from Scotland. His name was Jim Watt, a very nice young man, quiet and softly spoken with a Scottish accent. We were to have a meal in the restaurant in Leytonstone after the fight. I never got to the restaurant, as there was a bit of trouble with Maurice. He had been very sick after he had won, possibly something to do with what he ate. It was late and I had told Marie that I would have been home at least an hour and a half earlier. Jim and I became friends, and before each fight he would come to the shop with Terry, and have his lucky haircut. He became Lightweight Champion of the World. In his book, *Watt's my Name*, he mentions me. The misspelling of Patriarca is appalling, but it was nice of him.

I cut other boxers' hair, including Charlie Magri, who was also a boxing champion, and a nice lad. I did not cut Maurice Hope's hair. He became Middleweight Champion of the World, a very softly spoken man.

Terry was meticulous. On the night of Jim's fight (it was in Spain) the two fighters were in the Weighing Office. Terry asked Jim if he wanted a drink, an unheard-of thing, just hours from the fight. Terry picked up the water jug and poured Jim three-quarters of a glass and Jim slowly drank it. The other boxer and his manager looked on in amazement; they knew now that Jim had no weight trouble. Now, Terry had heard that the other boxer had spent some time in the steam room and skipping to shed weight before the weigh-in. He made Jim pee into a glass, and the water he drank was the same amount that he peed. It's all a game of out-guessing your opponent. Terry was a dab hand at it.

He brought Frank Bruno to the shop in E17 before he turned pro, but I never cut his hair. Frank was very quiet and did not say much – he never did. Terry did a lot for him, had his eye corrected, bought all his gear and took no money from him until Frank got going. Terry was a shrewd manager but sometimes too soft. I told him that he would be turned over in the end. 'Yes, I know,' he said. And he was, a few times. Bruno became European Champion and fought for the World Championship against Tyson. Of course he left Terry. Too many people wanted a share of him.

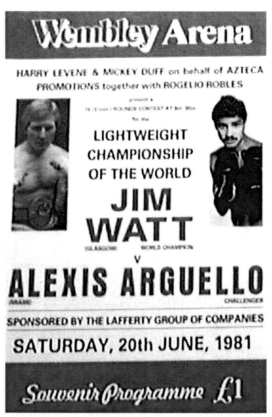

# Frank Bruno

**Sole Direction**
**TERRY LAWLESS**
**Phone;**

**4 Banyards**
**Emerson Park**
**Hornchurch**
**Essex**

# CHARLIE MAGRI
Flyweight CHAMPION Of The WORLD

Sole Direction
TERRY LAWLESS
Phone;

4 Banyards
Emerson Park
Hornchurch
Essex

196

# Jimmy Newman & George Dormer

I set off on my Lambretta scooter with George on the back to Streatham ice rink for his fight and to see Jimmy Newman fight Malloy for the British Welterweight Championship. The Newmans all lived in and around Walthamstow. When we first moved to E17 the family had a house a couple of doors from the barbershop. Their dad raced pigeons and would sell the ones that failed to win to my old man. They would end up as our dinner – talk about getting your own back! They would shoot the pigeons if they would not go into the loft, to remove the tag on the leg to log the bird in. The Newmans are all over E17, and are even related to my wife Norma. The family consisted of five boys and one girl, Barbara. The two older boys, Fred and Ron, I knew more as clients, but I knew Philly, Bob and Jimmy well. Bob was not the only one to shed a tear when I left Highams Park for Norfolk.

That night Jimmy was challenging Malloy for the Welterweight Championship of England. George Dormer was on the card. It was not George's night, and he lost his fight. Jim's fight with Malloy was close. If only Jim had gone forward earlier there would have been no doubt about the verdict. When it was finally given to Malloy, Jim Newman's brother, Philly, went mad, tearing around the hall shouting, 'We were robbed,' and worse. He grabbed hold of me, still shouting. I did not hesitate in agreeing with him. The family were all upset, just that little more. That's boxing! There were two fights left but George wanted to go home. I took him on the back of my Lambretta to West Ham. Next day he was erasing the bruises in the Turkish baths, a small place behind the police station, off Barking Road.

George Dormer once turned up in Highams Park, having found out where I had moved. It was a pleasant surprise to see him, as I had not seen him for quite a few years. He brought news from East-West Ham, and regards from my old clients. That was very nice of him. He was now working as a doorman at Canary Wharf, and very happy there.

It's amazing how many old clients keep in touch. They even

phone me after a lot of trouble in finding my phone number. A few even find time to see me in Norfolk. (I keep telling them that I'm not paying my brother's debts!) I like the ones who phone to see if I'm still alive! Jackson, a Judo instructor, has phoned me twice, though on the last occasion he informed me that Fred, the Judo instructor to whom I handed my club in Higham Hill Road, had died. That was a surprise as Fred had been a fit man. I expect another phone call from Jackson soon! (In revising this book, Jackson has not phoned. Are you still here?

Unfortunately the Whittingham Youth Centre where I once held my Judo class no longer functions. The centre was full with youngsters! Where do they go now? It seems to me that Walthamstow is going to pot. I hardly know anyone now. What a bloody shame!

I would visit a masseur quite regularly, to mend the torn tissues and aching limbs caused by Judo. He told me about a lady masseur who had a client, a JP, who paid her well. She would strip him naked and make him kneel down, then whip him while he would cry out, 'I'm not guilty! I'm not guilty!' He never said if there was sex after.

# Stoke Newington

I was a regular visitor to the Stoke Newington Dojo. It was in a four-storey house, with upper floors turned into flats, in very drab and dingy streets – we were always on our toes. We entered the building from the rear; an iron spiral staircase led you to the top floor and into the Dojo, mats laid, a stage at one end. It was worth the trouble getting there, as the practice was sharp and hard. Many times I had to crawl home in the thick fog of those days. How I got home safe is beyond me, as I'd find myself driving on the wrong side of the road (who said that air is not cleaner now than in those days?). I would go to the club to vent my anger, on my way to see Marie when she was in Mare Street Hospice. In Stoke Newington the Kray Twins had a notorious club. It was in there that they did a murder; I'm not sure if it was ever proved. I think it was Jack the Hat that had his chips above their club that was at the front on the ground floor. The Judo hall was three floors up. My old mate, Cliff, had acquired his first dan under the tuition of his mentor, Sensei Yamada, seventh dan. I was still a brown belt, and just about held my own with the rest of the Judokas. It was always full. On this night I gave this chap a good workout I got carried away and threw him everywhere. It was one of those nights that I could do no wrong. He retired. No sooner was I off the *tatami* than a Judoka asked for a *randori*. I turned and stepped back on the mat – as soon as my feet touched the mat I was flying through the air. I was shell-shocked – I could not keep my feet down and after a pounding I retired. I saw that he was a black belt and the mate of the one I had given a hard time to. You win some and lose some.

I returned the following week with one of the boys from the Tech. He and a young lady were on the *tatami*. I thought he was a bit rough with her, he being a blue belt, and I said so. He replied, 'If she can't take it, she should not be on the mat.' She was also a blue belt. I felt sorry for her and had a *randori* with her, taking it easy. On finishing the *randori* we bowed and left the mat. As we made our way to the dressing rooms she said, 'I enjoyed that. I'm going to have a shower then a good drink at the pub on the corner. What are you doing?' I said that I was going home; she looked at me and walked away. Marie at that time was very ill with cancer and I was going to go to the hospice that was only up the road from the club. It was in Judo that I could get rid of my frustration and anger!

We were all invited to the Krays' club downstairs; some of the boys went, but not I. They came up a few times to watch, but that was all the contact we had with them. It was a very good Judo club and the Judokas came from all over London.

Sensei Yamada was a very good instructor and was going round with everybody in *randori*, eventually coming to me. He was just a bit smaller than me. I wanted to prove myself and got stuck in. I went for a sweeping ankle (*de-ashi-barrai*); he moved his leg and instead of a sweep turned it into a kick! I hurt him, and he threw me into the air. I came down with him on top of me and he held me in a shoulder hold, pressing down on my chest. I was trying to break his hold when suddenly I felt my ribs pop. I tapped for him to release, but he held on longer than he should have done. I was in pain for weeks: he had popped some cartilage from between my ribs, and it's never gone back. Cliff said to me that I should have learned from him and not tried to beat him – there you go. What was I trying to prove?

Dave acquired his black belt from Sensei Yamada; he had to sweat for it. As I said it was a very active club.

Cliff, Dave, Terry Fields and I used to go to Mare Street police station, Hackney, and practise with the police, under a Japanese ex-world Judo champion built like a brick wall, who would be forever complaining about how he was robbed in South Africa by their champion. Then we would have to sit and watch a film of the fight. He was right, but it became boring.

He came to the Technical College in E17, and gave a display. I tried a *tomoe-nage* (stomach throw) on him and as soon as I put my feet down I was flying through the air. I tried the same throw on Sir Charles Palmer at the Leyton Baths. He had a big belly and my foot could not control his weight; I brought him down on his knees. I think I upset him, as he put all his weight in the throw and I was off the mat, nearly on somebody's lap! I did win my contest there, with a body drop.

That parade of shops near the lighthouse in Mark house Road, also had stories to tell, but they would not talk. My client, a friend in Judo, ran a chemist shop there. He accused me of using drugs, saying it was not possible for me to keep going all night at Judo, when they could not. What he did not understand was that mine was a reflex – I was not nervous, but they were. I could feel them tremble and see them sweat. As they got on and controlled their fears, they were more sure of themselves and it was harder for me to throw them. But when they were thrown, they hit the mat harder!

A café owner in Markhouse Road, Derek Gaisford's friend, also wanted to join my club, but I could not teach him to break his fall. He would dive to the floor with his head, and could not do a head-over-heels roll. He just charged the mat! He came for a few weeks but I told him to pack it in, as I could see he would do himself a lot of harm. It was in his café seven shops up from Elmo's barbershop that my brother visited revenge. Four chaps had aggravated his dog when the shop was closed by provoking him through the letterbox. The dog had a fit. Elmo came out of the back room of his shop and saw them enter the café. He took his time getting there, waited until they were seated round the table. He then proceeded to knock hell out of them. Moral: don't be caught sitting down!

I recall another who also could not somersault – a young lad with a back like a ramrod! I tried but his back was not supple. I inquired about him in the office, and found out that he had a rod next to his backbone to straighten his curvature of the spine! They should have told me, as I would have been in trouble. In the next training session I told him that I would have to have a doctor's letter stating that he could take part, knowing that no way would he take part in Judo again and that was the end of that. He could have broken his back when thrown – and I would have taken the blame.

# Defending the Jews

At a later stage – around 1973, when I had moved to Beresford Road – Stanley Brooks was no longer hairdressing and had taken up being a taxi driver. He asked me to help the Jews in Stoke Newington. The Orthodox Jews were being turned over by the blacks, who at that time were making their presence felt (the Jews were a soft touch). I went to the address of the house in Stoke Newington. Before entering I had to put on a paper skullcap. On entering the room, five of them were bearded and longhaired, dressed the same as the chap who opened the door to me. Sitting around the table they asked me questions. One got up and grabbed me from behind saying, 'What would you do now?' I'd show them. Someone else would arise, and take another hold. After a few more demonstrations, they hired me.

I was asked what I needed them to buy – the *tatami* (mats) and the Judoki (suits) – and we started in a gym off Stoke Newington Road, in an annex of the Jewish school. I took one of my students, Terry; he wanted to come as he had never mixed with Orthodox Jews before; neither had I. He came in handy, as the Jewish students were not young men. I found out that they did not like too much pain – to be fair, they were old. They were jewellers from Hatton Gardens and businessmen; some were very soft to the touch. When some were missing for a week or so, I asked why. He said, 'To Holland I have been.' That made my helper's eyes open wide, hoping that some would rub off on him! Somewhere along the line, he'd drop a hint that he liked anything gold! Cheeky sod!

I had some good laughs. In the first lesson, they came on the mat with their skullcaps or 'kippahs' on their heads held together with pins. I asked them to take them off but they would not have it. Then I asked them to remove their spectacles, and they looked at me in amazement, saying, 'Mr Ugo, if we took off our glasses, how could we see?' They kept them on most of the time, but I made them take them off when grappling on the ground.

Another time I was making them work, in fact sweating – they were all big chaps – one said to me, 'Mr Ugo, do you want us to come next week?' I replied, 'Yes,' and he said, 'Then don't work us so hard!' One had me pinned on the mat. I would always let them get a fair hold on me to encourage them, but this one wrapped his arms around me and said, 'Get out of that!' It was a vice. I said that he could not do much either. I knew that he could not keep the pressure on for too long; I just kept him busy until I felt it easing; then I turned him over. He told me he had been in the Jewish army – he was hard as teak! Students are all the same; they like to put one over you if they can. One had me from behind on the floor, and I could not shake him off. I offered him my neck by putting my head out, and he took the bait and went for it. I soon had him on his back and gave him a reverse strangle I never put them out; just enough for them not to find their feet, so that they staggered like a drunken man.

I got there early at the Jewish Hall one night, and I was taken aback on seeing the chap in charge, with his black Fedora hat and long hair, trying to bang his head against the wall. He gave me a sign to keep quiet; it was only then that I realised that he was praying. I hope they learned a few things. I doubt it. But I enjoyed it. They gave me a nice drink for Christmas and presented Terry, my helper, with a box of Terry's Gold chocolate. He was always talking about gold, hoping some would came his way; he tried, he really tried, and I think they saw the joke. Shame it ended, but nothing is for ever. I really enjoyed my time with the Jewish Judokas. I had many a good laugh and discovered new customs. I thought they were all the same, but the Jews from Walthamstow were a different part of the Jewish creed from Stoke Newington. One can never stop learning, can one?

In reality they were too old and slow for Judo. I think they would have been better at Karate. Judo is a reflex that takes years to acquire! But I must say, they were game.

# The Turkish Baths

I made a fair wage, hairdressing Monday to Friday, and I used to go to the Turkish baths in Bethnal Green every Saturday morning with a friend called Derek – more of him later. It was a roughish place; all types of people gathered there, even Turks! We would strip and get into a cold shower, get really wet, then wrap a towel around ourselves and so into the first hot room, with thick steam all around. You did not move quickly, as the steam was so hot that it would bite if you did. You placed a towel on the stone seat, as it was too hot for your bum. After a while you went for another cold shower to cool down, and then back into a hotter room: you trod carefully, slow motion, then plunged headfirst into the icy pool. Before you hit the water you were fighting to get out: I have never moved so fast! You had to go in headfirst, otherwise you could have a heart attack. Then you rest on a bed in a room like a dormitory and await your turn for a massage. I would listen to the chatter going on around me; a Jewish voice, 'Short-sighted, he bent to pick up half a crown in the street and picked up a dustbin lid!' Other voices, Greek, Turkish, you name it: it was all there. Later a Yiddish voice, 'So, who wants fish?' The money would be gathered, and the majority including us would be eating fish and chips. It came from the Jewish fish shop, just around the corner from the baths – nice and hot!

I used to talk about the baths in the shop. One of my friends asked if he could come. Alan Stringer was blonde with blue eyes, and so white when stripped that he looked like a milk bottle with hair. He waited for me to tell him what to do. I told him to have a cold shower to start with, so that the steam would not burn him. In we went into the steam room; the heat and steam held Alan back, but I prodded him forward. We put our towels on the long stone seat and sat very still; the steam was biting! I looked at Alan and I saw those blue eyes looking at me; and they were saying, 'What are you doing to me?' He could not take the heat and had to come out; he cooled himself, with a cold shower. He did not come again.

Martin, the ex-husband of my niece Christine, also wanted to try it, so I took him to the baths. Young and fair looking, he always thought himself tough. I told him to have a good cold shower. I saw some blokes looking at him, and kept my eyes open. The water was cascading down his face and naked body. This chap who looked like a Turk stood in front of him, five feet high by five feet wide it seemed, with his arms folded. Martin was enjoying himself under the shower until he opened his eyes and saw this squat man in front of him! His eyes opened wide and then quickly closed again. He started to rub his hands frantically over his face, hoping the man would disappear, but on opening his eyes he was still there. You could see that he was scared, your eyes will always give you away. I said, 'You can come out now Martin.' The Turk turned around, looked at me and walked away. Not that he was frightened of me. But I was confident in myself. Martin did not return to the baths again. He was always faint-hearted.

# Derek Gaisford

Derek and I would visit the deli to buy our own food to take into the baths, as we got fed up with fish and chips. After the hustle and bustle of the bath, we would settle down to a good meal, eating while sitting and relaxing on our beds. This Saturday morning, the masseur did not turn up. One of the chaps who was always at the baths had taken over the massaging. Derek went in first into the cubicle, while I rested on the bed. I had been in and out of the hot rooms, plunging into the cold-water pool. Fifteen minutes later Derek comes out in a fluster shouting, 'You're next! You're next!' His face was all red, and his eyes had a dazed look. I said, 'What's the hurry?' He said, 'He's waiting!' I went into the cubicle and this chap apologised saying, 'I'm sorry but I have no swab to rub you down with, I'll have to use my hands, is that OK?' I said, 'Carry on.' He started all right, and then I felt his hands where they should not have been, around my fishing tackle. I sat up and said, 'What the bloody hell do you think you're doing?' As if I did not know. He said, 'I told you I had no swab.' I said, 'Leave that alone and carry on.' I had a good massage! Derek had only a flushed face.

Derek had blonde hair – well, I used to touch it up for him plus give him a light perm, for which he would come to the shop every week. His face was knocked about a bit. He was a carpet retailer with a good business, which he worked hard at. He spent his hard-earned money on so-called friends. He joined my Judo club; I don't know how he used to last on the *tatami* as it was a two-hour session and he smoked all day long. His tongue was black! I was going on holiday to Malta and was asked by my friend CB Brown (fifth dan at that time) to visit Joe Abella, a Judo first dan, at this posh hotel, to convey his regards and deliver some paraphernalia on behalf of the British Judo Association to the Maltese Judo Association. Derek said that he and his wife, Florrie, would like to come to Malta as well. Why? First he wanted to take his girlfriend and said he would pay for the holiday. I said that there were only two bedrooms. 'You pretend Gill is your girlfriend,' he said, 'But she will sleep in my bed? And what if?' said I. 'What are friends for?' he said. I told him to forget it! (That's taking friendship just a bit too far.)

The three of us got to Malta. We were staying at my friend Vic Camp's apartment, very lush. I paid for it by leaving the money tucked behind the photo in the bedroom. At that time you were only allowed to take a certain amount of money abroad. I enjoyed meeting Joe Abella and we were made very welcome. Derek was always to the front; he was only a green belt but acted like a dan grade. They took us to their home and also took us for a tour around the coast on their boat – very enjoyable. Derek was stung very badly by mosquitoes, because he would lie on the bed in the nude and did not know what was biting him. They were all up his bedroom wall. Florrie did not get bitten, as she slept in her nightie I think. We left the wall splattered with blood, and it was all Derek's! Joe Abella's sister did not take to me at first (we were around their house for dinner) and she showed it! By all accounts she had had an Italian boyfriend and he had gone back to Italy without her. She came around in the end and was a very nice young lady. We had a very good time in Malta. I was sorry to be informed a few years later that Joe Abella had died of a heart attack. He was so young!

The flat above my shop in Gosport Road became vacant, as my mate had found a better place in Higham Hill to handle his food business. Derek wanted to rent it to set up his girl Gill. (Gill's husband was not around). I thought, better the devil you know. He did it up very well, carpets laid, furniture, and it worked well for him – until later on. I was a widower and he would always try to fix me up with a bird, get me to go to parties, pubs, boxing only if I took him. On the way home, we would have a big meal, usually in an Indian restaurant, in Lea Bridge Road; I could never finish the food. Derek always went over the top!

At a Greek restaurant just before Whipps Cross on the left, Ron, my brother-in-law, gave a birthday party for his wife Pat's Fiftieth. Derek and Florrie were also invited. The wine flowed and the food was good. As Derek could not pay (he always wanted to treat everybody), he put me in an awkward position by asking me if I was treating Ron by paying the bill. He spoke out loud and persisted with it. I had no choice but pay, with a silky smile on my face!

Derek asked me to go to Paris with him, saying I would pay for the petrol and drive and he would foot the rest. He was meeting a friend to measure for a big contract, laying carpets in a large office complex. He had booked a couple of rooms near the Bastille (nothing left of it, only a plaque to say where it had been). We arrived in Paris very early on a Sunday morning, a sign indicated left or right, north or south – I had no idea, nor did Derek. I took the right-hand turning. The street was deserted; then a man came around the corner and walked towards us. I waited and got out of the car. The chap stopped dead and looked at me. I said, '*Excusez moi*' in my best French. He turned around and was up the road like greased lightning. I looked back and Derek had his head out of the window. I said he had frightened the man, with his ugly face! He said, 'Not so: it was yours that did it!' I thought I was better looking? Eventually we found a policewoman, who was having a go at a foreign motorist. After that was settled she looked at me and said that foreigners should speak French. She thought I was French (until I spoke). Then two plain-clothed policemen came up. I made myself understood and one of them told us to follow them and took us to the hotel. It was very kind of them. Derek gave them a carton of cigarettes; he was always overgenerous.

In the hotel Derek started to look everywhere. I said, 'What are you looking for?' 'A way out in case there is a fire,' he replied. He had a point there. We tried to get into the Moulin Rouge, but the doorman said you needed a wallet like an accordion. Derek settled for a smaller place to meet his friend. We got there early and I was looking forward to my meal; but we were there too early and I had just one drink too many! Derek likes a drink; I drink very little. I remember meeting his friend and his wife and sitting around the table. The only thing that did not move was a big ashtray in the centre of the table. I did not take my eyes off it for the entire evening. I remember the lady saying something and I said, 'Please don't speak to me or I will spoil your meal.' How I kept everything down, I do not know.

On our way home to England I was driving, the roads straight and long, and I was belting it, as we wanted to get home. Derek started to open a new packet of fags when I said, 'There's a packet on the floor!' He said it was empty. I reached down to pick the packet up and, looking up, saw that I was on the wrong side of the road and racing towards me was a car! That car swung to the other side of the road, but behind him followed another. I drove for him, hoping that he too would follow the other car, as I was going too fast to swing to the left. Thank God he did. I looked at the rear and he was going all over the place: a good job there was no other car coming. Derek had pups. When we stopped for petrol he took over the driving. At customs, I suppose I was a bit cocky saying, 'You'll find nothing.' I did not know that Derek had put extra cigs in the boot of the car until the custom officer held the fags up. The officer said that he would let me off the fine, as the look on my face was genuine; so I only paid extra for the fags. Derek was a sod for his fags.

Derek was getting involved with a girlfriend, Rose, and told me that he loved her and she really loved him! 'So different from Florrie, she was alive!' 'What about your family?' I asked. 'They are old enough,' he replied. He would let his foreman bring his girlfriend, who was married, and use his love nest. But all has an ending. I was working in the shop and I could hear raised voices from above. I heard a thud – a body falling? I ran up the stairs and the foreman was laid out. Derek said, 'It's all right, Ugo.' I said, 'It looks like it!' The foreman had said something derogatory about his girlfriend, and that was that. A few weeks later Florrie and her daughter burst into the shop, which had three people waiting, and demanded, 'Where is he? I know you know, he has not been home.' I was taken aback, as were my clients who were waiting for their haircut. I said, 'Upstairs!' I thought she had found out about the flat, but she had not! She came round to see IF I knew. They were stunned when they saw the flat.

Florrie eventually got him home, but it did not end there; he left her soon after and went to live with his girlfriend. They moved to Clacton. It did not last too long: he had a very bad stroke and died in 1992. His young son, also called Derek, took the flat over. He had a couple of girls one after the other, eventually taking up with one called Susan. He told me that Susan said that he was a better lover than her ex-boyfriend. He was very proud of that. They had a lovely girl. Young Derek is living in Southend as a pawnbroker and is doing well. But he also ended the same way, on his own. He told me his lovely girl did not turn out so lovely after all. Life is full of twists and turns. I'll always remember young Derek; every Monday night, I'd yell up the stairs, 'Where's my bloody rent?' The answer was always the same: 'Spent!' I remember Susan for the lovely sandwiches she'd bring down for me when I was busy.

When they left (they got fed up with me shouting?) I re-let it to an up-and-coming client called Fred, who was in the food business. Fred used it as a business office. He had it for a while until his firm got cracking. His salesmen would be up and down through the side door. He became a millionaire and opened a factory in E17. When Fred and his foreman, Reg, found they were overstocked with bacon and it was going off, they put on white coats, loaded the van with the hams, and set off to different districts. Calling on the butcher shops that they passed, they sold all the bacon because of the greed of butchers looking for a quick profit. You have only to say, 'It came off the back of a lorry,' to make a killing. (The hams were not bad; they just had to be sold quickly!)

On the way to money, Fred got a good hiding for turning over an associate, again for selling bad hams. Two men were paid to give Fred a going over; they did it with a baker's paddle. They asked Fred how he wanted it, the hard way or the easy way? Fred told him to get on with it, whereupon the hit men picked up the paddle and proceeded to beat Fred with it. I saw him the next day; he had just come back from a visit to the Turkish baths to ease the pain. I said, 'You're mad!' He said, 'You have to take it now and then.' To become a millionaire, there was just a bit of pain on the way. Though my mate had dyslexia, he was a dab hand with mathematics. 'I've come to the conclusion that maths are more important than spelling – I can always get someone to write.' He did.

Eventually he got turned over by listening to people who were more persuasive than he! He told me that he's happier now that the bulk of the money has gone. He would say to me, 'Ugo, it's only stock.' I admired him to have got that high.

When I was keen on keeping fit, I'd run from Badlis Road to the Bell corner left up to the Billet roundabout, down Chingford Road turn right at the bus station, up to Forest Road, then home to Badlis Road, passing Lloyds Park in heavy army boots. Looking back, I was bloody mad! Some thought that I was a boxer, but I'd gotten over that period.

# Walthamstow Market

## The Cat Meat Stall

Sid, the cat's meat man, had a good business, a stall, on the corner of Willow Walk in the High Street. He and his son, also called Sid, were clients of mine. Young Sid broke away from his old man and started a cat and dog meat stall at the top of the High Street, Hoe Street end. He thought that he could do better than his old man. With younger ideas he built a strong trade and became a rich man. He had young George Bullock to get his meat for him from a farm – very secret – and stack it in a storeroom on the right-hand side of the alley behind the Granada Cinema. He had it well laid out, more like a butcher's shop. He'd cut the meat into manageable chunks, load it on to his lorry, and park the lorry in a blind alley off the High Street, by his stall. Young Sid became friendly with me – he liked strong men. He joined my Judo class in Higham Hill. Before that he would come with me to the Technical College in Forest Road to watch the Judo. There was a reason why he got close to me: he was not very good at Judo, and did not like pain but he stuck it out as he and some of the lads used me as an alibi, and did not always turn up for the Judo class. Some nearly got caught when their girlfriends or wives came to the shop to confirm if their boyfriends or husbands had attended my class. I covered for them – too many times, I'm sorry to say.

One husband came to see me, he had been recommended to me by someone in the High Street (I think it was Ernie Smith). He wanted me to teach him attacking Judo. I told him that it was not learned in a couple of weeks and took ages to get to the stage when it becomes a reflex. He turned around and walked out of the shop. I did regret not teaching him. I knew his wife, a nice lady who succumbed to Sid's pressure. I'm sure he would have

211

half-killed Sid, the bugger. (It's years before the reflex takes over; if you think what you are going to do, it's too late!)

In the end I had enough of making excuses and told them to sod off! I had a suspicion who was phoning my wife Marie, a 'breathing caller' she called him – just breathing heavily over the phone. I told her to slam the phone down on whoever it was. One day I was home at a time when I was not usually there. The phone rang and Marie answered; she gave me a sign. I took the phone and listened to the heavy breathing. I said, 'I think I know who you are. If I find out for sure I'll tie your balls around your f—ing neck.' The phone went dead. Marie had no more calls.

Sid had a flat in E17. I went there, when on better terms, up two flights of stairs; it had tricky landings and tight corners. After a drink he said, 'Where's my safe?' I replied 'I don't know.' He showed it to me, it was under the flooring. He said it was very heavy. He did not show what he had inside. 'Nobody will get it out!' he said. Funny thing is, a few months later, the boys had it away. It was witnessed by a milkman delivering milk to the flats. He told the police that, 'two blokes were having trouble loading it on to the van, and I went over and helped them. I thought that they were taking it for repairs. They made no fuss nor were they in a hurry in getting it into the van!' (I don't remember telling anyone about the safe.) Sid never told me how much he lost.

After a little bit of ducking and diving, I managed to get a stall in the High Street and employed women to run it, just to keep it ticking over until the council knocked all the houses down, and ruined a close-knit community. I found out where to get the cat and dog meat. Some meat I got from the boys who worked in Spittlefields market; other trays of brawn I got from a firm – bits and pieces by ducking and diving. I would get up early to set the stall that I pulled out from where it was kept overnight. I don't know why I did not let Butler, who pulled the majority of the stalls, pull mine. I kept a chest freezer full of meat at the back of the shop in Gosport Road. At this time I had let the rooms above the shop to Peter and Lesley Noble.

On the opposite side of the High Street to me was an ex-professional boxer from the Buxton Club, Alfie Price. He came to the club to help out with the training. He sold fruit and veg, and was a happy character.

*Alfie Price in 1971*

I also had a stall down the bottom of the High Street near Woolworth's. Peter Noble ran it with me for a while, but trade was slow and it did not last long. When the meat went off, I'd put it in bins around the High Street – not very nice of me!

It was when I had my stall opposite Buxton Road that I found how to treat meat that was going off. I'd gone into the butcher's shop, two shops from me, for a bucket of hot water. The stallholders helped each other out, as did the shops. The butcher was at the sink washing pork chops. I could smell the peroxide. He said it took away the smell. So, I tried it on my meat that had gone off. I put some in the water, and it fizzed away. I rinsed it in cold water – it looked very fresh. I sold this meat to a lady, who came back the following day for more. I had run out. She said, 'My dog loved it!' and pestered me for more. It worries me somewhat in what we buy to eat.

I'd work on the stall on Saturdays and I enjoyed it. Why a stall in the High Street? It was the hours, an early start and early finish, and also so different from working in the shop. One of my clients, Charlie Carroll, who became a trader in the stock market, said to me, 'Ugo, can I bring some of my friends from the city to see you down the High Street? They have not seen this side of life before.' He was a nice chap who made it good from poor beginnings and lived just round the corner in Edinburgh Road. I knew the family well. He was never shy in telling the stockbrokers where he came from. He followed me to Highams Park, coming all the way from the City by train, sometimes waiting an hour or more for his haircut, then back on the train to where he lived in the stockbrokers' belt. I said, 'Why not?' to his request.

I saw them approach from the corner of my eye. I started putting on an act, shouting, 'Nice fresh meat for your dogs,' and talking louder. He led his friends to the stall, all nicely dressed and said, 'I've brought my friends to see a side of life that they have not seen before.' They were all agog, seeing the meats displayed, particularly ox hearts hanging and dripping red with blood; they were defrosting. Ox hearts are very big and look good on display. I overdid it with my Cockney accent, but it went well. Charles told me later that they really enjoyed it. They would have done so, as the characters of those days you see now portrayed on television are nothing like the real thing!

## Market Traders Remembered

The High Street on Saturdays was packed to the brim with people buying, vendors shouting, throwing tomatoes up in the air, showing how firm and fresh they were. But they were not fresh; they would throw them in a certain way; after all, they were cheap – they had to be, otherwise they would not sell. An old soldiers' band, with their medals proudly displayed on their chests, played and marched, one old soldier on each side holding a hat for anything that was given. One beggar (that could be too strong a word) who had no legs would propel himself along on a square piece of wood, low on the ground, with roller skate wheels at each corner. With a small piece of wood on each hand, he would propel himself along the pavement quite fast, in and out between the multitudes of people. I never knew him to collide with anyone.

One of my clients who had followed me when I was off to Highams Park, in one of his sombre moods, told me of a predicament; he never made love to his wife before he married her. On his wedding night, he could not enter her, she being small. (Never heard of it before). They had to insert different sizes of glass phials, to stretch the womb. It took time. I'm glad to say it worked, (but what a predicament). Of course, it's between you and me.

Whom can you trust, when you're not at home? At your wedding, your mate, the best man, had somehow managed to prove to your new wife that he was the best man. While you were looking forward to it, after you stopped supping the drink. Maybe he did you a favour, as you would not be UP for it. The best man was not shy in telling me the nitty-gritty and how many times she yelped.

*Walthamstow Market, 1976*

There's a church spire, on the border of North Wales that is twisted. It got into that shape with the shock of a virgin being married there. It is said that it will only straighten when another virgin marries there.

Opposite Courtney Road at the bottom of the High Street, an Italian chap sold hot chestnuts. He would drive me mad with his broken English; I felt like tipping his brazier over every time I heard him. On the corner I'd watch this old girl, who sold rabbits, hook the head, cut round the neck, remove the paws, grab hold of the skin and pull it off like a glove. There was an escape artist outside the Chequers pub who would tie himself into a straitjacket and make a miraculous escape. In the winter, another Italian would sell hot potatoes outside the pub. Nice and big, he'd break them open and sprinkle with salt, enjoying it and at the same time warming your hands – lovely!

The biscuit stall man built a bungalow for his girlfriend. When she moved in, she did not want to know him and told him to sod off! The law did not permit him to evict her, so he hired a bulldozer and demolished the bungalow! There was a sarsaparilla stall outside the Carlton Cinema. Sarsaparilla is a mild diuretic. The drink was sold hot in the winter and cold in the summer. Is sarsaparilla available today?

It was Lieberman's café and snooker hall that the Krays took over as their headquarters. Michael (Mitch), one of my clients, had an affray in the billiards room, on the second floor. The minder at that time was Tommy Welsh (a.k.a. the Bear). He told them to clear off. Mitch was a bit of a hard nut and stood up to him. The Bear went to throw them out. Mitch got behind him, wrapped his arms around him and, trapping his arms, dragged the Bear to the edge of the stairs, saying, 'I'm going to throw you down, you f—!' The Bear replied, 'You don't want to do that, boy. I'll forget it.' Mitch let him go and there was no follow-up to the incident by the Bear. The Bear also threatened Terry Oldham, my next-door mate, over the phone. (He was paid by Terry's opposition.) Of course, Terry knew his voice; it always started with, 'Look here boy!' and then the threat! Terry said, 'I know it's you Tom.' Tom put the phone down. When they met in the shop, nothing was said.

Opposite old Sid's cat meat stall worked Ernie Smith on his fruit stall; he had three boys. One boy, John, is a PC and good at Judo, having reached the national youth finals, which were eventually won by Arthur Mapp. John and Robert from my club finished second and third. (I saw Robert at Chigwell police sports centre, and did not recognise him. He'd grown a beard and looked nothing like the lad I knew. I think he thought that I was ignoring him. Never – just getting old.)

Pocahontas is supposed to be buried in an old graveyard behind the flower shop – so I was told – opposite the Correction School. On the left-hand side of the High Street. In revising this book, I'm now told it's not true – who am I to believe? It seems that the correction centre needs to be reopened; it was well used in my younger days. My friends who keep in touch say how much the High Street has gone down the pan. I used to watch the eels outside Manzies pie and mash shop, which I frequented. People, including my mother, would buy them. I watched while he chopped a head from its squirming body. Just past the eel stall was the music shop. I recall the 'Wheels of Fortune' sung by Kay Star that was coming from the loudspeaker. I fell in love with it and still play it. Ray and Ron White and I reminisce about the old days, when we meet at Feltwell, Norfolk.

There was one shop that had two stalls on the pavement outside the shop selling similar goods to those sold inside the shop. The shop was open-fronted, with shutters that were pulled down when it closed. The stock spilled out on to the pavement, forcing people to walk nearer to the stock he had on the stall. The shop had the same system of paying as Davis's.

Davis's was one of the biggest shops, and sold ladies clothes and household linen. It was on the corner of Mission Grove. They also had a contraption for transporting money from the ground floor to a safe place out of reach. The thing you don't see now is when people bought items; they paid at the small counter that was at the right-hand side of the shop, then the assistant would put the money into a container, clip it on to a wire that ran to the top of the shop, pull a lever and the container would shoot to the top, where a glass-fronted box would be waiting to receive it. In this box of glass sat the governor, who checked the bill and money, placed the change in the container, pulled a lever and down it went. I think he felt that he was safe up there. On the other corner of Mission Grove, a client from the barbershop, had his tomato stall and also sold other soft fruits. He's the one whose legs would fly up when I applied the Pashana on his face after the hot towels. Behind him was the butcher's that had auctions on

Saturday nights to get rid of the meat that would be left over for the weekend. The old and not so old girls would push and shove to bid for the meat of their choice. It was in the dark of the evening but the hissing oil lamps would bring it to life! Tesco started in the High Street. It took over the Carlton Cinema. It was more like a warehouse than a shop, with everything stacked high and in boxes, with hardly any room for the shoppers between the aisles. The attraction was the cheapness! What a difference to the Tesco of today. I wish I had put my half-crown down in shares. Who knew what shares were then. Looking back, it was a stage and everyone had a part to play. The stallholders carried their money on their fingers or around their necks. One had a gold ring, on top a blob of hollow gold, inside a nice diamond. There were too many rogues on the lookout, seeing who was working down the High Street. Then, knowing that a flat or house was empty, they would pay a visit. I should know – my house was done, by someone I knew, but couldn't prove.

The cat meat stall down the High Street was getting me down; running two businesses took too much of my time. I told my mate Derek at the carpet shop that I was going to sell it. His wife Florrie had worked on it for a while to help me out, and he said he would buy it. I said that what with his carpet business, it would be too much for him, as it had been for me. No, he would not have it. He took my van over and his wife and young Derek got stuck in. The chest freezer went to the back of his shop. I was glad to get rid of it, as a friend of mine, Peter, who was renting the top floor above my shop, had had a nasty experience a few weeks earlier.

I had had the freezer behind my shop, as it had been thrown out of where it had been stored before. Peter phoned to tell me that he could smell the meat (in fact it stunk!). I told him to open the windows. On opening the shop on Monday morning, a horrible smell met me. Peter had not been able to get into the back room because it was locked. He was waiting for me to open the shop and told me that over the weekend they had been bombarded with bluebottles that were so fat they could hardly fly! I opened the back door and we went into an inferno of bluebottles that nearly covered the window that we opened to let them out. What had happened was that I had been sold a pup. The chap had delivered kidneys and offal that had gone off. I made an impolite phone call and he was round within the hour, but the smell lasted a lot longer.

So I was pleased to see the freezer go – or so I thought! Derek stuck it for a few months. He was meticulous with the fat on the meat, and would cut it all off so it took ages to serve. He ran my van into the ground and just pranced about, but his wife told him to stick with it. Derek asked me, 'Ugo, will you buy the stall back?' He was a friend, so I did, because I knew another chap who wanted it.

Elmo, whose shop was next to Derek's carpet shop, had his electricity cut off. As you know by now, Elmo did not know what a bill was. I think Sylvia was still there, but Derek ran a cable from his shop over the garden fence and plugged in. I bet my bottom dollar that Elmo never paid for the electricity that he used. I am told when the police searched Derek's or Elmo's shop for stolen fags, each would always throw them over the other's fence. I was given a wink that the police were to pay Elmo a visit. I phoned him just in time. Why? He had caused so much trouble for me!

# Terry Oldham

When Terry moved to Gosport Road, next door to me, he would ignore me; after all, I was an Italian! I did the same. He had a thriving trade as a tattooist. It was not long before he needed change and came into the shop and begrudgingly asked me for some. From then on, we got on well. He had the Dutch Hell's Angels come in droves one day. They parked their motorbikes on the pavement, blocking my entrance to the shop. I was not having that! I went into the tattooist shop, and asked them to move their bikes. Terry looked at me and spoke to them. They gave me a funny look, but moved their bikes. After they were gone, he told me who they were. They had been meeting up with the British Hell's Angels, and were a tough lot. But you have to stand up for yourself, otherwise people will walk all over you!

The word got around that the Asians were protesting about racism and were marching in Walthamstow. There was a certain amount of fear in the air. The majority of shops in the High Street closed; in fact, the road was dead. Most of the shops in Gosport Road closed, except for Terry's and mine. We were the only ones who stayed open. Terry and I stood in my shop doorway, defiant, waiting for the protest march. There we stood with arms folded, waiting for the masses to descend upon us. Only a few went by, taking no notice of us. That was our stand of defiance!

'Ugo! There's a bloke in the flat above my shop!' The boys had been stripping the lead, as the shops and houses were been demolished, and we were on the verge. Terry and I were the last to go. We rushed into Terry's shop – the bloke had come down and locked himself in the back room. I had no client in, so we went in from the back of my shop. He was in the scullery and there were bars across the window. 'Come out, you bastard!' says I. Terry had a go but he would not come out. Terry said, 'We won't hurt you!' The bloke replied, 'I don't trust him,' pointing at me. I got mad and threw a brick at him and he scampered away through the front of Terry's shop, never to be seen again. They were knocking down all around the shop. I was the last one to go, as the shop in Highams Park was not yet ready.

Terry the tattooist had moved to Highams Park, as Gosport Road was being demolished. I was still fighting for more money. Eventually I gave up and moved to an upstairs room that Terry found for me, next to his room that overlooked the main road; mine overlooked the back of the building. I was thankful for it.

His clients followed him and Terry did not lose out, as they would have followed him anywhere. Some of his clients will remember Terry for ever. One I recall was slowly having his whole body tattooed. I asked him why. He replied, 'I can't stand the white of my skin.' There is a young lady around who's had a tattoo around her private parts of flames surrounding it – where she failed to keep her knees together? But, that aside, his work is fantastic. The photo of him was taken by a professional (sorry about the poor copy), as Terry had a small part in the film *The Elephant Man*. The photo has been seen in America under different names. Bloody cheek! He never got a penny for it.

Alf, a long-time customer whom I'd known since I was a

lather-boy, also had a stall in the High Street – well he tried a few different places up and down the market. He sold flowers, then tins of fruit – anything that was saleable. Was it you that had a gold ring that in the centre that had a diamond hidden under a false motif? The stall workers in the High Street would wear their money around the neck and on their fingers. They would never leave it at home – why? The boys knew where they were, and nip round to the house and help themselves.

There were photos on the back door where the clients made tea, of Ron Todd and his old mate Scargill. One of my clients would throw darts at the photos – not through hate, just devilment! I was cutting a young lady's hair, dropped the comb and just stopped from grabbing it as it fell on her lap. 'Oops' I said, 'just stopped in time!' She said, 'I would not have minded.' I knew her husband well.

# Chanel Perfume

Alf's stall was not far from another friend/client, who sold grapefruit and oranges. He got friendly with the Kray Twins, who were just over the road in Lieberman's café-cum-snooker hall. He rented the Krays' flat so that he could be one of the boys. He told me he had bitten off more than he could chew after finding a gun hidden in a cavity behind a picture hanging on the wall – he was scared. He asked for help to be released from the flat! I passed him on to a friend and client, George W, who had already given me sound advice. The Krays took the flat back, but he lost his money. He was never a hard man, but you know how it is! He told me that he had a fright when he saw on *Police 5* they was asking people to keep an eye open for anyone selling perfume – and he had just bought the lot! He poured it all down the pan – he had the sweetest-smelling lavatory in E17! (He got some money back with my blades though.)

# The Giddins

## Liz Giddins

I started to court Marie when she knocked on the door of
29 Gosport Road. I had walked out (I still had to be home by ten
o'clock) and not gone back to a party at Meadows in the High
Street where she worked. Dad answered the door. 'A young girl is
asking for you.' It was Marie asking me why I had not returned to
the party. She did not know that I had to be home by ten o'clock.
I returned to the party. She did not care a fig for my father and
she showed it; she would come to pick me up at the shop. The
old man would give her a fag!

Marie's brothers were in the army, and Tom, her dad, in the
Navy. I was a bit apprehensive as I approached Mersey Road.
After all, Liz had warned Marie that I would sell her to the 'slave
market'. Who was I to meet? Eventually I went down the sloping
Mersey Road and knocked on the door, which Marie opened, and
I stepped into the passage of a Warner's flat. It was a very cold
night in February with a bitter wind. Marie and I walked down
the long passage. The paraffin heater was on, tucked in the bend
of the passage. The smell from the heater hung in the air. All the
rooms were on the left; a dining room, two bedrooms, the
scullery with a hipbath and a toilet. A door led you out to a small
garden. At the end, a half-glazed door faced you. In the sitting
room, Liz sat on a wooden chair in front of a coal fire with her
legs akimbo, determined to gather all the heat from the fire. None
escaped to the remote corners of the room.

I noticed the thick two-toned hair, grey and ginger, with a
brownish streak in the front caused by the cigarette that would,
more often than not, nestle between her lips, with the lower lip
jutting out to give it support. Sometimes the eyebrows would

have this brownish look as well. Free from make-up her face had a heavy look in spite of her features being small. Not a tall woman, but heavily built and a bit tubby, her whole appearance had strength and sturdiness. She always wore a wrap-around pinafore, which had a couple of pockets to accommodate the bits and pieces that she carried around with her, plus her fags. Her hands were broad and strong and bore the marks of hard work, and were adorned only by her wedding ring.

*Favourite pose*

Looking me up and down Liz said, 'I'll go and make the tea.' She rose from the chair and removed it from the front of the fireplace, in case you sat on it! Off she went into the scullery and after a rattle of cups in she came, handing me the cup and saucer, the cup doing a little jig. I quickly took it from her. No sooner had we drunk our tea than out came the cards. 'You like playing cards?' asked Liz decisively. 'Yes,' said I, hoping to please. 'Well, we'll play Kings,' she said, 'Penny in the middle and a penny a card.' Kings was the name that she gave to the game. Others called it Newmarket. After a few rounds of cards, out came the Ludo board. Liz liked to win and did not mind cheating. We turned a blind eye to it. She would scoop the pennies with a deep chuckle and a splatter of ash.

'I must take my teeth out,' she said, and did so, leaving only two teeth in her head. She told me that she lost her teeth making aeroplane wings during the 1914 war. I egged her on to relate her experience. 'Yes,' she continued, 'I worked at the Lebus Furniture Factory on the bank of the river Lea, at Tottenham. We used to get up early – there were five girls to a bed – and have a quick wash. Then we'd walk from Forest Road to the Standard and stop for a cup of tea – that was, if we had a penny to spare. Then along Forest Road to the Hale. We used to unload the barges on the river with the heavy mist around us and carry the wooden planks to a big barrow and pull it into the large sheds.' She lit a cigarette, the flame of the match dancing in front of her before she made contact and blew a cloud of smoke in front of me, continuing, 'In the factory the men built the wings of wood and we would glue the fabric on to the wings. When the cloth was dry we painted them with Shellac. It had a very strong smell, and of course we used to melt the big lumps of glue.'

She blamed the acrid smell of the Shellac for the loss of her teeth. She had lost them quite young. 'We often waved to the wounded solders as they went by on the train that passed by the sheds. They still had their bloodstained bandages around their heads and on their arms; straight from the front they were.' She told me of her stepbrother who came on leave from the front in France. When it was time to return, he did not want to go back! They got him to St James Street Station, and he threw his rifle on the track, saying that he would not return. He was calmed down, and off he went. He did not return, as he was killed in the big push.

Liz came from a family of thirteen children (that's a story on its own) and had five children of her own, three boys and two girls. Thank God for the two girls! Life was not easy. Tom, her husband, was in the Navy, money was short, but there was still time for a good laugh.

In time I had more respect for Marie's family than mine. We would go on outings – Southend, Brighton, Portsmouth and many other places. Many parties were held in Mersey Road. I have very fond memories. Norma was a little straw-haired girl, never shy in putting her hand down my pocket and getting money out. I used to pass Norma off as my daughter, and now I'm happy to say she is my wife.

Liz told me about her family. Liz's sister, Alice, had seven children that survived, having lost a boy at the age of fourteen years and a girl of nine months. Like a lot of families they were very poor, even more so because her husband Bill, a painter and decorator, drank a lot. They lived in a council house in William Morris Close, Walthamstow, which was off Forest Road opposite the police station. The houses all looked alike, and the close had a nice green centre where the kids played – if they had anything to play with, that is! It was usually skipping or touch, when you ran after your friend and touched them; he or she would then have to touch another player.

Alice's favourite trick was to buy goods from Northampton's in Forest Road, four turnings from where they lived or another shop called Blundels, promising to pay a certain amount each week until the goods were fully paid for. The things she bought went straight to the pawnshop, presumably to buy food for the family (although she liked a little flutter on the dogs). On the days that the 'Tally Man' came for his money, Alice made sure that she was out. He soon cottoned on to this and would vary his days. Alice usually made her escape via the back door while he was knocking on the front door. On one occasion he came round to Liz, looking for her. Liz gave him a few coppers to keep him happy for a while.

Marie and I would take Liz to the Hackney dog track, as she loved a bet, and sang all the way to the large stadium. The stairs from the arena led up to the tote, where she placed her bets. You always had to queue. By the time the bets were placed the roar would go up, 'They're off!' Liz would start descending the steps shouting, 'Come on, my son!' The roar would continue. 'Come on, my son!' I would watch fascinated: by the time she reached the rails the dogs would be on their final dash for the winning post. Liz would grasp the rail and lash her dog with her tongue as it hurtled by. If it won – joy. If it lost, she would claim the other dogs had blocked it.

Liz also loved wrestling. We took her to the assembly hall. Big Daddy was fighting that day. We got a seat at the centre next to the aisle. In one fight, one wrestler threw the other out of the ring. To say the least, she was upset. Out of her seat, she ran down the aisle, swearing, 'You dirty bugger!' and so on. She was stopped just before reaching the ring. She thought it was for real!

The funniest story that Liz told concerns the 'suit'. Bill had one suit to his name, which he wore on Saturdays and Sundays when he went to the Palmerston Pub in Forest Road, not far away, so that he did not have far to stagger home! The rest of the week this suit lived on a hanger behind their bedroom door, with a cloth draped over it. It did not take long for Alice to work out that she could pawn the suit on Mondays and retrieve it on Fridays, ready for Bill to wear on Saturday. She always left the braces hanging below the cloth to give the appearance that the suit was in its usual place. How long this went on for I don't know, but it came to an end when one day, mid-week, Bill thought he had left a ten-shilling note (fifty pence) in his trouser pocket. Alice ran round to me to see if I had any money, and we both went to the pawnshop to get the suit out, praying the ten shilling note was still there. Thank goodness the money was still in the pocket, ten shilling was a lot of money in those days.

As things improved (only slightly) Alice and Liz would now and then go to Temple Mills to have a bet, sixpence each way, on the whippets they raced there. At one time the popular song of the day was 'Nice work if you can get it'. They had been to the track and had a good win and sang that song all the way home. This was how we all lived during the twenties and thirties. Bill was at home, the front door never locked. At a knock on the door, he shouted, 'Come in.' A friend had come to see Alice. Bill never moved from his armchair. He asked her to make the tea, then drank it, still not moving an inch. She could not wait any longer and went. On seeing Alice the next day, she said how sorry she was about Bill. Alice said 'What do you mean?' 'Well,' she said, 'about Bill's legs, I did not know that he never had any.' Bill always sat on his legs, and being a lazy sod he never moved while she was there. I wish I could remember all the tales she told us.

Bill died at seventy-seven years of age and Alice lasted into her eighties. The children, who were now having better times, could afford to treat their mother like a queen.

# Tom Giddins Senior

*Tom Giddins*

My father-in-law, Tom, was an old salt of the sea. I first met him when I went to pick up Marie, and he was sitting outside the flat in Mersey Road. He was in his sailor uniform with a row of badges on his arm. He treated me well, and made me welcome. We became firm friends until he died. He was in the Royal Navy as a drummer in the 1914–18 war as a young lad and served in submarines and warships, which were fuelled by coal in those days. The Navy ships stopped for refuelling at the Falklands

Islands for the coal and other needs. Tom had only a few weeks left in the reserves when the Second World War broke out. He was one of the first to go in, and saw active service again from America to Russia.

Tom also had another relative in the Navy. I think his name was Bill. When the submarine HMS *Thetis* was sunk just inside Liverpool Docks, the only part of the submarine above water was the upturned hull. The sailors were all trapped inside. It was not made clear why the men were not rescued. They took so long to make up their minds that eventually the hull slipped under the water. It was a complete disaster. I think that there were only three saved. Luckily, one was Bill. I was told by Tom that the sailors picked names in a hat, and his was drawn. He got out by being fired out of the torpedo tube. Tom said Bill was never right in the head after that episode. I can't find his name on the death list.

HMS *Thetis* served in the Mediterranean after the incident and took the name of HMS *Thunderbolt*. It was sunk by the Italian sloop, under Capitano di Corvetta Augusto Migliorini, on 14 March 1943, exactly four years after going down in Liverpool harbour. I always say it's kismet.

## Tom Giddins Junior

When I first met Tom, the paratrooper, the war was still a going concern. He was around his mother's house with his mate, also a paratrooper. Marie let me in on knocking on the door. She was apprehensive going down the passage. There had been a discussion about me. Marie's brother took an instant dislike to me – I had just stepped into the room, and he tried to throw me out. Marie kicked him in the leg; there was a push and shove. I said, 'nobody throws me out!'(Pushing is all right.) I told Marie that I'd see her the following day.

Tommy Giddins asked to come to our wedding. Marie wanted him to come, and after a little pause, I agreed. It was as if nothing had happened – funny man. He took up boxing in the army. That got extra privileges, but he said he never got into the ring or threw a punch in anger. I believed him. You would go to the bar together, and he'd be first there with his hand in his pocket, but he was as tight as a drum and it would be me or his dad paying. His dad was ashamed of him. I would drink half pints he would have pints.

I got my own back on Tom, a funny bloke who could bring tears of laughter to your eyes. He came on holiday with us, when Marie was not in the best of health, to Switzerland. We had had a few laughs and a few drinks and were in our bedroom. He said that he felt good and could take me on. I said, 'Come on then!' Marie said, 'No,' but I thought it was payback time. I had no intention of harming him, though I dreamed of breaking his legs! I threw him on to the bed with a shoulder throw, and he bounced a couple of times. He called me a naughty name and came for me again – I did the same throw on to the bed. By this time, he had had enough with the drink and bouncing up and down on the bed – it got to him, as it would. He staggered to his room. Marie woke me in the middle of the night, saying that she heard a noise. I got up and, opening his bedroom door, saw that he was on the floor trying to wipe up the sick with his shirt. He looked at me and slurred, 'How did you know?' I told him to clear it all up. It stunk to high heaven – he had broken a small window. I apologised to the owner and to my mate, Vic Cocksedge, when I got back home, who had recommended me to his friend's Hotel!

# Reg Giddins

Reg, another brother, was the shortest man in the army. He served in Burma. He was quite cocky, not a likeable lad. He had no love for me, but would come for a haircut on his way to catch the train to Liverpool Street. That was until I said that I was putting up the price of haircuts. He took offence at that and stopped coming. Funny, as he never paid in the first place. He must have thought that I would be earning too much. I would have loved giving him one, but he was so short! I can understand their feeling towards me – they in the army, me an Italian. But they never stood up to me. Shame; I loved their dad, who was a real English man and a mate!

# Ron Giddins

*Ron Giddins*

My brother-in-law, Ron Giddins, was the youngest of the three boys and the best. While at school he was a very good swimmer. When I went to Mersey Road for a meal with the Giddins family, Ron and I would always fight for his mother's leftovers, picking the chicken bones and the dripping from Liz's cooking. The dripping would be dark brown; we would spread it on a thick slice of bread and just add salt – marvellous! Despite Liz's faults, like cheating at cards, waiting for me to sell the girls into slavery and smoking like a trooper, she was a wonderful cook. Her bread pudding – what can I say! Ron loved making a sandwich; as long as he had two slices of bread, what went between them was immaterial. His favourite filling was cheese with a Spanish onion, the onion having been soaked in vinegar.

Ron was called up for National Service and chose the Grenadier Guards. He was a very proud soldier, upright and tall, he looked the part. We visited him at Caterham. He told us that they had to pull together as a squad. If one failed – say by not having clean boots or belt not white enough – the whole squad would be punished for one soldier's carelessness. It was very strict, but he loved it.

Ron married his childhood sweetheart, Pat, in 1957. At his stag party the night before the wedding, someone spiked his drinks, and he only just made the ceremony. He looked dreadful but managed to get through it somehow. They had three sons; John was the eldest, and Dave a constable. Robert was very young and I did not know him too well.

As a young boy of five, John would be brought to the shop for his haircut by his mother. I'd sit him across the board, resting on the chair arms. He did not like having the haircut, and I would have to wrestle with him. His final act of defiance was to stick his two fingers up his nose and blow. Out came bubbles galore: not a pretty sight!

At the weekends his father would bring John to our home in Beresford Road, if I opened the door John would look up and say, 'I like you better than my other Uncle Ugo.' He could not connect me with the barber. I'd give him half a crown, but the other Ugo cut his hair!

I was very sorry to fall out with Ron in later years. We were both at fault, but neither of us would be first to say sorry. It was a great loss and sorrow to his family and friends when Ron died young, only sixty years old.

# Highams Park

**M**arie and I had finally bought a house at 104 Beresford Road, E17. We lived there until Marie died and I stayed on for three desolate years after that. On marrying my new wife, Norma, we purchased a house in Beech Hall Road, Highams Park. After some alterations, we moved in on our return from honeymoon in Malta.

Although I owned the freehold of the Gosport Road shop in 1980, the council had served me with a compulsory purchase order for the premises so that they could redevelop the area for housing. My previous neighbour in Gosport Road, Terry Oldham, who ran the tattooist shop, had moved into Hale End Road, Highams Park. He got me an office next to him, on the first floor. My clients followed me, but not too many, only the ones that I'd known for years. The shoe repairer over the road said I would not do well, as my shop was out of sight. I made a figure of a hairdresser in plywood, and put it on the side of the entrance of the passage that led to the first floor.

There were five businesses in the building; Terry's, my barber's, and a firm that cleaned anything. In fact, they were shit-shovellers, and told some good stories. They went to clear a blockage at this flat; the toilet bowl was filled to the brim, which finished with a curl in the centre! They had kept on using it, even though it would not flush. It sounds a rotten job, but it was very technical, believe it or not! On the ground floor, there was an estate agent's and a word processor office that went broke, and within hours, the word processor and everything that was moveable had vanished. I was slow again!

The office/barber shop was entered by a passage and a flight of stairs. The overheads were very reasonable and I was soon making a living, but having a long rest in between clients. All this moving about was costing money, but I had no choice. Norma and I had a holiday, and went to America while we still had some money.

It was not too bad; the rent was low, but the landlord was sly and untrustworthy. After a while, he had me moving downstairs, which was better for me, but I was not there too long before I was given my marching orders. I would not have moved, but I had no lease. The landlord got me a shop in the Broadway, just over the railway crossing. Again, I had to fit out the shop. Terry's old man did the work for me – Terry also had moved two doors from me in Winchester Road but now I had a lease for seven years! It was the best move yet. The shop was only five minutes from our house in Beech Hall Road, very handy. The shop turned into a little gold mine and was very busy.

When I moved in the shop was not completed but I knew my clients would not care. I did not expect strangers to come in and sit on empty boxes, but they did. Later I had ladies' salon combined with the gents', as the shop was too long for a one-man business.

A retired hairdresser with Italian parents asked for a job. I refused him, as I knew my clients would not have him cut their hair. He came back later and tried again. I did not open on Saturdays as I worked long hours in the week. I gave him an offer that he could not refuse – he would open the shop on Saturday, and I would take half of what he earned. His name was Ernie, and he was the nicest man in town! After a slow start, he was taking enough to pay for the expenses of the shop. He would bring the money to my house no more than ten minutes' walk away and split it down the middle, and he was happy as a pig in muck. I trusted him and he was happy.

His son, a bit slow, came to the shop with Ernie. He was a big fellow, not doing any harm, except maybe to his mind. He just sat there as if all was new to him. After some weeks, the lady hairdresser complained to me that he was upsetting her. 'How?' I inquired. She explained, 'He keeps looking at my bum!' But she did not mind my younger clients looking as she bent over, shampooing the ladies' hair. She wore very tight slacks, and the clients would watch her bum struggling to get out. To be writing this, I also must have had a good look. So Ernie did very well and was very honest, but his son never lost the vision of her bum!

# The Bear - Again

Tommy Brown, nicknamed the Bear, one of the Krays' men, was a pain. He had followed me from the shop in E17 to the Broadway. He would always be first, waiting outside the door early in the morning! He came from Tottenham, quite a distance for a haircut, shave and hot towels. He liked his shave close so he could not feel a bristle. After the hot towels, I would whack him hard under the chin and called it a 'massage'. He was a big man with a big nose that had been pushed around a bit. He took time to shave and I had to cut the hairs in his nose. I could not charge him fully, as he claimed the old age pensioner rate! He was a good seventeen to eighteen stone in weight. On the week that I was leaving he said, 'Boy, will you call a cab for me? There's one over the railway crossing, I don't feel like taking the bus back to Tottenham.' I phoned, he was picked up and I saw him for the last time.

One hour later the cab driver returned to the shop, very upset. He told me he had dropped Tommy off in Lordship Lane and, on asking for the fare, the Bear told him, 'Take it out of that!' pointing to his nose, and walked away.

The cabbie asked me where he lived so he could get his money. I told him I did not have his address, and that he was one of the Krays' minders, he should put it down to experience? He said to me, 'You booked the cab,' thinking I might pay. I told him to piss off, but I was sorry for him.

# Elmo and Money Again!

I had just moved into the Broadway, in Highams Park, from around the corner. It had cost me a small bomb. No sooner had I settled in then Elmo was on the phone from Scunthorpe. 'Please get me out of trouble, and send me £120 cash! Otherwise, the shop will be closed, and we will be all out in the street. It will only be for three weeks.' I could not argue, as I was busy, and the clients were hanging on to what I was saying. Even from that distance, he timed it right. Stressing it had to be cash he told me that he would send a box of chocolates to Norma. I phoned

Norma who, bless her heart, did not argue, although I got a telling off when I got home. On rewriting this book, I bet his family knew nothing about the supposed 'loan'.

Norma never got her chocolates, and I put the money with the rest – on the tab. Who reads these words must think that I'm a simpleton. If it were not for my family! I was told that I don't forgive but I must do, as I'm still in touch with Elmo's family, who had nothing to do with his habits. I bet he even borrowed from the girls.

Elmo died early, in 1996. His funeral at Scunthorpe Crematorium was a one-off, and demonstrated the other side to his character, of which you, dear reader, have had only a glimpse. The place was packed with a multitude of friends, and many mourners had to stand. The priest officiating had just begun to say a few words when an elderly chap near the front got unsteadily to his feet and interjected, 'That's not what we want to hear!' The priest wisely let him continue, and we were treated to the best drunken eulogy a friend could give. No one could have been offended by such a heartfelt tribute. The service finished with a rendering of 'Toot Toot Tootsie, Goodbye'! It was a fine and unique send-off.

# Ron Todd

Ron Todd was probably my best-known customer next to Terry Lawless. He lived in Edinburgh Road, just around the corner from the Gosport Road shop. I can't recall him in my early years, but he appeared when I returned to Walthamstow. I used to cut his and his brother Ben's hair. Ron had been a Marine Commando in Burma and saw action there. It was Ron who had guarded the Japanese General, Tomoyuki Yamashita, who surrendered in Burma. Ron said he was a very nice man, whom he taught to sing (It's a long way to Tipperary). By all accounts, he sang it as he marched to be hanged! It was a miscarriage of justice, as Yamashita was in charge of the army, not the Navy, which raped Manila – a dishonourable death for a solder to be hanged.

I found Ron a very honest man and I liked him. When he was

demobbed, he worked in Fords at Dagenham, and became a convener for the trade union, and did very well. From Dagenham, Ron rose high in the Transport and General Workers Union and was second to Moss Evans, whom he succeeded as general secretary. Ron followed me to Higham Hill, very proud of what he had achieved, and would arrive in a nice car driven by his chauffeur plus minder. I think he was not appreciated by his members when he lost out to his successor.

Since retiring, I met Ron and Moss Evans (now sadly deceased) in King's Lynn and they seemed very happy; they always liked a joke. Moss had been Mayor of King's Lynn. Ron Todd died on 2 April 2005. Can't say how sorry I was!

# Retirement

The last week in Highams Park in July 1989 was sad in a way but I was pleased to have reached my retirement. My neighbours in the shop bought me a tankard and Fred Andrews bought me a cut glass jug commemorating the date I retired. I was sorry yet happy to leave, with these words from the Bear ringing in my ears: 'Boy, when you get into a fight don't go down, or they'll kick your head in.' With these wise words, I closed the door and handed my keys to Andy, the Greek hairdresser, who had bought my shop.

After I sold the shop and house and made many journeys into Norfolk, we settled in a small Norfolk village, Tilney St Lawrence. I play golf with my wife, who turned into a good player and went on to become the Lady President at the Eagles Golf club. Who would have thought that? From E17 to playing golf as a club member – well I never.

# Postscript

## Declining Health

My doctor in Highams Park would say to me, 'Ugo, with every sport, there is a price to pay,' every time I went to see him for fractures on my legs, toes, ribs, collar bone. One morning after my Judo class on arising, I thought I was having a heart attack. I had this pain in the centre of my chest. He sent me to Chingford Hospital for an X-ray. The nurse had to have three takes in different positions to get a result. She said that my chest was too dense with muscle. I had fractured my sternum.

When I sold the barbershop to Andy, a Greek lad, just before I reached the age of sixty-five, I had been having trouble with my groin. I went skiing in Austria, and could not do the plough to stop. I put it down to Judo. The pain was in the groin; no way did I connect it with my hips. Two years earlier, I had packed my Judo club in and handed it over to Fred (first dan). I had retired from active Judo at the age of sixty.

After retiring from work, I went to see my doctor in Norfolk who put me on a painkiller, Volterol, as I could not sleep at night. Unfortunately, it affected my kidneys. It may have been because I did not usually take pills that they affected me. Fortunately, I only took half of the pills; otherwise, it could have been more serious.

I did not feel that I was ill; I was putting on weight and was playing golf no trouble. However, my golf shoes were getting tight. I took my temperature and it was over 100. I could not understand it – of course, the reading was wrong. From eleven and a half stone I went up to just over thirteen stone, but I did not feel ill. I was eating well, but as you have realised by now, I'm thick!

Lying in bed, I would tighten my stomach and then relax, then swish the water inside me around. My back was stone cold. That Friday morning I thought I'd phone the doctor to see what it was all about. He was on holiday. 'Was it important?' the receptionist inquired. I said, 'I'll wait until he comes back.' That Sunday Norma said, 'Phone Geoff [Our friend from Wanstead] to see if he knows something about it.' I did and explained my symptoms to him. He blew his top. 'I knew a girl who had that symptom, and she drowned when her lungs filled with fluid,' he said. Geoff phoned his wife's sister, Ann Margaret, in Wales, who was a nurse. On his return call, I was told to get in touch with my doctor straight away!

The doctor was not happy on arrival saying 'I have been up and down this road three times this morning!' He took my water sample and placed a small stick into it, still moaning. 'Can I use the phone?' the doctor then inquired. Within five minutes, he had arranged a bed for me in King's Lynn Hospital. I heard him say that I was in danger of a heart attack. Norma drove me to the hospital, post-haste!

The hospital was not geared for kidney troubles. All medication was stopped, as they were at a loss about how to treat me. I was only there for two days. The chap on my right died; they drew the curtains around the beds and wheeled him away in a boxed trolley. I had a peek through the gap. I was told that I was to be transported to Norwich. I was allowed home for the weekend. Norma laid on a big meal for me. I did not know what was in store for me on returning to King's Lynn Hospital.

On my return to the ward, I was told that my bed had been taken. Another bed was waiting for me on the bottom floor. These wards were in the bowels of the hospital. The staff nurse said, 'They're nice down there; anyway, you'll only be there for a couple of days.' They were small wards, just four beds each. One opposite me had a patient, the rest were empty. I spoke to the old man, who was strapped to the bed. He told me that he had been getting stiff for some time. Eventually he could not move and his wife looked after him. When she died, he was taken into hospital. He was very happy to be looked after. His bed was on a swivel, with a trapdoor under him to remove his waste. He was not depressed at all. He was a very nice chap; I felt for him.

A patient came and got into bed, a big chap, and not a word passed his lips. I thought, That's funny. Next morning the nurse said, 'Will you join the rest in the dining room.' In I went; they all stopped eating and stared at me. I could see the food hanging from their lips, and the food slopped around the plates. I saw an empty table and sat down. They then started to shove the food into their mouths. It seemed they were afraid that I would sit with them, and help myself to their food. They always had one eye on me. I quickly ate my breakfast, and made my way out.

The nurse asked how I got on with the other patients. I replied, 'They aren't all there.' She told me that quite a few had no other place to go to and would die there. I was now getting depressed. I asked to be moved, as I needed a bath. One of the nurses said, 'You don't need to move, we'll give you a blanket bath.' I thought better of it as they looked too keen. so I did not have one. The stiff chap and me were the only ones that spoke to the nurses. They were in their own private dreams. I was moved to the top ward, awaiting my departure to Norwich.

A not-so-young patient next to me did not speak, but seemed to like the banter between me and Barry in the bed opposite. He was also asked by the two young nurses if he wanted a blanket bath. He looked at me enquiringly. I said, 'Go on, give it a try.' He nodded his head. The curtains were drawn round his bed. I don't know what they were doing, but there was a lot of giggling and an 'Oh, Mr Brown!' One nurse poked her head out between the curtains, looked up and down the ward, closed the curtains and there was some more giggling.

When they'd finished the nurses gave me a wink, and off they went. Mr Brown not only looked clean and bright, but had twinkling eyes and a happy smile. I asked, 'Well, how was it?' He looked at me and gave a big smile. When his visitors came, like a silly sod I said, 'He had a good blanket bath by two nurses.' Mr Brown was still smiling, but his visitors did not take kindly to my insinuations. I thought, Keep quiet, Ugo!

I had thought I'd heard it all in the hairdressers, but the male nurse told me what happens at night in Norfolk. It wasn't a rare sight to see a male coming into the casualty with a bottle stuck up his rectum, or with his penis sucked into a vacuum nozzle that wouldn't let go. In the hairdressers, I'd been told that 'fisting' was the going thing and asked, 'What the hell's that?' And I was told: apparently it was performed in public in a Hackney pub that queers frequented! It's hard to believe, but one bloke would make a fist and push it, up to the elbow, into the other bloke's arse. So I definitely believed the nurse's stories. Had I been there longer, I would have had more to tell, as they liked a little chat to shorten the night hours away.

Norma visited without fail, and brought some oranges. I never knew before how nice they tasted. When Norma went, the depression set in again; the darkness could not hide my fears. The next morning I was taken to Norwich Hospital. I never did have a blanket bath! Shame!

# Norwich Hospital

The only one to come and see me regularly was my Norma. She came three times a week. David Day, a golfing friend, travelled with Norma to the hospital to keep her company. He came a few times and I thanked him for that. It's a long way from Tilney St Lawrence – 300 miles a week. Norma never failed to turn up. I was now in a six-bed ward. Doctor Hamilton arrived with five other doctors; one was Spanish. Dr Hamilton was having trouble in pronouncing my name, but the Spanish doctor put him right. After the examination and a long discussion with the other doctors, Dr Hamilton said, 'We will put him under...' I can't remember what. The other doctors all looked up sharply at Dr Hamilton. A notice was put over my bed that said, 'nil by mouth'.

I was under heavy sedation. I would find myself sitting in a chair by my bed; all of a sudden my head would lurch forward and my teeth would snap! If anybody had been within striking distance I would have bitten something off! I was a bit high and the smell of urine was in the air. I asked the nurse if I could have a shower, as I'd seen other patients making their way to the shower room. I was having trouble passing water and waste. The hot shower made me pee – I just let it go! You have to be in the same situation to find such happiness in having a pee.

My friend Fred Breyer came from Hadleigh; I did not expect him, but there you go, friends. I heard a voice asking for me and I turned my head. I could see the desk where the staff nurse kept an eye on us. Fred was speaking to the nurse. The nurse pointed to my bed, and Fred looked at me. He turned to the nurse and I heard him say, 'I have known Mr Patriarca for over forty years, and that's not him!'

I was lying on the bed; it was hot. Only that morning I had asked the doctor to tie my feet to the bed rail, as I felt that I was about to float to the ceiling. My wife told me the previous day that she thought that I was looking very ill. I beckoned to Fred, who was shocked at my appearance – more so, when he saw the size of my belly. I can't remember if I showed him my scrotum: it was the size of half a football. I don't think Fred was into scrotums! While we were talking they wheeled this chap in, still in his own bed (I wondered why they had taken the other bed away), and put him into the empty space near the window. As soon as he was wheeled in he was indicating that the TV should be facing him. His wife turned the TV around. I thought, There's an 'I'm all right Jack' attitude.

Within half an hour Fred and I were both shouting for the nurse. 'Nurse, nurse!' Fred was shouting, 'He's having a heart attack!' The fellow's wife was in tears. In rushed the staff nurse, pushing a red button on the way. Doctors rushed in, followed by a male nurse pushing a gas cylinder, curtains drawn around the bed – bedlam. Fred went to the cafeteria for a cup of tea to calm down. He returned to the ward and said that he had spoken to the man's wife, who was also there to regain her composure. When Fred drove out of the car park of the hospital he drove straight through the park barrier! He did not stop until he arrived home.

There were two old blokes in the ward; the one on my right would say, 'I can't hear the chuck wagon; are they late?' He would strain his neck to see down the corridor. The other would reply, 'The cook had one too many last night.' This was from the far corner of the room. The response was, 'I'm just about ready for it.' They spoke as if they were still in the trenches in 1914, but here the only thing on their mind was FOOD!

I must thank Dr Hamilton and his staff for their care; he and his team worked hard on me. My wife Norma wrote a nice letter to the hospital, thanking them for the care they gave me. Also Ena, who offered her kidney if it were needed – that I shall remember!

I had to have five steroids a day at a high strength. I went to Boots; the poor man did not know which way to turn. 'Are you sure this is right?' he asked. My wife said, 'We have just come straight from the hospital.' They said, 'Go to King's Lynn Hospital and get them there.' He was so nervous that I felt bad. King's Lynn would not give us the prescribed pills, as they were prescribed by Norwich hospital. Eventually we found a pharmacist in Gayton. She had them only at half strength. That was the strength they were allowed to sell. I ended up taking ten a day. It takes some swallowing.

But I am still alive and enjoying life.

# And Finally...

Before completing this book, I wrote to the *Walthamstow Guardian* to ask my old clients and friends if they had any old photos of the High Street and surrounding areas. I was overwhelmed with phone calls and letters that brought back memories of a time when I was a young boy of eight or nine. I have displayed some of these letters opposite to finish this book. I must thank one and all for their interest and hope they will not be too disappointed with the result. So to you all, I shall think of you; and to those who did not reply – the same to you!

'The same to you!' is what I would write on the bottom of my card when notifying clients of my holidays. The card was always up in good time, but the clients would not read it. They often told me that they were caught out, as they had read the last words from the notice. In the end George Burgess made a stand-up figure of a barber, who looked like me, holding a placard stating when I was going and returning, adding, 'If you don't like it, lift the card.' One day a lady brought her kid for a haircut and kept looking at the card. All of a sudden she leapt from her chair saying, 'I must see what's under there.' I tried to stop her, but it was too late, and she saw what George had painted in bright red – 'Bollocks!'

*Some replies from Walthamstow*

Printed in the United Kingdom
by Lightning Source UK Ltd.
128956UK00001B/84/P